C000283496

HISTORY

OF

WAR

IN

MAPS

Published by Collins
An imprint of HarperCollins Publishers
Westerhill Road, Bishopbriggs, Glasgow G64 2QT
www.harpercollins.co.uk

HarperCollins Publishers
1st Floor, Watermarque Building, Ringsend Road, Dublin 4, Ireland

First edition 2022
© HarperCollins Publishers 2022
Text © Philip Parker 2022
Maps © see Acknowledgements on p224

A catalogue record for this book is available from the British Library

ISBN 978-0-00-850649-0

10 9 8 7 6 5 4 3 2 1

Printed in Bosnia and Herzegovina

If you would like to comment on any aspect of this book,
please contact us at the above address or online.
e-mail: collins.reference@harpercollins.co.uk

collins.co.uk

HISTORY

OF

WAR

IN

MAPS

Philip Parker

Contents

"A plague upon it!
I have forgot the map."

Hotspur in *Henry IV, Part I*, Act 3 Scene 1

William Shakespeare, 1597

Introduction

Warfare is the continuation of politics by other means, or so declared Carl von Clausewitz, the great 19th-century Prussian historian of military theory in his *On War*. And central to the conduct of both politics and war is knowledge of the landscape in which the struggle for power, be it the violence of the battlefield or the even darker arts of the demagogue, play out. There is no better tool for the ambitious politician seeking to extend his country's borders or the general devising the best lines of advance, a place to avoid an ambush or high ground which might give that vital edge to his troops than a map.

The crystallisation of knowledge in graphic form, maps have performed many functions since the first rudimentary scratches on rocks and bone during the Neolithic period and the first more finely delineated plans of fields and townscape from Mesopotamia in the 3rd millennium BC. Most of these earliest maps would have been of very limited military use. The Babylonian map from the 6th century which portrays a stylised view of the world – mainly Babylon, and its satellite city-states, with realms of permanent darkness beyond an enclosing world river – or the medieval European *mappae mundi* replete with biblical sites and fantastic beasts such as manticores and Minotaurs may have been sources of instruction or amusement, but they could never have been used to plot the movements of armies.

Ancient generals must have relied principally on the local knowledge of guides to shape their decisions. It is clear that the Romans had access to some form of more detailed mapping: the 4th century historian Vegetius in his *Epitoma Rei Militaris* advises that "A general . . . should have an exact description of the country that is the seat of war, in which the distances of places specified by the number of miles, the nature of the roads, the shortest routes, byroads, mountains and rivers should be correctly inserted." However, other than the incidental marking of town fortifications on the Peutinger Table, a late Roman itinerary map, nothing of a military nature has survived.

Perhaps commanders or their scouts made ephemeral sketches to help with battlefield deployments, but none of this has come down to us. The gradual increase in the

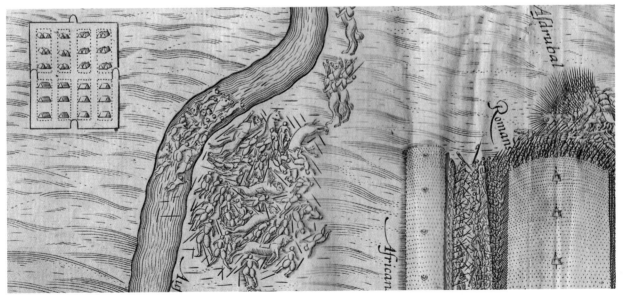

The Battle of Cannae (216BC), shown in Emanuel Bowen's 1732 map (see pages 26–27), was one of the Carthaginian general Hannibal's greatest victories against the Romans.

sophistication of cartography, especially after the diffusion of movable-type printing in the 15th century, still did not produce maps which were of the scale, or containing the detailed information about the state of roads, location of river crossings or situation of mountain passes, which a general needed.

It was not until the mid-17th century that we have maps which were surveyed for overtly military means. One example is the *Delineatio generalis camporum desertorum vulgo Ukraina cum adiacentibus provinciis* created in 1648 by Guillaume le Vasseur de Beauplan to help King Ladislaus IV of Poland plan campaigns against the Crimean Tatars from his eastern territories in Ukraine. Long before that, however, another form of military mapping had emerged, one which forms the focus of this book. These maps which told the story of battles or campaigns, whether for propaganda purposes in disseminating news of victories (or putting a positive spin on defeats), to satisfy the growing thirst for contemporary and historical information as the printing press made books cheaper and more accessible, or, more recently, as simple matters of record.

Most of the more than 70 maps in this volume are contemporary (or nearly so) with the conflict which they portray, providing a unique insight into how those battles were understood at the time. They reveal, starkly, the choices (and the mistakes) which influenced the outcome of the engagement: the complexity of the fighting at the climactic American Civil War battle of Gettysburg in 1863, the ingenuity of the military engineer Sébastien le Prestre de Vauban in devising trench systems at the Siege of Maastricht in 1673, or the envelopment and destruction of a British force by the Zulus at Isandhlwana in 1879 are all far more comprehensible in cartographic form than text alone could achieve. Many of the maps are artworks in their own right. The skill of the engravers and mapmakers in evoking the battlefield – such as the 1732 map by the Welsh cartographer Emanuel Bowen of the Battle of Cannae in 216BC, one of a handful of later and antiquarian maps covering eras of military history where no contemporary maps exist, or the exquisite surveying that produced the Mawangdui Garrison map around 168BC, the very earliest piece of military cartography in existence from anywhere – shows

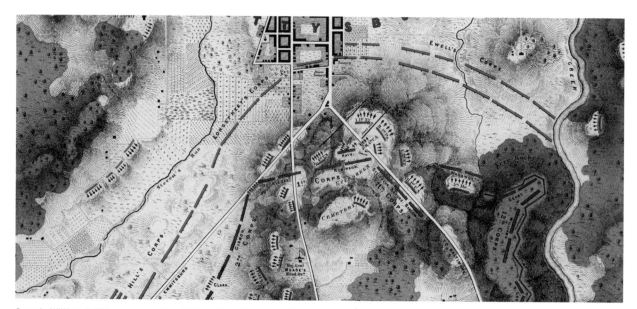

Captain William H Willcox's map of the 1863 Battle of Gettysburg (see page 124) captures the fighting at a critical moment in the decisive battle of the American Civil War.

that the cartography of war has produced more than merely functional mapping.

The span of time covered by the maps in this book is immense, from the clash between Egyptian and Hittite chariot armies at Kadesh in 1275BC to the Russian intervention in Ukraine's Donbas in 2014 and the flare-up of that conflict in 2022. Yet the challenges facing the generals have remained in many cases the same: how to recruit, train and manoeuvre armies of increasing size, how to deploy increasingly destructive offensive weapons (from spears to area-obliterating ordnance), how to deliver maximum force to the enemy's weakest point and how to outwit and confuse an adversary as to one's intentions. Those wars have been fought for a variety of motives, from the acquisition of resources, be they human or mineral, in the name of religion and ideology (with the defence of the "nation" being an increasingly important subsection of the latter) or through ambition or the simple lust for power.

The key to all this is knowledge, its analysis and the will to act on it. Whether in a raid on a neolithic village to seize grain or enslave its inhabitants or in a 21st-century hybrid war involving drones, crypto-strikes, irregular forces and the propaganda power of fake news, superior information is always an advantage. Maps remain key to leveraging that advantage, and in an era in which digital cartography can be created and updated at lightning speed, their importance for the military is likely to grow.

And as a means of understanding conflict, of mapping battles and wars for a more general readership, maps will retain their unique power. It is my hope that the maps presented here will give a flavour of some of history's most significant conflicts, of the armies and generals who have fought them, the tactics they have adopted, and the consequences for their peoples of victory and defeat.

The 2015 map (see pages 220-21) shows the progress of Russian-backed forces in taking over Ukraine's Donbas region in a conflict which presaged a much wider war seven years later.

ANCIENT
AND
MEDIEVAL
WARFARE

1275BC–1500

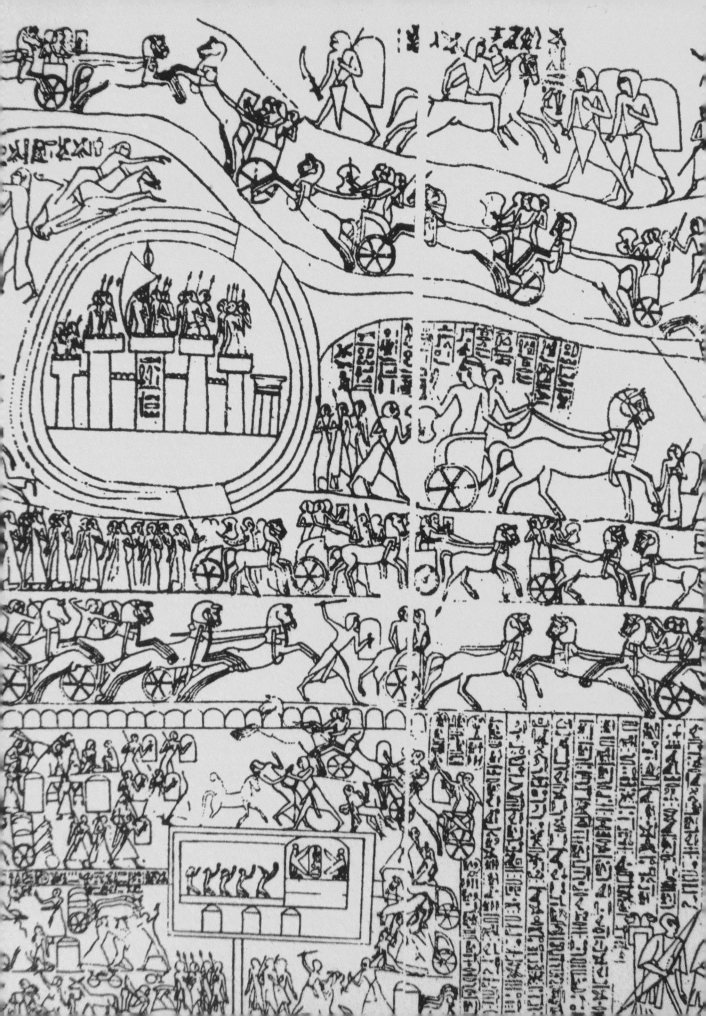

Battle of Kadesh

The image depicts a New Kingdom Egyptian army on the march. Redrawn from the temple of Ramesses II at Abydos it shows part of the force that won a famous victory for the pharaoh, or so he claimed.

The foot soldiers and chariots massing for the battle at Kadesh in western Syria were part of an expeditionary force that Ramesses led through Gaza into Palestine in the summer of 1275BC, intent on capitalising on a successful campaign in the region the previous year. He planned to crush Egypt's bitter rivals, the Hittites, once and for all, and establish his rule in an area in which his predecessors had dabbled for over 200 years.

At the core of his 35,000-strong army was a force of 2,000 chariots divided between four divisions: Ptah, Amun, Re and Seth. A technology borrowed from the Hyksos nomads who had ruled Egypt for over a century before the start of the New Kingdom around 1550BC, the chariots were the ancient equivalent of a battle tank. They moved far more rapidly than infantry, were able to manoeuvre – wheeling and turning to confuse the enemy – and acted as a mobile firing platform, bearing archers deep into the opposition's lines.

Ramesses' advance was at first largely unopposed as he headed towards Kadesh, the key to unlocking the Hittite heartland. As he came close to the city, his confidence in taking it increased when two captured Hittite spies revealed that their king, Muwatallis, was still far away in Aleppo. Without waiting for the rest of his army, Ramesses made camp with his Re division on the west bank of the Orontes, ready to attack the city the next day. Unfortunately, the spies' information was a double bluff, as they had been planted by the Hittites precisely to mislead him, and Muwatallis and his 40,000-strong host were actually hidden in gullies just outside Kadesh.

Just as the Egyptians were settling in, Muwatallis struck, sending his own chariot force crashing into Ramesses' camp. The Hittite chariots were heavier, as each carried three men – two archers and a charioteer – rather than the complement of two in their Egyptian equivalent. Their impact sent the Re division into flight, and their momentum carried them on into the Amun division, which had almost reached Kadesh and was now faced with hundreds of Hittite chariots smashing into its line of march.

All seemed lost, but with a prayer to the god Amun, Ramesses set about rallying his troops and launching several small counterattacks. Their morale stiffened by the courage of their pharaoh, the Egyptians rallied until the arrival of the Na'arum, a mercenary unit, and the Ptah division, which tipped the balance of numbers back in their favour. The lighter Egyptian chariots were also able to outpace and outmanoeuvre the Hittites, harrying them and stopping them approaching the Egyptian lines. Fatally, Muwatallis held back from committing his infantry reserve stationed in Kadesh, which could have pinned the Egyptians to the Orontes, and so by the time dusk fell, he found that victory had been snatched from his grasp.

So it was the Hittites who withdrew from the field, back towards Aleppo. Ramesses prudently retired to Egypt. He had not captured Kadesh, nor had he inflicted a decisive defeat on Muwatallis, the bulk of whose army was intact. Yet being seen to be victorious was almost as important as the reality of a victory and so he ordered celebratory inscriptions and friezes to adorn temple walls throughout Egypt, bearing resounding proclamations such as "I made slaughter among them, and there was none that escaped me". As well as being probably the largest chariot battle ever fought, Kadesh was perhaps the first example of spin, of war propaganda claiming a victory for what was in fact most likely an inconclusive draw. It ultimately led to another innovation, the first known peace treaty between two major powers, signed between Ramesses and Muwatallis's brother Hattusilis III in 1259BC. The treaty agreed an end to the seemingly interminable hostilities between Egypt and the Hittites and set the boundary between them. Each agreed to come to the other's aid if an outside power attacked them. It was a fitting coda to the "victory" that both sides had claimed at Kadesh.

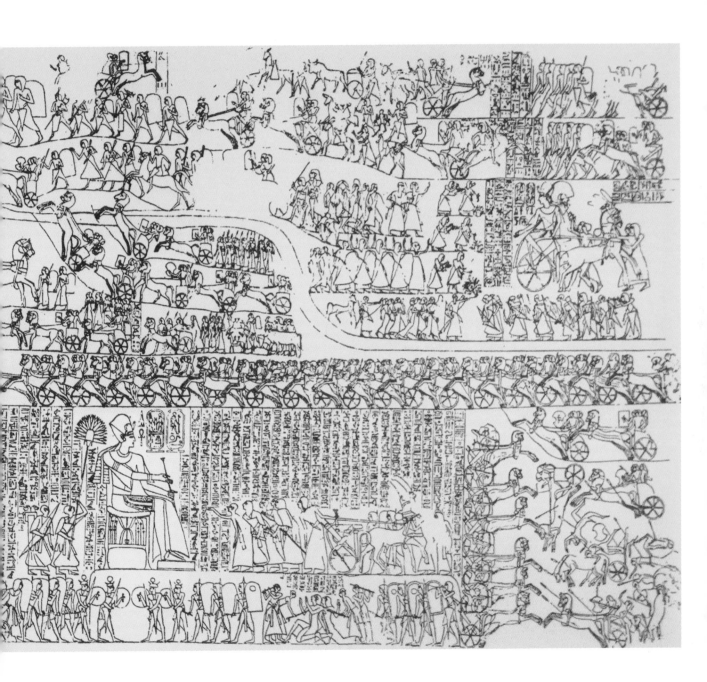

Battle of Marathon

Greek warfare was a brutal, bloody and highly choreographed affair, fought between phalanxes, units of heavily armoured infantry drawn up in compact formations up to eight ranks deep. They were composed of land-owning yeoman farmers armed with long spears, which the first three ranks used to thrust against their opponents, and short stabbing swords. Protected by bronze breastplates, greaves and the *hoplon*, a round shield which gave them their name, the hoplite phalanx pushed against the opposing side, hoping to use the momentum from the back ranks to force their foes back and the spears of the front ranks to open up a gap to prise the other phalanx apart. Each hoplite relied on the shield of the man on his right to protect his vulnerable spear-wielding flank. It was dangerous, but democratic.

Hoplite battles tended to be short, on pre-arranged battlefields in open ground. They ended when one side fled, only to be allowed to return to collect and bury their dead with honour. But then a new foe appeared, and one who did not play by the time-hallowed rules. The Persian king Darius I, ruler of a vast empire that stretched from the Aegean Sea to Central Asia, had been angered by a revolt of the Greek-speaking cities of Ionia in western Asia Minor in 499BC, and in particular by the support they received from the city-states of mainland Greece, including Athens.

Bent on revenge, in 490BC Darius dispatched an enormous naval expeditionary force. The Athenians, whose territory lay right in the path of the Persian armada, were left terribly exposed when their Spartan allies delayed sending reinforcements because of a religious festival and other city-states dithered, fearing to anger the Persian leviathan. Led by the generals Callimachus and Miltiades, the 10,000 Athenians hoped to prevent a Persian force more than three times their number from advancing inland from the beach at Marathon, where they had landed, towards Athens itself. Taking up a blocking position by a grove dedicated to Hercules, the Athenian commanders watched with horror as a section of the Persian force, including much of its cavalry, re-embarked and headed for a now unprotected Athens.

Their reaction, which caught the Persian commander Datis entirely by surprise, was to attack. The phalanx was ordered to advance at the double, crossing the distance to the beach with such speed – despite their heavy armour – that the volleys from the light archers and slingsmen which would normally have decimated them, barely dented the wave of hoplites which had now thinned its rear ranks to allow it to match the width of the Persian line. Even so, the Greek centre collapsed as it impacted Datis's line, but this caused the Persians to move forward, which allowed the Greek wings to envelope them and fall on their unprotected rear. Panicked, the Persians turned and fled, leaving thousands of their number dead in the marshes that had constricted their battle line. The Athenians, in contrast, lost just 192.

The Athenian hoplites had won a resounding victory. Their fight was not yet over, as they had to return to defend Athens and would need to fight off a second Persian invasion ten years later, but it showed what a disciplined phalanx could achieve against theoretically overwhelming odds. Marathon became one of the most celebrated military encounters of the ancient world, and the Greek victory the subject of intense scrutiny both by Herodotus, the "father of history" who chronicled the conflict, and by later historians. The map of the battle was engraved by the French cartographer Ambroise Tardieu. It is taken from the *Voyage du jeune Anacharsis en Grèce* ("Voyage of the Young Anacharsis in Greece"), a fictionalised account, published in 1788, of the travels of the 6th-century Scythian Anacharsis, sometimes counted among the "Seven Sages of Greece". It was written by Jean-Jacques Barthélemy, a French scholar most renowned for being the first to decipher an ancient script, when he successfully read an inscription in Palmyrene, a language of ancient Syria, beating the much more famous Jean-François Champollion, who unlocked the secrets of Egyptian hieroglyphics, by almost 70 years.

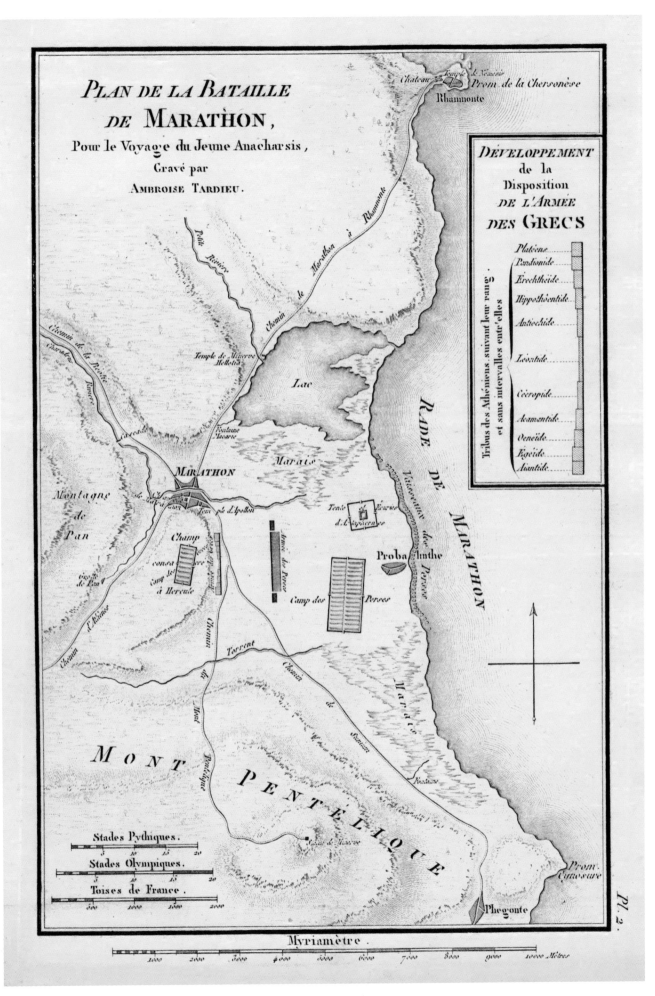

PLAN DE LA BATAILLE DE MARATHON,

Pour le Voyage du Jeune Anacharsis,

Gravé par

AMBROISE TARDIEU.

DÉVELOPPEMENT de la Disposition DE L'ARMÉE DES GRECS

Tribus des Athéniens suivant leur rang, et sans intervalles entr'elles

Platéens
Pandionide
Erechthéide
Hippothoontide
Antiochide
Léontide
Cécropide
Acamantide
Oenéide
Egéide
Ajantide

Prom. de la Chersonèse
Château — Temple de Nemesis
Rhamnonte

Chemin de Marathon à Rhamnonte

Petite Rivière

Temple de Minerve Mellotis

Lac

RADE DE MARATHON

Marais

Fontaine Macarie

Montagne de Pan

MARATHON

Temple d'Apollon

Grotte de Pan

Champ
consacré
Camp des
à Hercule

Armée des Grecs

Tente d'Artapherne

Probalinthe

Camp des Perses

Intervalle des Perses

Torrent

Chemin

MONT PENTÉLIQUE

Temple de Minerve

Prom. Cynosure

Phegonte

Stades Pythiques.
5 10 15 20

Stades Olympiques.
5 10 15 20

Toises de France.
500 1000 1500 2000

Myriamètre.
1000 2000 3000 4000 5000 6000 7000 8000 9000 10000 Mètres

Pl. 2.

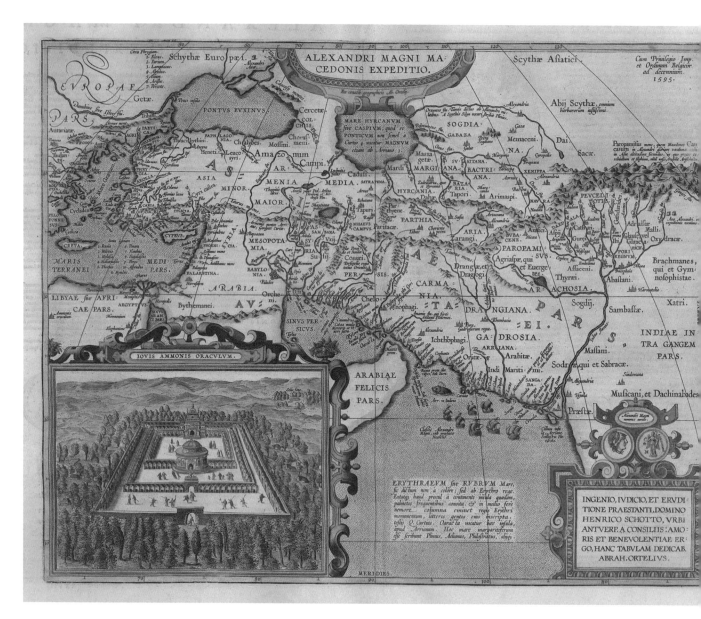

ALEXANDRI MAGNI MA
CEDONIS EXPEDITIO.

Ex conatu geographicis Abr. Ortelij.

Cum Privilegio Imp.
et Ordinum Belgicor.
ad decennium.
1595.

IOVIS AMMONIS ORACVLVM.

ERYTHRAEVM five RVBRVM Mare,
fic dictum non à colore; fed ab Erythro rege.
Extatq; haud procul à continenti inula quandam,
palmetis frequentibus confita, & in medio feré
nemore columna eminet regis Erythri
monumentum, litteris gentis eius inscripta.
teftis Q. Curtius. Darie ca uocatur hec infula,
apud Arrianum. Hoc mare in/exparitiferum
effe feribunt Plinius, Aelianus, Philoftratus, atqui

INGENIO, IVDICIO, ET ERVDI
TIONE PRAESTANTI, DOMINO
HENRICO SCHOTTO, VRBI
ANTVERP. A CONSILIIS: AMO
RIS ET BENEVOLENTIAE ER
GO, HANC TABVLAM DEDICAB.
ABRAH. ORTELIVS.

Battle of Gaugamela

The intricate hand-coloured map shows the Persian Empire into which Alexander the Great, King of Macedon, burst in 334BC at the start of an astonishing four-year campaign in which he overwhelmed the Persian Achaemenids, one of the ancient world's mightiest empires. The map was drawn by the Flemish cartographer Abraham Ortelius, whose *Theatrum Orbis Terrarum* ("Theatre of the World"), first published in 1570, was the first real modern atlas. Over time, Ortelius added the *Parergon*, a supplement to the atlas containing historical maps and including this one of Alexander's expedition, which dates from 1595.

Although the resources Alexander commanded were vastly outweighed by those of Darius III, the Persian king of kings, he was able to draw on the experience of the Macedonian infantry phalanx, armed with the 20-foot-long *sarissa*, an extended version of the traditional Greek hoplite pike. Projecting forward from the front of a formation eight or sixteen ranks deep, it created a lethal barrier which was next to impossible to break into. Combined with this, the heavy Macedonian cavalry gave Alexander's men a mobility which the tactical genius of their commander exploited to full effect to outmanoeuvre his numerically superior Persian foes.

Having defeated the local Persian satraps at Granicus in western Asia Minor, Alexander then advanced slowly eastwards, finally encountering Darius at Issus on a narrow plain in northern Syria (shown on the map between the Taurus Mountains and the Mediterranean Sea). The next two years were spent mopping up and asserting Macedonian control of the Levant and of Egypt, where Alexander visited the oracle of the god Ammon in the desert oasis of Siwa, the site illustrated by Ortelius in the southwest corner of the map: the audience with the priests there left a lasting impression on the Macedonian conqueror, giving him the belief that if he was not a god himself, his victories were divinely ordained.

By the summer of 331BC, Darius had replenished his army, while Alexander was on the march eastwards, crossing the Euphrates river and then the Tigris as he pushed into the heart of the Achaemenid Empire. Harrying attacks by the Persians forced Alexander north towards Arbela (now Arbil in Iraq), where Darius's host was arrayed around a hill called Gaugamela ("the hump of the camel"). The two armies remained within striking distance of each other for ten days while a series of fruitless embassies passed back and forth between them. Only on October 1 did Alexander attack, sending forward his army in an oblique line to confuse Darius. On the right his heavy cavalry sucked Darius's Bactrian and Scythian horses forward, opening a gap in the centre through which the Macedonian phalanx crashed, while on the left Alexander's most trusted lieutenant Parmenion held off a concentrated Persian attack.

As the thud of the sarissa shafts against the phalangists' shields spooked the enemy horses, the sheer momentum of Alexander's infantry assault penetrated deep into the Persian line. Darius, fearing capture, fled, followed by thousands of his men. The battle might almost have swung the other way, as Alexander's advance, coupled with reinforcements sent to aid the hard-pressed Parmenion, had opened up a gap in the Macedonian ranks through which thousands of Persian cavalry surged. Had they swung around and attacked Alexander from the rear, rather than plundering the Macedonian camp, then Darius's cause might have been saved. Instead, while the rest of the Persian army crumbled, Mazaeus, the commander facing Parmenion, fought bravely on, probably thinking he was winning, until Alexander's main force arrived and it became clear the king of kings had fled. Then he too retired.

The defeat was crushing. As well as those killed on the battlefield, thousands more Persians and their allies were cut down as they fled. Darius lost as many as 40,000 men from his original complement of over 200,000, while Alexander's casualties were as little as 1,000, from an army a fifth the size of that of Darius. Although the Persian ruler fought on, his authority was shattered, and in July the following year he was murdered by Bessus, the satrap of Bactria, who had fought by his side at Gaugamela and who now claimed his throne. It was a short-lived reign, however, for by the next year Alexander had killed Bessus too and, despite some resistance in the east, was generally acknowledged as the king of kings. It had been an arduous journey from the first crossing of the Hellespont into Asia Minor, but Gaugamela had proved the climax of the campaign which Ortelius so colourfully documents.

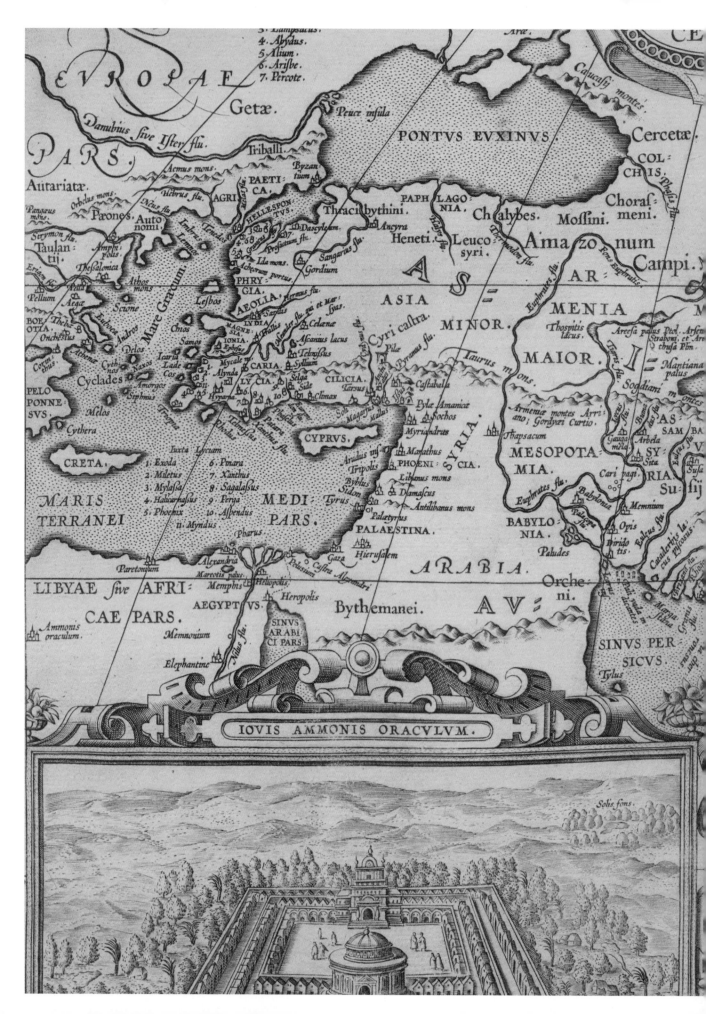

IOVIS AMMONIS ORACVLVM.

Qin Wars of Unification

The Chinese state achieved a level of sophistication and maintained a sizeable centralised bureaucracy with few equals in the ancient world. Its conduct of war and its use of cartography show its parallel abilities to marshal forces on a huge scale and yet to pay attention to the smallest details in defending its domains.

The map, found in a lacquer box inside the tomb of a noble – possibly a general of royal descent – was unearthed during excavations at Mawangdui in China's southeastern Hunan province. It dates from around 168BC, during the early years of the Han dynasty, when Chinese unity was scarcely half a century old. Two other maps found with it covered general topographical and administrative divisions in the Kingdom of Changsha, a sub-fiefdom of the Han Empire, but this one, known as the "garrison map", is different. It shows the border with the southern tributary kingdom of Nanyue, a flashpoint for the Han dynasty under which it was compiled. Around 39 inches by 30 inches in extent, it is a virtuoso piece of compilation, drawn up originally in three colours, and with symbols for military posts (25 of them, nine on strategic mountaintops) and information on the number of households in each village and whether the local population was loyal or likely to be hostile. It also marks non-Chinese indigenous groups (indicated by the term *pu* for chieftain). Settlements and military posts are coloured in red or black on the original of the map. There are even symbols for watchtowers where messages were passed by smoke signals, an underground tunnel and the location of the main army units (including the three frontline armies of General Hsu along the border). The map, in short, provided everything that the emperor and his senior advisers needed in determining how to defend this troubled frontier region.

The Han maps form part of a long-established tradition (of which these are among the oldest survivors, after a set of 4th-century BC maps from the Qin kingdom) which dates back at least to the Western Zhou dynasty (1041–771BC), who maintained two separate cartographic bureaus. When Zhou rule collapsed, China gradually dissolved into a patchwork of feuding statelets in the Spring and Autumn Period (770–476BC) and the even more chaotic Warring States Period (476–221BC), during which it has been calculated there were no fewer than 358 separate wars between the rival Chinese kingdoms.

These armies could be huge, mobilising vast reservoirs of manpower, with infantry at their core – heavy infantry armed with halberds, spears and axes and lighter (but probably deadlier) crossbowmen flanking them, supported by more mobile troops, at first chariot-borne, but by the 5th century BC largely on horseback. China's many wars during the period yielded a significant corpus of writing – one which can be paralleled in the ancient world really only from the Roman Empire. These include most notably Sunzi's *The Art of War*, a complete manual for the aspirant general, most likely composed around the 6th century BC, which counsels the selective use of force, ensuring the enemy is weakened before striking, and champions the power of deception.

The bloodiest clashes occurred in the linked series of wars in which Ying Zheng, the king of Qin, defeated the remaining Chinese states (by then reduced to six) between 230 and 221BC. Cunningly, he allied with states further away from Qin to defeat his nearest neighbours, beginning by swallowing up Han in 230BC. Zhao fell next, despite stout resistance by its capable military commander, Li Mu.

By now, with Qin armies reaching as large as 600,000 men, the surviving states were seriously alarmed and resorted to less conventional means to defeat Ying Zheng. Knowing of the Qin ruler's intense interest in maps as an aid to his conquests, the king of Yan, which was next in line for a Qin invasion, sent an agent, Jing Ke, who pretended to be a turncoat. He only gained an audience by claiming to be bringing a map of strategic installations in the Yan kingdom, but wrapped in it he had concealed a knife. The assassination attempt failed, and Ying Zheng used it as an excuse to send an army against Yan. Wei and Chu fell next, which left only Qi, in the far north.

In 221BC Ying Zheng conquered that too, and now the master of all China, he declared himself Qin Shi Huangdi, the First Emperor and founder of the first dynasty to rule a united country. As he and his successor in the Han dynasty realised, detailed knowledge of strategic regions had played a great role in his victories, and maps had been key to acquiring this. Maps had made an empire.

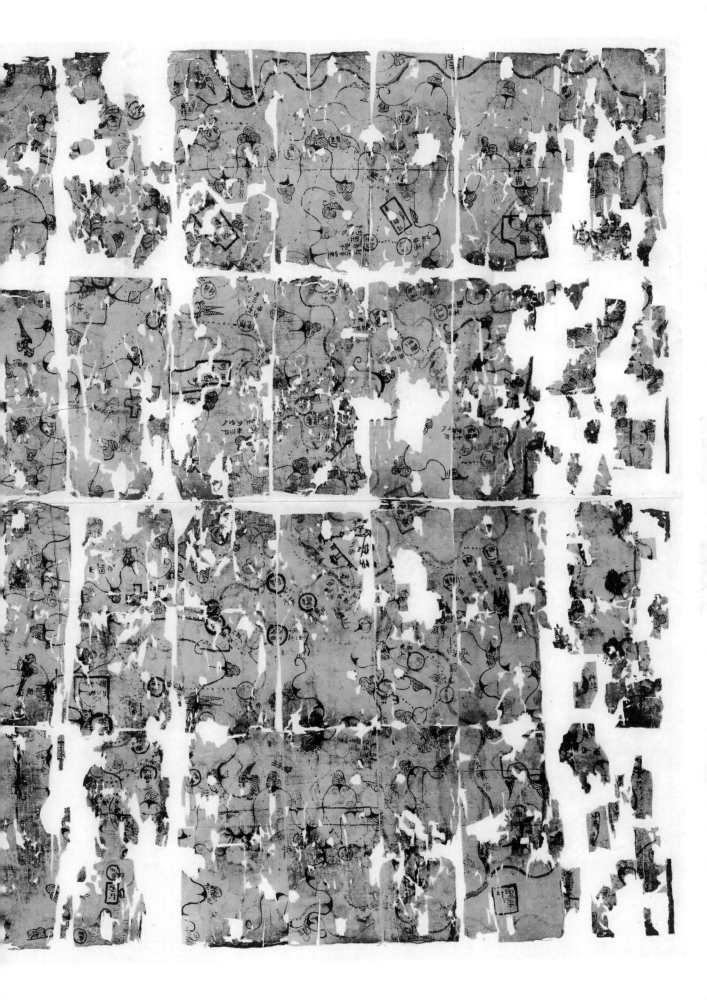

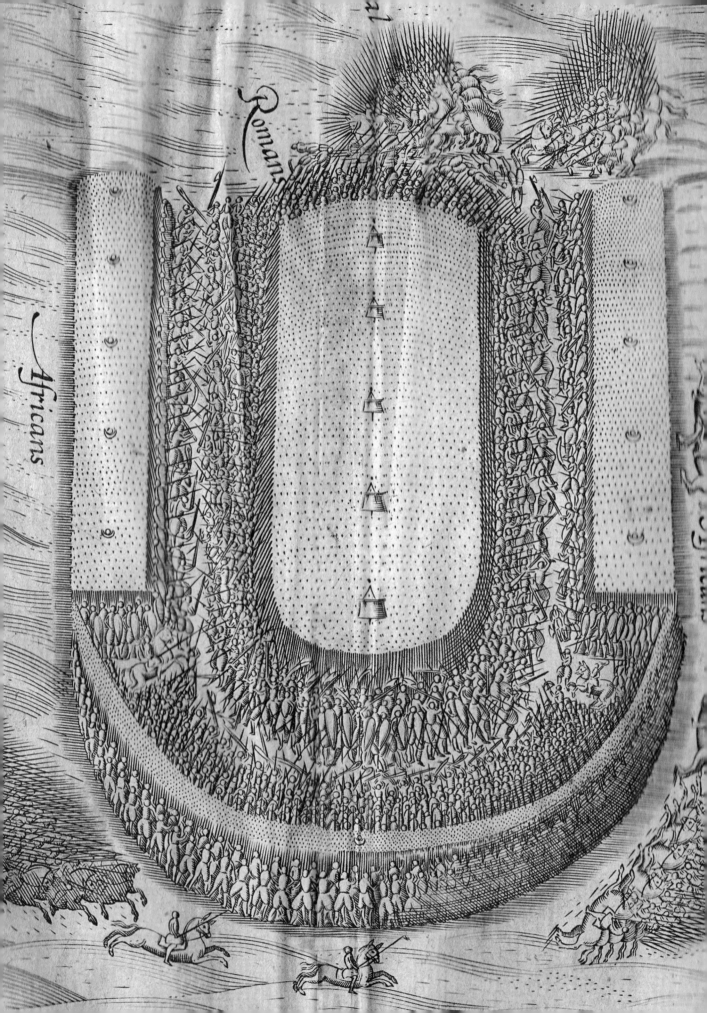

Romans

Africans

Battle of Cannae

Rome's history seems a tireless ascent to greatness, its legions' triumphs punctuated only by occasional bouts of internecine warfare until, after a thousand years, a tired empire succumbed to an irresistible tide of barbarian invaders. Yet it was not always so. The 18th-century map by the Carmarthen cartographer Emanuel Bowen – whose other notable works include *Britannia Depicta*, one of the first portable road atlases of Britain – shows the scene of Rome's greatest military disaster, which almost accelerated the fall of its empire by seven centuries.

The troops at the base of the U-shaped mass of soldiers are Carthaginians, from the army which Hannibal had led over the Alps in 218BC, achieving a feat which none had thought possible and which caught the Romans unawares. Conflict between Rome and Carthage, a city in modern Tunisia, had brewed for two decades since the First Punic War between the two cities ended in 241BC with a partial victory for the Romans. The Carthaginian recovery, by dint of building a new empire in Spain, made a new clash almost inevitable, and by the summer of 217BC the Romans were smarting from defeats at Hannibal's hands in battles at Trebia and Lake Trasimene.

Tapping their almost inexhaustible will to recruit fresh troops until their opponents wearied of war, the Romans doubled down by raising eight legions (rather than the customary four) for the campaign season of 216BC. Leading them would be that year's consuls, the veteran Lucius Aemilius Paulus and the inexperienced Gaius Terentius Varro. Commanding between them 80,000 men (including cavalry and skirmishers), they would have been confident of victory against an enemy on whom months in the field would have taken their toll.

By now, having turned aside from a direct assault on Rome, Hannibal was campaigning in southern Italy, and in early June he crossed over the Aufidus river (in modern Puglia), halting near the small town of Cannae. There, he waited for the Romans to make the long, hot, dusty march southwards to meet him. By late July they had arrived, but the first few days were an awkward dance of march and countermarch as the Roman system of alternating command daily between the two consuls caused confusion as to their tactics. This allowed Hannibal to station his 40,000 troops facing north and in command of the critical water source of the Aufidus, while the Romans were forced to face south into the scorching heat of the libeccio wind, their advance constricted by a narrow valley.

Roman armies during the middle Republican period fought in maniples, a modified form of phalanx, with the least experienced troops, the *hastati*, in the front ranks, the more seasoned soldiers, the *principes*, in the next line, and the veteran *triarii* at the back, only to be committed at times of crisis. Cavalry were stationed on the wings. Hannibal placed his least experienced troops, the Gaulish and Spanish infantry in the centre, with the more effective Libyans flanking them and his cavalry also on the wings.

After initial inconclusive fighting by light skirmishers, the Carthaginian left-wing cavalry engaged the Romans, eventually driving the Roman horses from the field. By then, however, the main battle had begun, the Roman maniples pushing hard against Hannibal's Gauls. The Carthaginian line buckled and bent inwards, just as Hannibal knew it would, and the Romans were sucked into a trap. Surging forward in a compacted mass, they found the Libyan infantry folding in onto their flanks and then the Carthaginian cavalry sealed the rear. Pressed against each other, the Romans could barely move, let alone pivot to face the attack from behind. Grim hours followed as the Carthaginians methodically cut down their trapped opponents. Few Romans escaped the sea of blood inside which they were sealed. Varro had been with the cavalry and got away with around 370 of his command, while about 3,000 infantry evaded the envelopment. The Roman historian Livy calculated the Romans losses at 70,000 dead, which would make it the worst loss suffered by any army in a single day in military history.

Hannibal was utterly triumphant, the Roman Senate dejected and fearful. Yet Hannibal demurred from marching on Rome, and a new Roman strategy of prolonged defensive manoeuvres marshalled by Quintus Fabius Maximus Verrucosus, nicknamed "Cunctator" (the delayer), gave them time to rebuild their forces and, 14 years after Cannae, inflict a final defeat on Hannibal at Zama in North Africa, which brought an end to the Second Punic War. Hannibal himself fled and died in exile in Bithynia in 183BC, his fame long outlasting his achievements. For Emanuel Bowen, there was an even sadder end. Cartography had not brought him riches, and in 1767 he died in abject poverty. Only the fineness of his map-making ensured his posthumous renown.

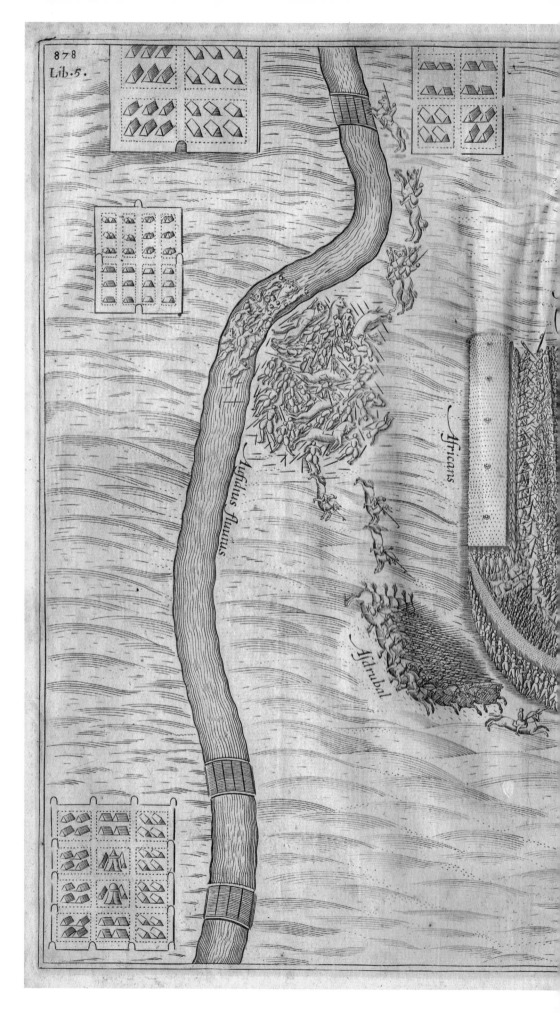

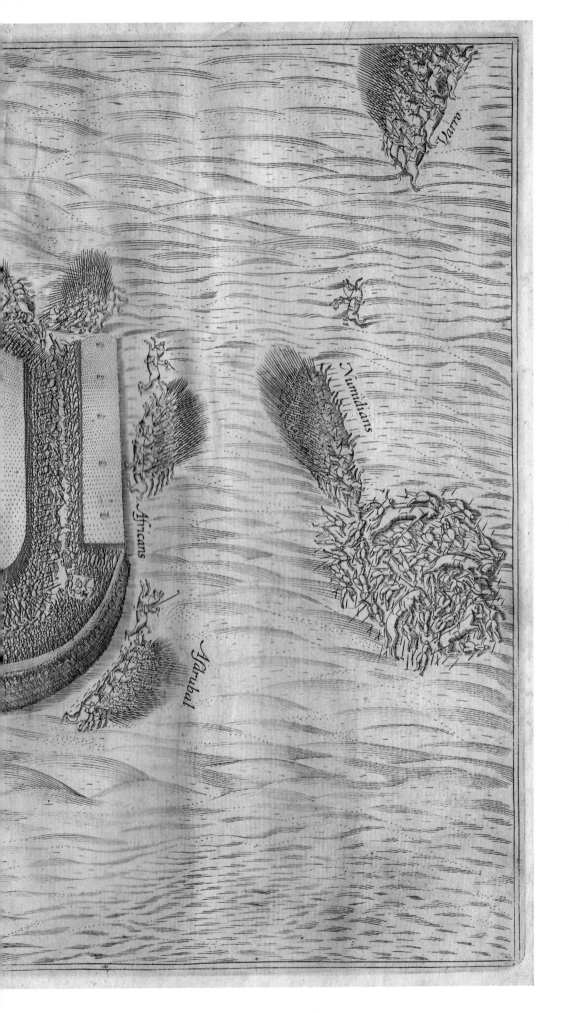

Battle of Actium

The Roman navy always played second fiddle to its far more formidable land-based legions, enjoying a brief burst of glory during the Punic Wars against Carthage (see page 25) in the 3rd and 2nd centuries BC, but then, as Rome faced little significant maritime threat in the Mediterranean, subsiding to the status of anti-piracy squadrons and troop transports. The greatest danger to Rome's growing might came to be civil strife, and in particular the devastating civil wars which erupted in the mid-1st century BC. In the culminating battle of these, the two fleets which faced off at Actium off the west coast of Greece are shown on the map by the French cartographer Jean-Baptiste Bourguignon d'Anville. Something of a prodigy, he composed his first historical map of Greece at the age of 15, and with the patronage of the influential Duke of Orléans, ended up as geography tutor to King Louis XV.

The encounter in the summer of 31BC, illustrated by the map, decided the fate of the entire Roman world. That world had dissolved into chaos after the assassination of Julius Caesar in 44BC, as his killers, led by Brutus and Cassius, fought to restore the Republic in a brutal civil war against the dead dictator's allies Octavian and Mark Antony. Although victorious, relations between Antony and Octavian worsened from testy to downright hostile amid accusations that Antony intended to gift several Roman provinces in the east to his mistress, Cleopatra VII of Egypt. While Antony gathered an army of 19 legions and dispatched them to Greece, together with a fleet of 170 ships that were reinforced by Cleopatra and an Egyptian contingent, Octavian raised a counterforce to prevent Antony from crossing over to Italy.

Antony's host and flotilla tarried too long at their base near Corcyra (on Corfu), which allowed Octavian's general, Agrippa, to seize key positions and blockade the enemy legions near Nikopolis and to choke off Antony's fleet's escape route from the Gulf of Ambracia (his fleet shown to the east on this map of the battle). Concerned by growing defections from his army, Antony finally decided he had no choice but to break out, abandon the invasion of Italy and consolidate his position in the eastern provinces.

Antony burnt those of his ships he had insufficient sailors and marines to man, which left him with mostly heavy hexaremes ("sixes") and ennereis ("nines") whose larger number of rowers were needed to propel their massive bulk. Just after dawn on September 1, the fleet advanced, with Antony on the right and Cleopatra's squadron at the rear. Sea battles in the Hellenistic and Roman worlds commonly degenerated into a miniature version of land fighting, with the ships used as troop platforms, as archers and slingsmen issued volleys of projectiles, some of them combustible, and ships tried to ram each other, either to sink the opponent or to allow the troops they carried to board the opponent's crippled vessels.

Antony had ordered his ships to carry sails, always intending to use them to make a rapid escape once clear of Agrippa's fleet. But he had miscalculated: Agrippa extended to stop Antony's ships from escaping around his flanks, and Antony's heavier ships found themselves outmanoeuvred and surrounded by Agrippa's lighter vessels, which pummelled them with missile fire. Then, at a critical moment, Cleopatra's squadron slipped through a gap in the line, escaping into open water beyond the bay. Now heavily outnumbered and with many of his ships badly damaged or sunk, Antony transferred to a small, fast vessel and joined Cleopatra in her flight to Egypt.

Although Antony had extracted around a third of his fleet and avoided capture, the sight of their commander and his mistress abandoning them did nothing for the morale of Antony's legions, still besieged by Agrippa's army. Their general, Publius Canidius Crassus, rapidly negotiated a surrender and Antony's legions in Syria and Cyrenaica (in northern Africa) also disbanded. So, although both Antony and Cleopatra reached Egypt safely, by the time Octavian's pursuing force reached there in the summer of 30BC, he faced virtually no opposition. After a failed attempt by Antony to escape to India, both he and Cleopatra took their own lives. Thanks to Actium and its aftermath, Octavian was now master of Rome and within three years would be elevated to the status of its first emperor.

Roman fleets continued to operate, and with a strong force based at Ravenna providing the spine of imperial Rome's naval muscle, the *Classis Britannica* ("Fleet of Britain") patrolling the Channel and smaller contingents enhancing security along the Rhine and Danube frontiers, there would not be another naval encounter in the Mediterranean to match Actium for over a thousand years.

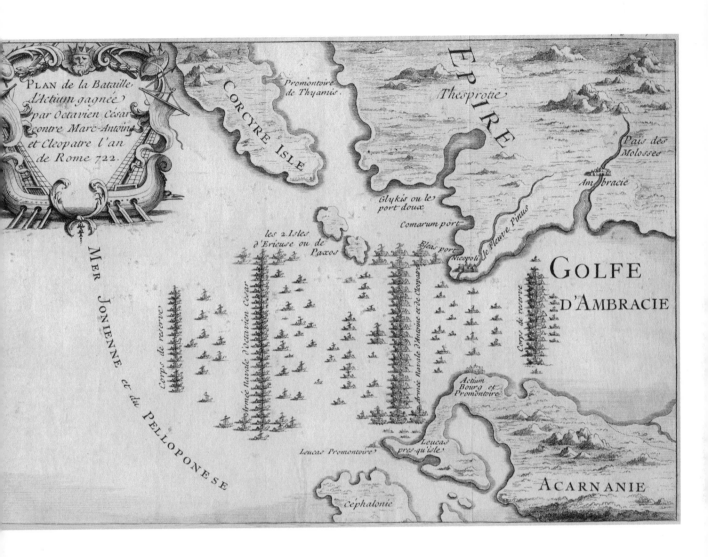

PLAN de la Bataille
d'Actium gagnée
par Octavien César
contre Marc-Antoine
et Cleopatre l'an
de Rome 722.

EPIRE

CORCYRE ISLE

Promontoire
de Thyamis.

Thesprotie

Pais des
Molosses

Ambracie

Glykis ou le
port doux

Comarum port

les 2.Isles
d'Ericuse ou de
Paxos

Efeas port

Nicopoli le Fleuve Pinus

GOLFE
D'AMBRACIE

MER JONIENNE et du PELLOPONESE

Corps de reserve

Armée Navale d'Octavien Cesar

Armée Navale d'Antoine et de Cleopatre

Corps de reserve

Actium
Bourg et
Promontoire

Leucas
pres-qu'isle

Leucas Promontoire

Cephalonie

ACARNANIE

VISIGOTHS
powerful under Alawarick, retreat
before the Huns 36 under Alavivus
and Fritigern.

After Attila's death in
the Pannonian Village
his kingdom ends

GEPIDÆ. 460. 567.
The Kingdom founded by Arda-
rick, overthrown by Kunimund
the Lombard.

Danube

OSTROGOTHS. 455. 553.
Found a powerful kingdom in
Italy, under Tejas, are subdued
by Narses.

Adrianople 378
Visigoth
Valens

BLACK

Constantinople

Dnieper

powerful und
thrown by the
Asia, and

The Hic
after t
93. N
and
as

Consenza
Alarick 410 Ataulph,
his successor pa
through France into
Spain.

Corinth

AN

SEA

Battle of Adrianople

By the mid-4th century, Rome had endured for over a thousand years since the traditional date of its foundation in 753BC, and, despite its many trials – plague, civil war and the insistent pressing of barbarian tribes against its frontiers – the poets and panegyrists who praised its emperors confidently expected it would last another millennium still. Yet the map shows differently; the former frontiers of the empire are festooned with labels showing the progress of a host of invaders: Huns, Ostrogoths, Visigoths, Franks, Vandals and Alans, as they dismembered the empire and set up their own kingdoms on its former territory.

The map, created by British lithographers Day & Haghe, illustrates an edition of *The History of the Decline and Fall of the Roman Empire* by the great 18th-century historian Edward Gibbon. His confident assertion that "If a man were called to fix the period in the history of the world, during which the condition of the human race was most happy and prosperous, he would, without hesitation, name that which elapsed from the death of Domitian [AD96] to the accession of Commodus [AD180]" led subsequent generations rather unfairly to regard the next two centuries of the Roman Empire as an uninteresting stub.

By 376, the empire did face serious new challenges. The migration of the Huns, a nomadic group with a reputation for ferocious savagery, had driven other groups – Goths, Alans and Vandals – westwards towards the Rhine and Danube frontiers of the empire. Groups of Goths began trickling over the Danube into the Balkan provinces of the empire, which by now was ruled over by two emperors, one for the east, and one in the west, in acknowledgement of the impossible task of a single man ruling its enormous extent. The Roman army too had changed. The 5,000-strong legions, bolstered by smaller non-citizen auxiliary units, had been replaced by a more flexible organisation. Along the frontier, fixed garrisons of less well-equipped *limitanei* (or border troops) were supplemented by an elite field force of *comitatenses*, whose units were smaller than the old legions, more diverse, and included an increasing number of Germanic auxiliaries.

The Roman commander on the frontier, Lupicinus, had taken advantage of the situation by mistreating the Goths as they crossed, extracting bribes from those he allowed through and stranding others without food. Finally, large numbers of Goths broke through: the Tervingi, led by Fritigern, and a rival group, the Greuthingi under Alatheus and Saphrax. For the next two years they rampaged through Thrace (now part of Bulgaria, Greece and Turkey), at times coming uncomfortably close to the Byzantine capital of Constantinople and attracting defectors from Goths enlisted in the Roman army.

In the summer of 378, the eastern emperor Valens called for help from his western colleague Gratian and set out to meet the Goths. On hearing that the Goths were encamped near Adrianople (present-day Edirne in northwest Turkey), he chose to cut them off, judging his force of around 20,000 sufficient without waiting for Gratian, who was just a week's march away.

The forced march had tired the Roman troops, but when they arrived close to the enemy camp on August 9, they found far fewer Goths than they had expected. Fritigern seemed to have only about 10,000 warriors, roughly half the number Valens commanded. This was because Alatheus and Saphrax were out conducting a raid with the bulk of the Gothic cavalry, so Fritigern stalled, pretending to negotiate a settlement and setting light to the dry grass on the plain around Adrianople to add further discomfort to the Roman troops' march-weary legs.

Valens's patience snapped and he ordered a general advance, but the first units, of the Imperial Guard, were held by the Goths drawn up inside a protective line of waggons. Then, as the Roman left wing surged forward ahead of the rest, they came crashing into Alatheus and Saphrax's returning Gothic cavalry. The Romans were surrounded and cut down in their thousands. Only a small force escaped (which did, though, include the senior Roman general Richomeres), leaving their emperor, Valens, dead on the field.

The loss of the eastern empire's main field army left it horribly exposed to further Gothic predation. Adrianople was said to be Rome's greatest disaster since Cannae but, despite the predictions of doomsayers, it did not turn out to be the empire's funeral pyre. It was to be the western part of the empire that buckled first, its provinces overrun one by one by the barbarian groups displayed on the map (see overleaf). The east, in contrast, rebuilt after Adrianople, its provinces in Egypt, Syria and Asia Minor largely shielded from barbarian attacks. It would, in truth, last for another thousand years, just as the poets had predicted.

BRITISH MUSEUM

376. HUNS advance from inner Asia to the Volga, and cause by their invasion of the Alans and Goths the Great Migration. After 434, Attila, the scourge of God, unites the scattered hordes, and leads them to Chalons 451 and against Rome 452. The Kingdom ends with his death. 454.

Wolga

Kama

SEA

G O T H S about 200 after Chr.

Tanais

G O T H S already powerful 215 in the reign of Caracalla and 273 and are divided somewhat later into Visigoths and Ostrogoths, West and East Goths.

ALANS driven before the Huns enter Pannonia & unite themselves to Radagasus

Jaik or Ural

OSTROGOTHS powerful under Hermanric 350 overthrown by the Huns 376 pass into Thracia and Asia Minor

Wolga

VISIGOTHS powerful under Alamrick retreat before the Huns 376 under Alavivus and Fritigern

Attila's death... ...onian Kings... ...an ende

Don

SEA CASPIAN

DE 460. 507... ...m founded by Auda... ...wn by Runimund

Danube

Dniester

G O T H S ...some supposed to be their original abode

...THS. 455. 555. ...ful kingdom in ...as. are subdued

Adrianople 378 *Visigoths Valens*

B L A C K S E A

Constantinople

Cyrus u. Kur

Araxes

HIONG NU The Hiong Nu (according to Desguignes & Gibbon) after the loss of their kingdom in China B.C. 207. 93. A.C. move in two divisions as the Enthalites and Hajathalites South West over the Oxus, as Huns North West over the Volga.

...sa ...10 Ataulph. ...cessor pr... ...in France...

Korath

Tigris

Euphrates

SEA

Damascus residence of the First Caliphs. 762.

Bagdad founded by the... ...ur residence of the ...sword Caliphs. 762. 1258.

Cairo founded 970

ARABIANS under Mohammed † 632. conquer the World, Abubekr 632. Omar 644, Othman 655. Ali 660.

Battle of Hastings

It was the last hurrah of the Vikings – or at least of their Norman descendants – who had terrorised northwestern Europe for over two centuries, of the Anglo-Saxon kingdoms which had dominated southern Britain for twice as long and of a style of warfare which characterised them both. The Battle of Hastings (or Senlac, as it is called on Edward A Freeman's finely drawn map, printed in 1869 for the third volume in his *The History of the Norman Conquest of England: Its Causes and Its Results*) was one of the greatest turning points in English history.

The English host, led by King Harold Godwinson, defended long and hard that day in October 1066 against a Norman army under Duke William, whose invasion a fortnight earlier had been in pursuit of a claim to the throne that the Anglo-Saxon ruler vigorously disputed. As the great-nephew of Emma, the wife of King Aethelred the Unready of Wessex, William had a tenuous claim by blood. More importantly, he swore that he had been promised the throne by Edward the Confessor (who had spent his youth in exile in Normandy) and by Harold Godwinson himself, who spent time at William's court in 1065 as a guest-cum-captive after being shipwrecked off the northern French coast.

After Edward's death in January 1066, William was furious when the English nobles chose Harold as their next king. His hopes of the English crown seemed irretrievably dashed when another rival claimant, Harald Hardrada of Norway, landed near York in the summer, defeated the English militia sent against him and seemed set to snatch the prize. Yet Harold made a forced march to meet him and scattered the surprised Viking host, killing both Hardrada and his own traitorous brother Tostig, who had joined forces with the Norwegian king.

Almost immediately, news reached Harold Godwinson that a Norman fleet had disembarked over 7,000 invaders, and he was forced to make a week-long forced march back down south to meet William. As a result his men, largely composed of the *fyrd*, the Anglo-Saxon levy, reinforced by

a central core of *huscarls*, or elite bodyguards, were weary. After a fitful night's rest they drew up atop the thousand-yard-long ridge of Senlac Hill, north of Hastings, forming themselves into a shield wall. Their long kite-shaped shields, bristling with spears, formed a formidable barrier to any Normans who made it up the slope. Along the line too, some huscarls were armed with large axes for close-quarter combat and the richer ones with protective suits of mail armour.

The Normans were not so differently attired from their Anglo-Saxon foes, though William's force had a larger contingent of cavalry and archers, both of which would prove decisive in the later stages of the battle. At first the volleys which William ordered his archers to unleash and fitful infantry charges up the slope made little impact on the shield wall. Then a contingent of Bretons on William's left flank broke and fled, provoking a section of Harold's army to set out in pursuit, where they were cut down when the Normans rallied. Seeing this, William ordered a series of feigned retreats which further thinned the ranks of the shield wall as elements of Harold's army fell into the trap. Final victory, though, was gifted by the archers, who unleashed a further storm of arrows, one of which seems to have struck Harold in the face, inflicting a wound which, if not mortal, removed him from the battle line and caused the Anglo-Saxons to waver, break and flee. As was the way with many medieval battles, the mass of casualties was inflicted as the English sought to escape, cut down by pursuing Norman knights.

The Witan, the Anglo-Saxon royal council, tried to offer the throne to Edgar Aetheling, a distant relative of Edward, but he was too young and commanded little support. So the English nobles and churchmen one by one submitted to William, and by Christmas Day he had been crowned king. He brought not only a new dynasty to England, but new ways of ruling – with the construction of wooden and then stone castles to cement his control – and of warfare, as well-born cavalry became the core and shock troops of the royal army for the next 200 years.

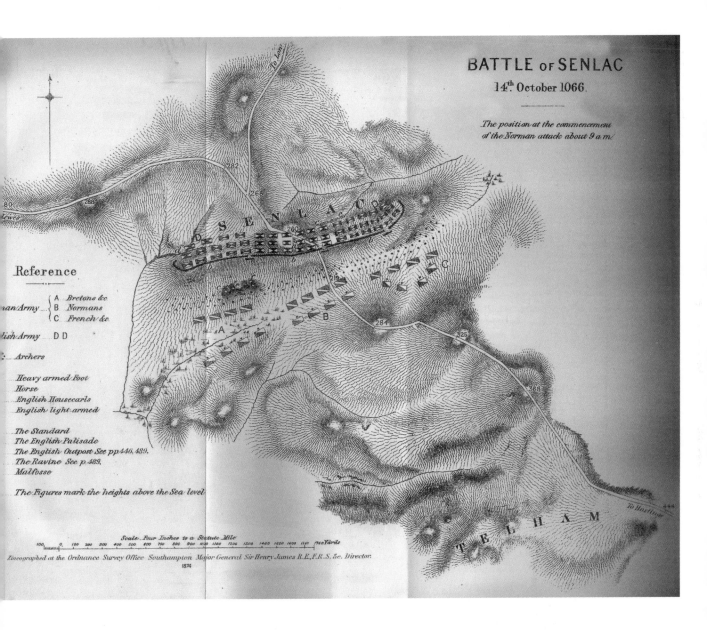

BATTLE of SENLAC
14th October 1066.

*The position at the commencement
of the Norman attack about 9 a.m.*

Reference

Norman Army {
A. *Bretons &c.*
B. *Normans*
C. *French &c.*
}

English Army D D

Archers

Heavy armed Foot
Horse
English Housecarls
English light armed

The Standard
The English Palisade
The English Outpost See pp.446, 489.
The Ravine See p. 489.
Malfosse

The Figures mark the heights above the Sea level

Scale Four Inches to a Statute Mile
100   0   100 200 300 400 500 600 700 800 900 1000 1100 1200 1300 1400 1500 1600 110 1760 Yards

Zincographed at the Ordnance Survey Office Southampton Major General Sir Henry James R.E., F.R.S. &c. Director.
1874

SENLAC

TELHAM

To London

To Hastings

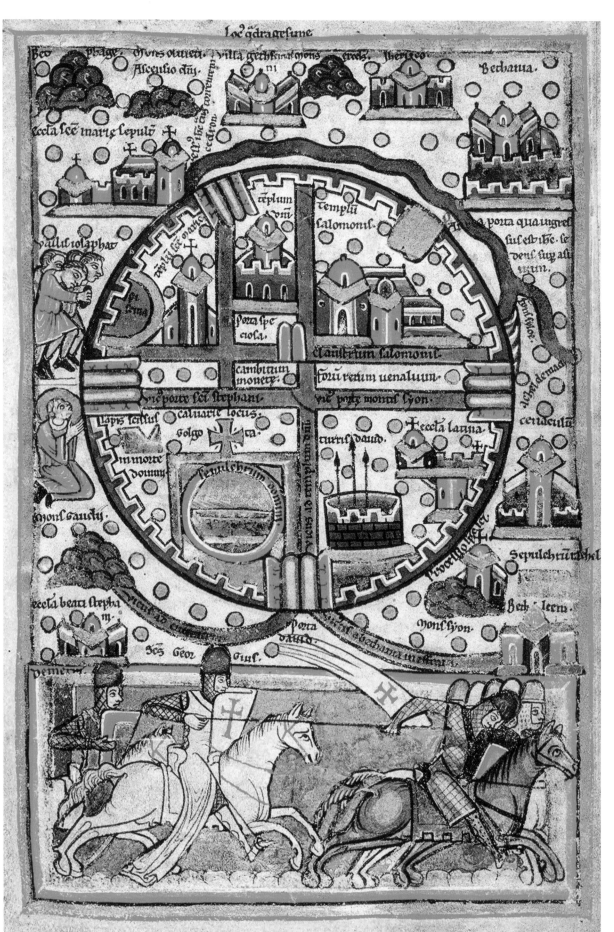

Siege of Jerusalem

The map is a stylised image of Jerusalem, its status as a Holy City for Christendom underlined by the sacred sites it shows, such as the Holy Sepulchre, topped by a cross and enclosing the sarcophagus said to have contained the body of Christ. Yet at the foot of this page from a late 12th-century psalter another side of piety is presented as the soldier-saints St George and St Demetrios, attired as medieval knights, help their side win a victory against a Muslim foe.

The capture of Jerusalem was the primary object of the First Crusade, an armed pilgrimage assembled to seize the city from the Muslim rulers who had controlled it for over four centuries and who had latterly made life difficult for Christian pilgrims visiting the holy places. It was, though, the appeal of the Byzantine emperor Alexios Komnenos in 1095 for western assistance against the Seljuk Turks pressing against his borders that prompted Pope Urban to preach the crusade, promising a remission of sins for any who took up the cause.

Thousands of knights led by Godfrey of Bouillon, Count Raymond of Toulouse and the Norman warlord Bohemond Guiscard responded, swearing a crusader oath and heading towards Constantinople, preceded by an untrained, humbler rabble whose "People's Crusade" was cut to pieces almost the moment it entered Seljuk territory. The main crusader force, sent rapidly on its way by Alexios, fearful they might attack his city, was forced into a six-month-long trek across Asia Minor. The heavily armoured knights, the shock troops of the age, were unbeatable if they charged a static enemy, the impact of their couched lances almost impossible to withstand, but the Seljuks were nimble, largely avoided pitched battles and harried outlying contingents of crusaders all the way.

Most of the crusade was therefore taken up with sieges. The crusaders' leaders were experienced with these, but transporting siege engines was laborious and constructing them on site required hard-to-locate materials, and the logistics of encircling a well-fortified town often taxed the attackers more than it did the defenders. A protracted siege of Antioch from October 1097 to June 1098 almost broke the crusaders' spirit; only the fortuitous discovery of the holy lance said to have pierced Christ's side at the crucifixion and the alleged miraculous intervention of St George (shown on the map) inspired them to a final effort, which took the city.

The crusaders were forced into yet more gruelling sieges as they fought their way down the coast towards Jerusalem. The need to leave garrisons in newly captured towns such as Tortosa in Syria meant it was a depleted and demoralised force that arrived at Jerusalem on June 7, 1099. Its Fatimid governor Iftikhar ad-Daula had only 400 cavalry and a few thousand infantry to defend its extensive walls, but the 11,000-strong crusader army struggled to encircle the city or feed itself, and a lack of timber to build siege engines or ladders hampered attempts to break down or storm the walls. Only the lucky arrival of six Genoese galleys at Jaffa, two of which were dismantled to build massive siege towers, offered a solution. The leviathans, packed with crusaders, were laboriously hauled towards the walls and, though attacks on July 13 and 14 failed, the next day Godfrey of Bouillon's tower reached the northeastern fortifications of Jerusalem near the Damascus Gate, spitting out Greek fire (an early form of napalm) and crossbow bolts as the defenders were blinded by a change in wind that sent choking smoke in their direction.

The crusaders forced their way onto the walls and soon thousands of their comrades were pouring into the city, subduing last-ditch resistance at the Al-Aqsa Mosque and Tower of David, and slaughtering thousands of innocent civilians, hardly discriminating between Muslims and local Christians. Once the massacre was over and those of the Fatimid defenders who had been spared – including Iftikhar ad-Daula – had been expelled, the crusaders began reshaping the city, building new churches and lavish monuments over Christian holy places. They elected Godfrey of Bouillon as the ruler of a new Kingdom of Jerusalem, one of four crusader states (along with Edessa, Antioch and Tripoli) that would maintain a crusader presence in Palestine in some form until its very last stronghold, Acre, was taken in 1291.

Battle of Crécy

The compressed French battle lines, hemmed in by a dense mesh of contours, are a clue to how their superior numbers lost one of the defining battles of the Hundred Years' War, a prolonged conflict between France and England for the right to the French crown.

Compiled by Samuel Rawson Gardiner, a scholar better known for his work on constitutional history and the English Civil War, it appeared in his 1907 *School Atlas of English History*, ironically three years after the two countries finally patched up their centuries-old enmity in the Entente Cordiale alliance aimed against Germany.

The conflict had its roots in the bitterness of the English monarchs at the loss of their last possessions in France in 1214 under the disastrous stewardship of King John. When Charles IV of France died in 1328 with no male heir, Edward III of England tried to assert a claim to the French throne through his mother Isabella. The French nobility rejected his claim, which ultimately led Edward to invade northern France in 1337 and began a war which would stutter on, with long breaks, until 1453.

Most of the fighting was in the form of *chevauchées* – extended raids in search of plunder and to prise loose the control of opponents over their territory by destroying its security – and pitched battles were relatively rare. When Edward invaded again in 1346, he expected little opposition, landing at La Hogue in Normandy on July 12 and sacking Caen two weeks later. But then the French struck back, blocking his route to Paris and hemming him against the Somme and Seine rivers.

Finally, at Crécy in Picardy, Edward decided to turn and fight his pursuers, despite their numbers being double his own 6,500-strong force. He chose his ground well, arraying his troops along a 500-yard-long ridge. In the front line were two battles of dismounted men-at-arms commanded by Edward's son, the Black Prince, and the Earl of Arundel, with the rearguard battle under his own command. Deployed on the flanks were units of Welsh archers armed with longbows. These weapons required long, hard training to use, but their superior range and rate of fire compared with those of the crossbows carried by Genoese mercenaries the French king Philip VI had employed gave the English a decisive advantage.

A rainstorm on the morning of August 26, just before the battle, wet the strings of the Genoese, which made their crossbows hard to operate, and when they were sent to the front, their pavises (large, oblong protective shields), were left behind in the baggage waggons, which made them sitting ducks for the volleys of arrows unleashed by Edward's archers. At this critical moment, Philip lost control of his army, and the heavily armoured French knights, impatient to smash the English line, charged up the slope. Funnelled by the hills to either side onto a narrow front, they became rapidly entangled with the floundering Genoese. Harried by longbow fire and the impetus of their charge dulled by the slope, their horses' hooves mired in mud and corpses, the French attack slowed, and few even reached the top of the ridge. With little tactical imagination, the same scene repeated itself fourteen more times as the day wore on, each charge more desperate, less effective, and more costly than the previous.

Adding to the chaos were five ribauldequin, an early type of cannon, which Edward had brought along, which peppered the French with heavy stone balls. Late in the evening, Philip gave up and fled, leaving thousands of his knights dead on the field. In the aftermath of the battle, Edward was able to advance on Calais, capturing it after an eleven-month siege and gaining a lodgement on the French coast which would serve as a main base of English operations for the rest of the war and remain in English hands until 1558. The victory too had shown that the days of mounted chivalry were numbered and that, effectively deployed, mixed units of dismounted men-at-arms and longbowmen could blunt and outfight armoured horsemen. And it marked a shift in the European balance of power: as the Italian poet Petrarch remarked, "In my youth the English were taken to be the meekest of the barbarians. Today they are a fiercely bellicose nation. They have overturned the ancient military glory of the French."

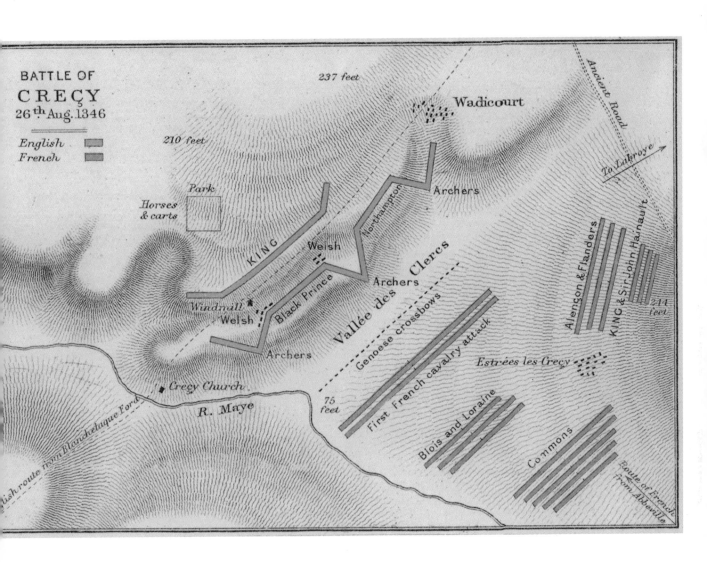

BATTLE OF
CRECY
26th Aug. 1346

English
French

237 feet

210 feet

Wadicourt

Ancient Road

To Labroye

Park

Horses
& carts

KING

Welsh

Northampton

Archers

Archers

Clercs

Windmill

Welsh

Black Prince

Vallée des

King & Sir John Hainault

244 feet

Alençon & Flanders

Archers

Genoese crossbows

Estrées les Crecy

Crecy Church

R. Maye

75 feet

First French cavalry attack

Blois and Loraine

Commons

Route of French from Abbeville

English route from Blanchetaque Ford

The Fall of Constantinople

The heavily stylised representation of Constantinople, painted in 1537 by the Romanian artist Toma of Suceava for the monastery of Moldoviţa, lays great stress on the city's fortifications. Well it might, for the mighty triple-layered walls had repelled attempts to capture Constantinople ever since their construction under Emperor Theodosius I in the late 4th century. Avars, Persians, Arabs, Rus' and Bulgars all had believed they could storm them, and all had failed.

Only in 1453 did the ancient magic of Constantinople's saintly protectors crumble under the assault of a new threat, along with the religious processions of intercession shown in the fresco and the hard stone walls themselves. Artillery was the threat, and this too was portrayed by Toma. The fire spewing forth from the massive cannon to the right pummelled the walls to rubble, literally beneath the gaze of its horrified defenders, including a crowned and bearded Byzantine Emperor Constantine XI.

They would never have got near, had not the Byzantine Empire been reduced to a shadow of its former self by the 15th century, controlling tenuous slivers of territory in the hinterland of Constantinople. Most of the rest had been overrun by the Ottoman Turks. When in 1451 an ambitious new sultan, Mehmed II, ascended the throne, he resolved to capture the city, a sparkling prize wedged precariously between his other possessions. Gradually he throttled it, building a fortress, Rumeli Hisarı, on the Bosphorus to stop relief forces or supplies reaching it during the siege which he eventually launched in April 1453.

He brought with him a vast army of around 80,000 men, including regiments of the elite janissaries, and around 170 cannons, among which were several huge artillery pieces built by Urban, a Hungarian engineer who had offered to build cannon for the Byzantines, but whom Constantine XI had turned down on grounds of cost. Inside the city walls were, as the Byzantine historian George Sphrantzes counted, a mere 4,773 Greek defenders and a few hundred foreigners. Yet the city's walls were reasonably well maintained and, with an additional contingent which arrived from Genoa under Giovanni Giustiniani, it seemed they had just enough manpower to defend the land sections, while the sea walls were denied to the Ottoman attackers by a great metal chain strung across the Golden Horn which prevented Turkish ships approaching.

By April 5 the bulk of Mehmed's army had arrived, but even though Urban's cannons spat out stone balls of a prodigious size – weighing up to 1,000 kilograms – that smashed gaping holes in weaker sections of wall, the Byzantines managed to patch these up, reinforce other areas with bales of wool and hay, and fight off several attempts to storm the gates. Then, on April 22, Mehmed ordered a road made of logs to be built across Galata, the small peninsula opposite the city, and along this the Ottoman fleet was rolled, past the chain and into the Golden Horn. Now forced to defend the sea walls too, the overstretched Byzantines faced an impossible task, and when Mehmed ordered a final attack on May 29 following another epic bombardment by Urban's guns, there were simply not enough defenders to face them.

As a result, a party of janissaries managed to enter via an undefended minor portal near the Blachernae gate. More Ottoman attackers followed, and in chaotic fighting to repel them Giustiniani was fatally wounded and the defenders' morale collapsed. Somewhere the emperor died, having, it was said, removed his imperial purple buskins (or slippers) to prevent his being identified. After three days of looting, Mehmed call a halt to the mayhem and rode in triumph through the city streets to the ancient church of Hagia Sophia (which he declared a mosque).

The fall of Constantinople marked the extinction of the final fragment of the Roman Empire, after more than two thousand years, and also the closing of an era when cities and their rulers could shelter behind stone walls, confident that, if well supplied and not betrayed from within, they could withstand all threats and assaults by outsiders. In siege warfare, artillery was now king, and warfare entered a period of adaptation both in sieges and, as portable gunpowder weaponry became available, on the battlefield.

Battle of Murten

The lakes, woods and hills around Murten in western Switzerland seem the dominant elements in this engraving by the German artist Johann Andreas Pecht (1773–1852), which appeared in Franz Ludwig Haller's *Darstellung der merkwürdigsten Schweizer-Schlachten vom Jahr 1298 bis 1499* ("Description of the most remarkable Swiss battles from 1298 to 1499") and which chronicles one of the key encounters in the establishment of Swiss independence against the designs of Charles the Bold, the ambitious Duke of Burgundy.

Burgundy suffered both from being squeezed between an increasingly powerful France to the west and the shifting constellation of German states in the Holy Roman Empire to its east and from its limited resources in territory and manpower. Charles the Bold, who became duke in 1467, took drastic measures to combat this, reforming the Burgundian army by creating mixed companies of around 900, composed of cavalry, foot soldiers, arquebusiers and crossbowmen, enforcing rigorous drills and training, and even providing uniforms (blue and white with a St Andrew's cross). He undertook campaigns against King Louis XI of France on the Somme, the archbishopric of Cologne on the Rhine, and then, in 1475 against Duke René of Lorraine, all in the name of strengthening Burgundy's vulnerable borders.

By then, Charles's alarmed neighbours had united to form the League of Constance to hold him in check, bringing the cantons of Switzerland, led by Berne, into alliance with the towns of the Rhineland. The Burgundian duke's ambitions now focused on Savoy, lying between Switzerland and Italy, and to conquer this, he needed to subdue the Swiss. In principle the small cantons should have been easy for Charles's well-equipped army to brush aside, but the Swiss, organised into an Eidgenossenschaft (Confederacy), benefited from a common language and a determination to defend their homeland. In contrast, the multinational Burgundian forces included a large element of mercenaries and were often difficult to co-ordinate.

The Swiss had also specialised in a form of infantry warfare that was challenging for opponents to overcome. Armed with large pikes and supported by archers and handgunners, they formed into a version of the Greek phalanxes of old, which were hard for cavalry to penetrate or lighter infantry units to dislodge. The Burgundian fortunes against them were mixed. Charles took Grandson on Lake Neuchâtel in late February 1476, but his hanging of the surrendered garrison stiffened opposition and he was roundly defeated in a battle outside the city a few days later.

Poor reconnaissance had been a major contributory factor to the Burgundian defeat there, and, though an undeterred Charles pressed on with his campaign, he failed to learn any lessons from this early failure. When he faced stiff resistance, he moved on to try to take Murten. It seems that he was trying to goad the Swiss into attacking, to relieve their beleaguered countrymen inside the town, which was subjected to a tight siege. The Burgundians established a strong palisade, the Grünhag ("Green Hedge" – marked "2" on the map) to the east of Murten, manned by archers and arquebusiers, to create a deadly killing field when the Swiss approached.

By June 21, Charles doubted the Swiss were coming, and a heavy rainstorm convinced him that no attack would occur in the coming days. So he stood down most of his troops, leaving only a skeleton force of 2,000 Burgundians and Italians to defend the Grünhag. Yet the Swiss were almost upon him, and the vanguard of 5,000 pikemen burst out of the dense woods where they had been concealed. Within minutes, they had smashed through the startled defenders of the green palisade.

More and more Swiss arrived and soon over 20,000, including cavalry, were overrunning the hastily re-assembled Burgundian units. An Italian mercenary captain named Troilo put up some resistance, and a unit of English archers managed to shield the efforts of the rest of Charles's army to escape. But hemmed in by the advancing Swiss, whose forest of pikes deterred any attempt to blunt their momentum, and pressed against the lake, many of the Burgundians were simply trapped and perished in uncoordinated last-ditch stands.

Charles the Bold did get away, though several thousands of his soldiers lay dead on the field. It was a crushing defeat. He had lost his chance to take Savoy, and now key allies such as Galeazzo Maria Sforza, Duke of Milan, began to desert him, as power inexorably ebbed away before his final defeat and death at Nancy a year later. For the Swiss it was a triumph, an affirmation both of their independence and of the effectiveness of the pikemen who would dominate European battlefields for almost a century.

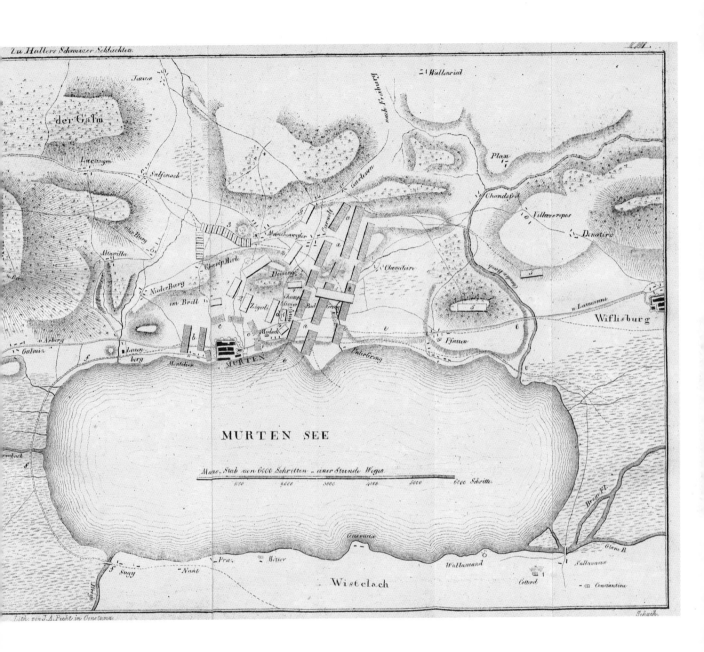

MURTEN SEE

Maass Stab von 6000 Schritten = einer Stunde Weges.

1000   2000   3000   4000   5000   6000 Schritte.

Wistelach

THE
GUNPOWDER
REVOLUTION

1500–1775

Battle of Pavia

The lavish painting by German artist Rupert Heller shows troops of the Imperial Habsburg army breaking into the walled hunting ground of Mirabello to confront panicked French troops (a few sporting unlikely headgear) in one of the most decisive battles of the Franco–Italian Wars, a series of conflicts between the French Crown and the Habsburgs for control of northern Italy which dragged on from 1494 to 1559.

In October 1524, Francis I of France mounted his second expedition to Italy. He crossed the Alps with a force of 40,000 men, easily capturing Milan. Rather than press on, however, Francis attempted to take the town of Pavia, which had been garrisoned by 5,000 Habsburg mercenaries under Antonio de Leyva. But the siege became bogged down, and Francis stubbornly refused to bypass it, giving time for an Imperial army under Charles de Lannoy to move northwards to relieve it.

Lannoy and his men arrived in early February 1525, but their task seemed initially very hard, as the French camp blocked access to the east of the city, where de Leyva's garrison was still trapped. Weeks of desultory skirmishing yielded no breakthrough and, fearing new French reinforcements might force him to retreat, Lannoy marched a large force at dead of night along the eastern perimeter of the Mirabello wall. He hoped to break into the hunting park which the wall enclosed and where the French troops were sheltering, at an undefended point. At its northern apex, near the Porta Pescarina, his engineers began breaching the wall, but it was thicker than they expected and so it took until nearly 7am to make a large enough gap for two columns of Imperial forces to pour into the Mirabello and fan out southwards.

Alerted by scouts to the din the Imperial engineers were making, a French cavalry unit under Charles Tiercelin dashed northwards to face the intruders, but the dense blanket of mist which enveloped the park in the pre-dawn gloom – a literal "fog of war" – confused both him and a unit of mercenary pikemen under Robert de Florange, the Marshal of France. As a result, a force of Imperial arquebusiers under the Marques del Vasto made it to Castle Mirabello largely unimpeded and easily stormed it.

While de Leyva punched his way out of Pavia to tie up the Duke of Alençon's section of the French army, the Imperial forces moving southeast through the park were experiencing greater difficulty. The Imperial light cavalry was scattered by Tiercelin when finally the mist began to lift, while the artillery that had been hauled laboriously through the breach was captured. Then, just as he seemed close to victory, Francis made a fatal error. Seeing the Imperial heavy cavalry being decimated by his cannon fire, he decided on a charge to finish them off.

This meant the French artillery had to cease firing to avoid hitting their own side, and Francis's charge, while it scattered Lannoy's opposing horsemen, carried him far beyond his own lines. As the Imperial army regrouped and even more troops entered the breach in the park walls, the French king found himself isolated and surrounded, with De Vasto's arquebusiers pouring in fire from one flank and Georg von Frundsberg's *landsknechts* (mercenary foot soldiers) blocking off retreat to the rear. The French knights were constricted into an ever-smaller space and cut to pieces, despite a fierce last-ditch resistance by the "Black Band", a group of landsknechts fighting for the French. Francis was unhorsed and found himself surrounded by a mob of enemy infantry. It was only through the personal intervention of Lannoy that he was captured alive.

With their sovereign lost, Tiercelin and Florange retreated from the park, and Alençon, who had been facing de Leyva outside Pavia, fled the battlefield. It was a disaster for the French. Francis was imprisoned in the fortress of Pizzhigettone near Cremona and then hauled off to Madrid, where he was bullied into signing a treaty giving up all claims on Imperial territory in Italy (concessions, though, which he repudiated the moment he was freed). The battle itself had proved the worth of handheld firearms on the battlefield, as the Imperial arquebusiers played a key role in containing the French cavalry. While the Italian wars only ended in 1559 with a set of treaties that largely confirmed Imperial holdings in Italy, the face of the battlefield would never be the same again.

L' ASSEDIO E BATTERIA DELL ISOLA DI S. MICHELE A DI XXVIII DI GIVGNO.

Dopo' la presa di Santermo fuggirno molti rinegati dalli quali se infere che il Bassa uoleua battere le fortezze con 60 pezzi imaginandosi in pochi giorni ridurle tutte in pole
Questa Isola di S. Michele e posta dalla lingua de Italia nella quale era superiore l'Armiraglio Fra Pietro de Monti et Fra Pietro Giustiniani.

A. Castello S. Angelo.
B. Il Borgo.
C. Posta di Prouenza.
D. Il Saluatore.

E La Catena.
F. L Isolotto.
G. Lo iprone dell'Isola e le molina.
H. S antermo gia preso da Turchi.

I. La Fronte dell'Isola di S. Michele.
K Il Galeone che fu pigliato ai Turchi.
L Ponte che si passaua dall Borgo all Isola.
M Catena di antenne fatta da i nostri.

N. Archibusieri alla scarpa dell fosso.
O L Arteglieria che conducono da Santermo.
P Batteria di 3 canoni che batteuano il borgo e S. Angelo.
Q Punta di Dragutt doue stauano 4 canoni che batteuano Salermo.

R S Margherita doue stauano 6 canoni et
che batteuano la fronte di S Michele e Pr
S Il Curadino doue stauano 13 canoni che i
S. Michele cioe la cortina.

T La Burmula doue stauano 2 cannoni che tirauano a S Angelo et al Borgo. V La Mandra con 3 canoni che batteuano S. Michele. 2 B arche co doite pietra p dare l'assalto al speront. Y Batteria di 3 canoni che tirauano al sperondel uole Z L'Armata del Turco doue di S.

Siege of Malta

The image, from a late 16th-century Italian engraving, is dramatic. A massed battery of Ottoman Turkish guns fires at the island opposite, whose harbour walls are crowded with the defenders of the Order of the Knights of St John. It portrays a critical moment in the defence of Malta against the armada amassed by the Ottoman sultan Suleiman the Magnificent.

Suleiman was already master of the eastern Mediterranean, but Malta presented an obstacle to his ambitions to extend his sway to the west. Also standing in his way were the Knights of St John, who had taken up residence on the island after their expulsion by the Ottomans from Rhodes, their previous home, in 1522. The Order's Grand Master, Jean de la Valette, perhaps provoked Suleiman too much when he raided Ottoman-held Djerba in North Africa in 1560, and with retaliation only a matter of time, the Knights set to a programme of upgrading Malta's defences, building two stout fortresses at St Elmo and St Michael on the tips of peninsulas jutting out into the island's Grand Harbour.

On May 19, 1565, the long-feared attack came. More than 190 ships led by Admiral Piyale disembarked around 40,000 troops on the southwest of Malta who then marched across the island to set up camp opposite the Grand Harbour. The initial Ottoman assault was delayed by disagreement between Piyale and the army commander Mustafa Pasha, as to which fort to attack first, but the initial blows finally fell against St Elmo. Blasted, bombarded and assaulted several times, the 1,500 defenders held out heroically for nearly a month, but, with the ramparts reduced to rubble, they perished almost to a man in chaotic hand-to-hand fighting on June 23.

The Ottomans then turned to St Michael, beginning with a series of bombardments. It is this stage of the fight which the engraving shows. The fortress is protected by a chain (E) to stop Ottoman boats flanking it, while a wooden bridge gave access to the other main surviving stronghold of the Knights at Birgu. The defenders' morale was briefly raised by the arrival of 700 reinforcements who had slipped onto the island past the Ottoman fleet, but they could do nothing to prevent the Turks building a log road to roll ships into the Grand Harbour, so avoiding a large artillery battery stationed at St Angelo (and reprising the tactic of Suleiman's ancestor Mehmed II at Constantinople in 1453).

Significant losses inflicted when the Ottoman fleet then did sail too close to the St Angelo battery deterred a direct assault, so Mustafa Pasha ordered his artillery to pound the walls of St Michael and Birgu, hoping to bludgeon them into submission as he had done to St Elmo. But the defenders held firm until August 20, when a combined barrage and landward assault almost broke into the city. Only after desperate fighting were the Ottoman janissaries expelled. Another assault at the start of September was similarly thrown back, but, despite the bodies of Turkish troops which choked the foot of the walls, the defenders could ill afford the casualties they suffered, and de la Valette understood they were almost at breaking point.

Then, salvation came for the Maltese. The relief force which had been laboriously assembled by Don Garcia de Toledo, viceroy of Sicily, finally arrived on September 7. Ironically, Mustafa Pasha had already decided that there was no longer any chance of taking the island before the onset of winter and had re-embarked most of his army, ready to sail back to North Africa. But hearing of the new Christian force, he landed a detachment again, though it was rapidly scattered by a charge from Garcia's knights.

It had been a close-run thing, but even in the gunpowder age well-defended and well-supplied fortresses could resist if they had some hope of relief. For Suleiman, the Siege of Malta and a defeat in the naval battle of Lepanto off Cyprus six years later marked the end of his dreams of becoming lord of the Mediterranean. Ottoman ambitions instead were turned to advances on land, in the Balkans, where even a century later they came close to taking Vienna (see page 68).

Siege of La Rochelle

The engraving shows the stoutly fortified city of La Rochelle on France's Atlantic coast under siege by the forces of the Duke of Anjou – who are shown firing at the fortifications with batteries of cannon protected by barricades – during France's 16th-century Wars of Religion between Huguenots (French Protestants) and Catholics. Inspired by a French original by the artist François Desprez, the Italian compiler clearly shows his sympathies by referring to the defenders of the city as "gli Eretici Ribelli" ("the Heretical Rebels"), a sentiment which shows the bitterness of a conflict that was already a decade old.

Protestantism had gained a significant foothold in France after the Reformation, but its adherents, the Huguenots, were still a minority, albeit a large one. By the 1560s a series of religious killings had flared up into sporadic warfare, and in 1572 Catholic leaders became alarmed after King Charles IX permitted the marriage of his sister Marguerite of Valois to the Protestant Henri of Navarre. As tensions heightened, the Huguenot leader Gaspard de Coligny was assassinated in Paris, very probably with the connivance of the Queen Mother, Catherine de Medici, which sparked a general massacre of Huguenots on August 23. Angry mobs killed around 3,000 Protestants in Paris and thousands more in the provinces.

Many survivors fled to towns with Huguenot majorities, such as Nîmes and Montauban. La Rochelle in particular became the focus of Protestant resistance, its inhabitants refusing to accept a new royal governor, Armand de Gontaut, baron de Biron, when he was sent to take up his post in September. The king demanded their submission, and when the city's leaders refused, he ordered Biron to lay siege to it. The blockade was at first half-hearted. Negotiations conducted by François de la Noue, a Protestant envoy sent from the court, further delayed matters; and divisions in the Catholic camp, many of whose leaders felt an attack on La Rochelle would inflame rather than resolve the situation, meant that only on December 4 did Biron begin to surround the city from the landward side. Even then the royal army's 20,000 men could make no headway against the mere 1,200 trained soldiers and several thousand townsfolk manning the ramparts, and Biron's lack of a fleet meant that supplies reached La Rochelle relatively unhindered.

Matters became somewhat more serious in February 1573, when the impatient king sent his younger brother Henri of Anjou with a strong contingent of artillery to force the city into submission. Despite heavy bombardment from Henri's 42 siege guns, which began on March 22, the walls stood largely firm – though a part near the bastion de l'Évangile collapsed. Eight major assaults between April 7 and June 11 all failed, incurring significant casualties and capturing only very minor outlying strongpoints. One sortie by the defenders even reached the royal camp, nearly destroying it and causing further embarrassment to Henri, who had lost 10,000 of his men in battle and roughly the same number to disease.

With only half his force remaining, Henri was perhaps relieved when news reached him in late May that he had been elected king of Poland. He rapidly opened negotiations with the defenders, and on July 6 the siege was lifted and Henri began a slow progress to Poland (which he reached in January 1574, only to turn back around six months later when he learned Charles IX had died and he was now king of France).

La Rochelle's resistance led to a peace in July 1573 which conceded toleration for Huguenots, but only there and in Montauban and Nîmes. Even this limited concession broke down, which led to further bouts of warfare until the accession of Henri of Navarre to the throne in 1589 was followed nine years later by the Edict of Nantes, which granted general toleration to the Huguenots. La Rochelle was to suffer again, though, in 1627–28, when another siege during a period of renewed Catholic–Protestant clashes provoked by the Thirty Years' War ended in the city's capitulation. And when, finally, Louis XIV revoked the Edict of Nantes in 1685, once again outlawing Protestantism, many Huguenots fled to Britain. Their resistance in the 1572 siege of La Rochelle might have brought them victory, but it did not bring them peace.

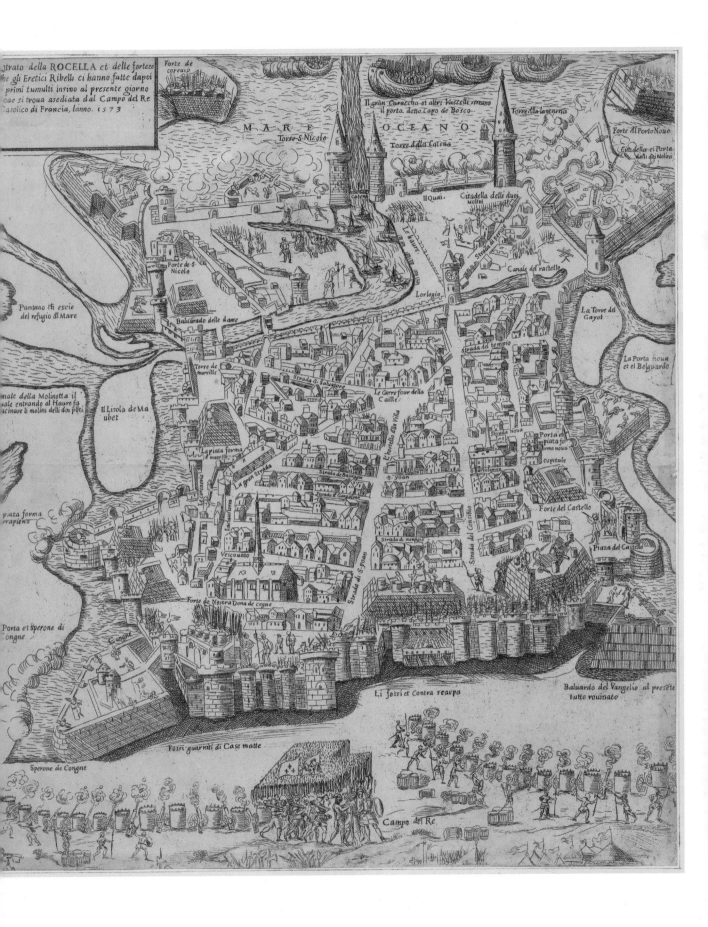

…trato della ROCELLA et delle forteze
…he gli Eretici Ribelli ci hanno fatte dapoi
…primi tumulti insino al presente giorno
…oue si troua asediata dal Campo del Re
…atolico di Francia, l'anno. 1573

Forte de coreuio

Il gran Caraccho et altri Vastelli seruno il porto, detto Capo de Bosco

Torre della lanterna

Forte Al Porto Nouo

Cittadella et Porta delli dui Molini

MARE OCEANO

Torre S. Nicolo

Torre della Catena

Il Quai

Cittadella delli duoi Molini

Strada di Pirou

Canale del rastello

Forte de S. Nicolo

Pantano ch escie del refugio di Mare

Baluardo delle dame

Lorlogio

La Torre del Gayot

Torre de morcille

Strada del tempio

La Porta noua et el Belguardo

nale della Molinotta il uale entrando al Haure fa acinare li molini delli doi puti

Il Lisola de Ma ubet

Strada S. Saluatore

Le Carre four della Caille

Strada Noua

Portà et piata for ma noua

L'ortello alla Villa

Ospitale

La piata forma d'mcrille

La gren strada

Strada de Battagia

S. yoan

S. Bartolomeo

piata forma rapieno

Strada di Gogolon

Strada di menguio

Forte del Castello

Vescouato

Strada del Castello

Piaza del Castello

Porta et sperone di ongne

Strada di S. yoan

Cougne

Forte de Nostra Dona de cogne

Baluardo del Vangelio al presète tutto rouinato

Li fossi et Contra scarpa

Fossi guarniti di Case matte

Sperone de Congne

Campo del Re

Battle of Sekigahara

For over two and a half centuries the Tokugawa shoguns ruled Japan, for much of the time keeping the country insulated from foreign influence (and safe from the type of European encroachments which overwhelmed India and sapped the power of the Qing dynasty in China). The unification of the country which made this era of tranquillity and cultural flowering possible was crowned at Sekigahara, the battle depicted on the 19th-century Japanese silk painting. It shows the fighting at its height, seen from the north, as the forces of Tokugawa Ieyasu struggle against those of a coalition led by Ishida Mitsunari, the banners of the contending samurai houses (those of the Tokugawa in the centre foreground) prominent on the battlefield.

The road to Sekigahara had been a long one. Japan had nearly been unified by Toyotomi Hideyoshi, whose death in 1598 threatened to unravel his pacification of the country after decades of civil war. His chief lieutenant Tokugawa Ieyasu rapidly sidelined Hideyoshi's son Hideyori, but many of Hideyoshi's former retainers objected to his presumption. They coalesced around Ishida Mitsunari, who formed a "Western Army" to punish Ieyasu and restore Hideyori. Both sides seized strategic castles, but Mitsunari's advance to Ogaki Castle, uncomfortably close to the imperial capital of Kyoto, forced Ieyasu's hand, and he laid siege to the Western Army force there.

Mitsunari held out obstinately, and so Ieyasu was forced to turn to subterfuge, seeding a rumour that he was about to attack Mitsunari's home domain and then seize Osaka. With his heartland seemingly under threat, Mitsunari slipped out of Ogaki, but he did not get far, as the Eastern Army, expecting his move, caught up with him at Sekigahara on October 21, 1600. The Western Army entered the narrow valley around the village first, seizing the high ground overlooking the village, while the Tokugawa alliance stationed itself around the village's crossroads. Both sides had around 80,000 men, and Mitsunari hoped to use the bulk of his force to pin Tokugawa down in the valley, then send the Kobayakawa and Mori clans down from the ridgetops to surround Ieyasu and cut the Eastern Army to pieces. Mitsunari was unaware, though, that Koboyakawa Hideaki and Kikkawa Hiroie – on behalf of the Mori – had both been in secret contact with Ieyasu and pledged to stand aside when the battle began.

At first a thick blanket of fog held the two sides in place, but at around 8am it lifted and Ii Naomasa and Fukushima Masanori's samurai charged the Western Army, setting off a bitter struggle in which volleys of matchlock fire alternated with hand-to-hand fighting using traditional *katana* swords. Ieyasu then reinforced his left flank to support Naomasa and Masanori's assault while also starting a new attack on the right. By 10am, though, both Eastern Army attacks had become stalled in the muddy ground.

Mitsunari now saw his chance to land a decisive blow, ordering the lighting of signal fires to set off the predetermined attack by the Kobayakawa from Mount Matso. And so, down the slope Hideaki's 15,000 warriors charged, but instead of charging the Eastern Army, they turned on their "allies", slamming into the Otani and Ukita samurai. In the confusion, several more Western Army samurai clans took the opportunity to defect, and Mitsunari's right flank collapsed completely. As he was forced back, he sent frantic messages to Kikkawa Hiroie to intervene, but Hiroie remained resolutely immobile, both blocking other Western Army clans from advancing and threatening a total collapse if he followed Hideaki's lead and defected.

By 2pm Mitsunari understood his position was hopeless and retreated with his surviving retainers. A few units, notably one led by Shimazu Yoshihiro, fought a desperate rearguard action and then performed a near-suicidal charge through the Tokugawa lines to escape. Many of the Western Army leaders had been killed or had killed themselves. Mitsunari was captured three days later and executed at Kyoto along with a number of other clan leaders. Ieyasu's victory was total, the resistance to him shattered. Two years later he was elevated to the rank of shogun by the Emperor Go-Yozei (whose power was strictly ceremonial). Among his edicts were the forbidding of arms to commoners and the enforced residence of *daimyo* (clan chiefs) for part of the year in the capital, where he could keep a closer eye on them and root out possible conspirators. Apart from an uprising in 1637 (in part supported by daimyo who had converted to Christianity), the next two centuries saw little warfare in Japan. At Sekigahara, gunpowder weaponry and traditional samurai swordsmanship had combined to create a bloody killing field in which 40,000 died. Now peace descended.

▶

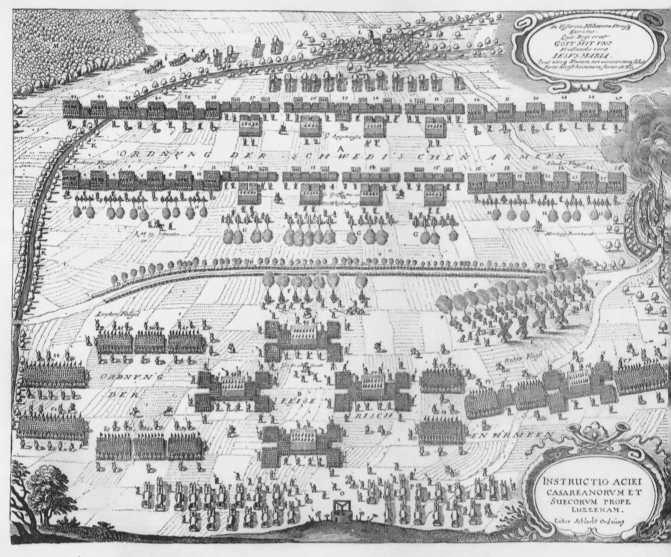

Battle of Lützen

The Swedish army of Gustavus Adolphus (at the top) faces the Imperial forces of Albrecht von Wallenstein, their battalions divided by the Leipzig to Lützen road, in this engraving by the Swiss-German publisher Matthäus Merian. He included it in his 1633 edition of the *Theatrum Europaeum*, a journal devoted to notable happenings in the German-speaking lands.

The battle at Lützen in Saxony on November 16, 1632, was certainly worthy of inclusion. Germany had already been ravaged by nearly a decade and a half of fighting in the Thirty Years' War. Originally sparked by a Protestant revolt in Bohemia against the Catholic Habsburg Holy Roman emperors, it soon metamorphosed into a continent-spanning conflict which pulled in Spain, France and a constellation of German princes. By 1630, the Protestant cause was under severe pressure, but then the Swedish king Gustavus Adolphus responded to the desperate pleas of his co-religionists and in July landed with 13,000 troops at the Baltic town of Peenemünde.

Gustavus's tactical genius won him a series of early victories, including one at Breitenfeld in September 1631, which went a long way to shoring up the Protestant cause. Exploiting the power of gunpowder weaponry, he formed his army into brigades of around 500 men, two thirds of them with modern matchlock muskets and protected by the remaining soldiers bearing long pikes, and in the infantry brigades he deployed light 3-pounder cannons which could be drawn by single horses. Yet he also understood the power of shock, encouraging his cavalry to charge at a gallop, rather than the stately trot and turn at pistol distance - the *caracole* - that had become the norm.

In autumn 1632 the new Imperial commander Albrecht von Wallenstein, a grizzled veteran who had risen from jobbing mercenary to Imperial count palatine, had reined in the Swedish advance and taken up winter quarters in Leipzig. On hearing that Wallenstein had sent a detachment ahead under General von Pappenheim, Gustavus, who had been steadily pushed north into Saxony, decided to turn and fight, emboldened by his numerical superiority, with 18,000 troops to Wallenstein's reduced complement of 13,000.

The battlefield on which they met was not promising for the Swedish king's hope of a mobile battle, with the marshy ground near Lützen and the Mühlgraben stream meaning that the Swedes would be funnelled south of the two. Both sides formed up according to prearranged plans, which enabled more rapid deployment but made less efficient use of the terrain. Neither side was in the massed squares shown on the plan; these bulky square phalanxes of 3,000 men had long been abandoned. Instead, the Imperialists formed up into longer rectangles up to 26 deep, with musketeers in the front to create a rain of fire and screens of dragoons, Croat light horse and Polish Cossacks to exploit any weakness. The somewhat thinner Swedish lines, with German allies on the left and the cavalry on the right, were supported by a superior artillery contingent.

The battle opened as the Swedes marched north of a canal and unleashed a massed salvo to soften up the Imperialists. The Swedish cavalry than smashed into Wallenstein's left flank, while the infantry moved against the Imperial centre and right. But Gustavus's deployment had been hampered by early morning mist hanging over the marshy landscape and was not complete until 11am. So, just as the Swedes seemed to be gaining the upper hand, von Pappenheim, whom Wallenstein had frantically recalled when he heard of Gustavus's approach, arrived to join the fray. The Swedish infantry were swept away, although the death of von Pappenheim, struck by a musket ball, almost blunted the Imperial revival. The battlefield was becoming chaotic, with disorganised units and a pall of smoke making visibility almost impossible. While Gustavus was trying to rally his infantry, he stumbled into an enemy cavalry squadron, was shot in the arm and fell from his horse, which dragged him to his death.

Unaware of their king's demise, the Swedes had at first rallied, while their German allies advanced against the Imperial centre, driving it off a windmill-crested hill and turning Wallenstein's captured artillery against him. Around 5pm the Imperial commander had seen enough; although von Pappenheim's reinforcements were still arriving, he ordered a retreat. Both sides claimed victory, but each had suffered terrible losses: Imperialist casualties were around 6,000, those of the Swedes scarcely less. Though the Swedes fought on, without Gustavus's guiding genius the Protestant side never quite regained the ascendancy and the Thirty Years' War stumbled on for another 16 years until finally it was ended by the Peace of Westphalia. What the battle did prove was the role that effective direction of firepower and the use of field artillery could have when combined with cavalry that exploited breakthroughs. In that, Gustavus Adolphus's legacy lived on.

Battle of Naseby

Without the two lines of troops facing each other, it might have been a bucolic scene, framed by hedges and windmills, with a prominent ridge dominating the terrain just north of the small Northamptonshire settlement of Naseby, around 6 miles south of Market Harborough. The engraving is by Robert Streeter, an English artist better known for his ceiling decorations of the Sheldonian Theatre in Oxford. It shows the forces of the New Model Army, recently constituted in an attempt to instil discipline into a slightly flagging, if still largely victorious Parliamentary cause against the King Charles I's Royalist troops in the Civil War between king and parliament which had dragged on since 1642.

As Serjeant-Painter to Charles II, Streeter might have been distressed to depict one of the greatest reverses suffered by his master's royal father, for at Naseby the last gasp of a possible Royalist revival was snuffed out. Defeat at Marston Moor in 1644 had prised the north from Charles I's grasp, but strong Royalist presences in the southwest and around Oxford – the temporary royal capital – still offered a platform for a recovery. On May 30 the king's talented, if impetuous nephew, Prince Rupert of the Rhine, captured Leicester, a victory which led to a misplaced surge of confidence and the dispatch of part of the Royalist army north to regain Yorkshire, and southwest to reinforce the king's supporters in Somerset and Devon.

By now Sir Thomas Fairfax was on the march from Oxford, which he had been besieging. He commanded 13,000 New Model Army troops, including 5,500 cavalry, twice the size of the diminished force that the king and Prince Rupert could muster. Despite the intention that the New Model should be a reformed force, there were concerns about discipline – one commentator remarked, "I never saw so many drunk in all my life" – but they moved with surprising speed, and by June 11 Fairfax was within 12½ miles of the Royalist camp. Sporadic clashes broke out between the two sides' patrols, while Fairfax cut off an attempt by Charles to retreat back towards Leicester.

The morning of June 14 brought a morale-sapping fog and saw the Royalists drawn up on a ridge between Little Oxendon and East Farndon. Fairfax's men were sheltered (and concealed) behind Naseby Ridge (towards the bottom of the engraving), with a strong detachment of dragoons hidden in Sulby Hedges on the Royalist right. Fearing his position was actually too strong and might deter the Royalists from fighting altogether, Fairfax pulled back slightly, sucking Prince Rupert into just the sort of headstrong charge which had lost him the Battle of Edgehill right at the start of the Civil War in 1642. His wild charge took him far beyond the Parliamentary lines to their baggage train, which he wasted time in plundering. The Royalist infantry meanwhile charged the Parliamentary centre and despite inferior numbers pushed back the New Model infantry under Major General Philip Skippon in a brutal hand-to-hand encounter. It was only the intervention of Cromwell leading the Parliamentary horse on the right wing, and Colonel John Okey whose dragoons now burst out of the shelter of Sulby Hedges, that overwhelmed Charles's infantry, many of whom simply threw down their weapons and ran. Only Prince Rupert's Bluecoat Regiment (so-called from the colour of their tunics) resisted until they were trampled and clubbed into submission.

Seeing the disaster unfolding, Charles tried to lead a last-gasp charge of his personal lifeguard but was restrained by the Earl of Carnwath, who warned him, "Would you go upon your death Sire?" Even the return of Prince Rupert, who had finally rallied his cavalry, came too late, and the remaining Royalist cavalry fled towards Leicester, leaving the foot soldiers and hundreds of camp followers (including soldiers' wives) to be slaughtered along the road.

The king had lost his last large military force, and soon his remaining strongholds fell into Parliamentary hands, beginning with Leicester on June 18, with Prince Rupert handing over Bristol in September. Without artillery and experienced troops, and with the ignominy of his personal correspondence having been captured at Naseby (which exposed his attempts to broker alliances with Catholic monarchs in Europe), Charles I tried to set his enemies against each other by surrendering to the Scots at Newark in May 1646 and promising to establish a Scottish-style Presbyterian church in England if they joined his cause. It all ended in his trial and beheading on a cold winter's morning in January 1649. The walk to the executioner's block, though, had begun nearly four years earlier, at Naseby.

THE DESCRIPTION OF THE ARMIES O

Sᵗ Tomas Fairefax his Excellency, as they were

the Fow

Dust Hill

Prince Rupert

Prince Maurice

Sir Barnard Astley

His Tertia

The Left Wing Commanded by Commis Generall Ireton

Maior General Skippon

Coll: Butlers Regement

Coll Com Vermudens Regiment marded by Maior Huntington

Comand Generall Ireton

Forlorne hope of Musquetters

Maior Generall

Sir Hardres Wallers

Coll Riches Regement

Coll Fleetwood Regement

The Reserve of the Station

Leiutennant Coll: Pride a Reserue

Rupnill Hill

Fanny Hill

The Mill Hill

Leane Leate hill

The traine guarded with firelockes

NASBYE

Streeter fecit

Printed for John Patridge

AND FOOT OF HIS MAJESTIES, AND
rall bodyes, at the Battayle at NASBYE;
of June 1645.

Prince
Regiment Ruperts
of foote

Collonell How
ard Horse

The Lord Bard
Tertia

Sir George Lysle
Tertia

Sir Marmaduke Langdale and The Newarke horse

The Generall

Coll Mounta
gues

The Generalls Regt

The right wing of horse commanded
By Liutenant generall Cromwell

Coll Whalleyes
Regt

Coll Hamm ond a Reserue

Coll Rainsboro ugh Reserue

Sir Robert Pye

The generall deuison of
the life guard

Coll Rossiter

Coll Shiffeilds de uision

Sir Robert Pye

Coll Fines

The life guard horse

Coll Fines

Coll Rossiter

place this mapp betweene fol: 2 372

Siege of Maastricht

The map shows a siege that launched one illustrious career and ended another. Produced by the Franco-Italian engraver Francesco Collignon, the second of three generations of artists who made their living in Rome creating images of the city's rich heritage of religious and secular art, it portrays the Siege of Maastricht in 1673, with projectiles from the French batteries landing in the centre of the beleaguered town, whose strategic position straddling the River Meuse in Flanders made it an attractive prize and whose capture gave France's Louis XIV his greatest victory of the 1672–78 Franco–Dutch war.

The French king had won the town once already, during the 1667–68 War of Devolution against the Dutch, but was forced to give it up by the Treaty of Aix-la-Chapelle which ended that conflict. Louis's ambition was to secure France's northeastern frontier by seizing the Spanish Netherlands, and the equally firm determination of the Dutch Republic (which bordered it to the north) to resist him sparked another war in 1672. During the *Rampjaar* ("Disaster Year"), French forces struck deep into Flanders but bypassed the fortress-town of Maastricht. By 1673, though, its position athwart the French lines of communication had become a serious irritation, and Louis ordered its capture.

To direct the siege, Louis XIV called on the services of Sébastien le Prestre de Vauban, one of history's most talented military engineers, who had begun his career inauspiciously, on the wrong side of a rebellion against the king in the 1650s, but who by 1672 had risen to become royal director of fortifications. Bypassing the normal hierarchy of command (which would have left the siege's conduct to the army commander Henri de la Tour d'Auvergne, vicomte de Turenne), Vauban ordered the building of a massive circumvallation, a trench surrounding Maastricht which prevented the defenders from sallying forth.

Against Turenne's 50,000 men, the Dutch garrison commander Jacques de Fariaux had just 5,000, and the defences of Maastricht had been allowed to become dilapidated. Nonetheless, Fariaux was reasonably confident when the first French troops arrived on May 17 that he could hold out until relieved. He reckoned without Vauban's ingenuity. Aside from innovations such as ricochet firing – by which artillery fired at a low angle, the projectiles skipping along the ground like stones to dislodge wall-mounted defensive guns – his approach was summarised by "burn more powder, shed less blood", then careful degrading of the defenders' ability to resist, before a final assault.

To this end he ordered the construction of a series of parallel trenches linked by zigzagging smaller ditches (marked "D" on the map), which allowed the French to move around unhindered by Dutch fire and to creep gradually closer to Maastricht's walls. By June 24 these parallel trenches were complete, and a force of 2,500 assembled to attempt to storm the walls. A volley of cannon fire announced the attack, among whose leaders were James Scott, Duke of Monmouth, the illegitimate son of King Charles II, and Charles de Batz de Castelmore, comte d'Artagnan, who commanded a unit of royal musketeers. A colourful character who had served his royal masters as a spy, dashing musketeer and senior officer, d'Artagnan had jumped at the chance of real combat after a frustrating stint as governor of Lille. Yet just as the French assault seemed about to succeed, early the next morning the Dutch struck back, driving the attackers from the walls. At the height of the fighting, d'Artagnan suffered a fatal wound in the neck from a musket ball.

Fariaux's triumph was short-lived, as the French artillery continued to pound Maastricht relentlessly. He knew another attack might well succeed, so on June 30, rather than subject Maastricht to the uncontrolled plundering which was the lot of towns taken by storm, he negotiated a surrender, by which the remaining garrison was allowed to evacuate unhindered and the townsfolk would be spared.

The fall of Maastricht, far from signalling the end of the war, heralded its expansion, as the Austrian Habsburgs joined their Spanish cousins in opposing the French, while the Dutch continued their obdurate resistance. Finally, when it looked as though Britain would join the anti-French coalition, Louis came to terms: by the Treaty of Nijmegen in 1678 he was confirmed in possession of a large swathe of the Spanish Netherlands, but crucially not Maastricht, which was returned to the Dutch.

Vauban's career continued to prosper, the more than 150 fortifications he built for Louis (such as Besançon and Neuf-Brisach) being among the finest examples of military architecture anywhere. That of the comte d'Artagnan had an unexpected coda, since he provided the model for Alexandre Dumas's fictional version of the musketeers' commander in *The Three Musketeers*, so becoming the most illustrious casualty of the Siege of Maastricht.

Limme

Maestricht 11-30 Iune 1673

4

TV

Strada Sittart

Meersen houtem

S. Martino Porta
ferrata

Op debeek

Meersen houf

Golgen hauff

Hochter Porta

Mosa fluuius   Mosa fl.

Demer mase

S
Haren

Porta della Croce

H

M

R

L

Septentrio

F

Strada di Marseikc

D

D

Porta Brussel

D

Kitbel fl.

K

Kouwemberg

L

C

A Maestrick
B Wiick
C Circonuallatione
D Trinciere e approcci
E Batt.ia di 10. pezzi
F Batt.ia di 8. pezzi
G Batt.ia di 6. pezzi
H Batt.ia di 5. pezzi
I Forr. S. Pietro
K Bombe n.o 4.
L Bombe n.o 3.
M Ponti di Barche
N Quartiere di Sua M.a
O Quart. del Duca d'orleans
P Quart de Montal
Q Quart. de Duras
R Quart de Lorges
S Quart. del M.ro di Campo
T Quartieri di diuersi

N

D

Peterson

Monte
Dousberg

ri

Si Stampa in Roma da fran.co Collignon nel Parione con licenza de sup.

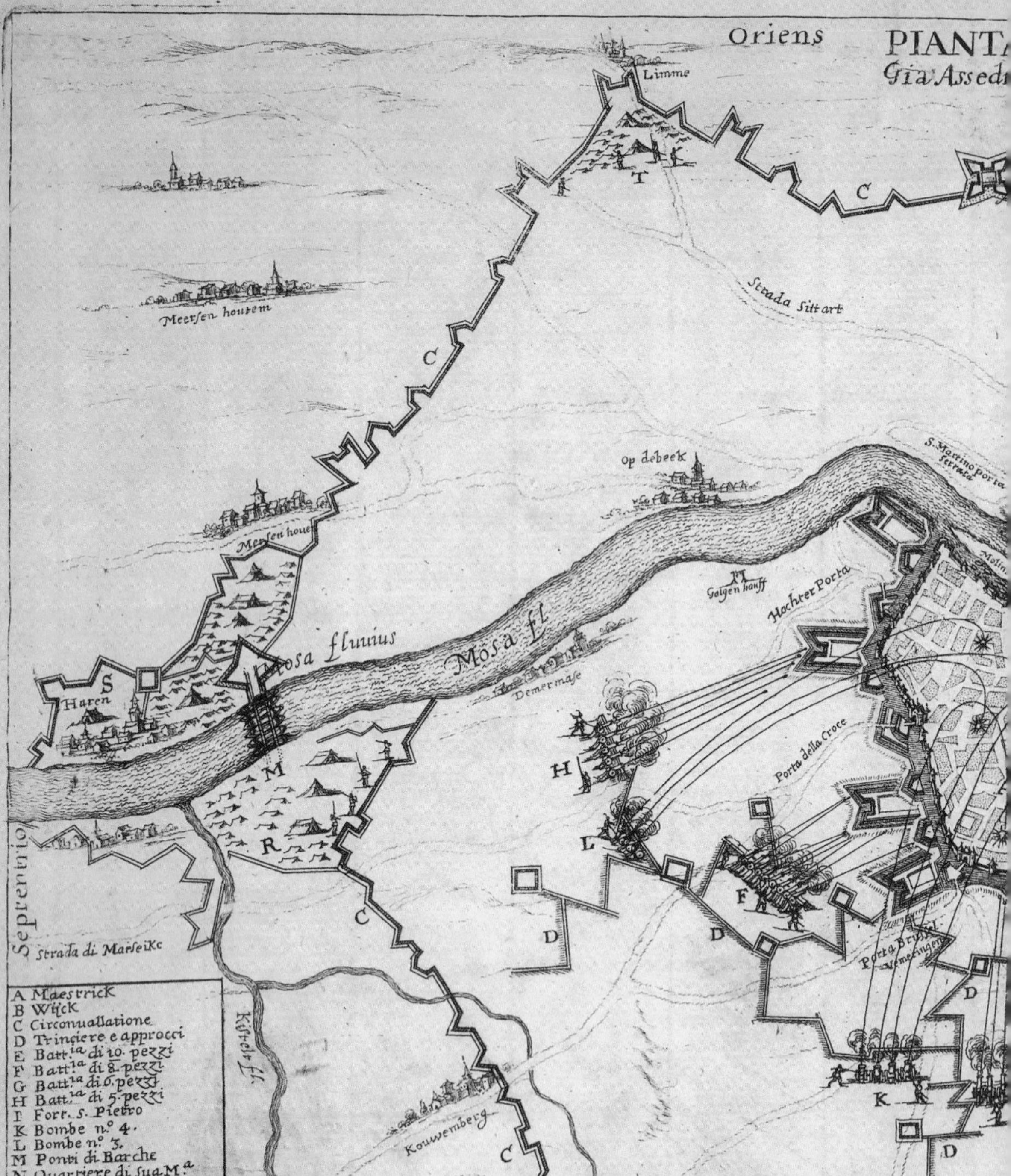

CITTÁ DI MASTRICH 1673.
...o dal Rè Christianiss.° LVDOVICO XIV.
...sa alli 30. del detto

Siege of Vienna

The map shows the critical moment in one of Europe's most decisive battles. Produced by the Bolognese print and map publisher Giuseppe Longhi, who was active in the second half of the 17th century, it shows masses of Ottoman Turkish troops, including the elite janissaries ("Gianizzeri" on the map), attacking the city of Vienna from the south, while on the north bank of the Danube a relieving army of Poles ("Polachi") and Bavarians musters.

Vienna's fall in the summer of 1683 would have marked a new phase in the long Ottoman expansion into southeastern Europe which began with the capture of Gallipoli in 1354. An earlier failed siege of Vienna in 1529 left the boundary between the Ottomans and the Austrian Habsburgs stalled in Hungary and the region plagued by protracted border skirmishing between the two sides. An uneasy peace in 1664 was broken when an ambitious new Ottoman vizier, Kara Mustafa Pasha, came to power. Taking advantage of Habsburg incursions into Hungary, he convinced his master Sultan Mehmed IV to mount a counterstrike to capture Vienna, the imperial capital of their foes.

The host of over 150,000 which set out from Belgrade, including large contingents of Transylvanian and Hungarian Christian allies, was formidable indeed, causing Emperor Leopold to flee from Vienna and the main Habsburg army, under Charles of Lorraine, to retreat to the west of the city. This left Ernst Rüdiger von Starhemberg, commanding around 10,000 professional soldiers and an assortment of citizen militia, to defend Vienna. He was assisted by the eminent German military engineer Georg Rimpler, who reinforced the city's defences by hurriedly constructing new firing positions and building a series of wooden palisades.

The main Ottoman forces reached Vienna on July 14. Kara Mustafa was short of siege artillery, with only 150 guns, and so simply blowing breaches in the walls followed by a massed assault was not an option. Instead, he began a slow process of attrition, having his engineers dig mines which were then detonated with explosives (one is shown as "mina" on the map). The process was painfully slow, although the loss of Rimpler, who was fatally wounded in August, and the temporary incapacity of Starhemberg from heatstroke and exhaustion deprived the city's defenders of crucial leadership. By early September the Ottomans were conducting more than probing attacks – on September 2–3

the crucial Burg defensive position was lost, and a week later Turkish engineers detonated a mine under the Löbel bastion, reducing it to rubble.

It seemed as though the city was about to fall, but Kara Mustafa had been just a little too cautious. While his forces were tightening their noose around Vienna, Emperor Leopold and Charles of Lorraine were conducting frantic diplomacy to assemble a coalition to save the city. They succeeded in recruiting Saxony, Bavaria, Baden and Swabia to the cause as well as, crucially, Jan Sobieski, the king of Poland, who was given overall command of the allied force of 80,000 which approached the Vienna hills on September 12. On hearing of their arrival, Kara Mustafa detached a large part of his own army to face the threat, leaving just enough besieging troops to stop Starhemberg breaking out. The battle, around the Kahlenberg mountain – on which the allies lit bonfires to signal to the besieged inhabitants of Vienna that salvation was at hand – began with a tussle between the German contingents and the Ottomans around the villages of Nussdorf and Heiligenstadt. Kara Mustafa managed to contain the German advances, but he had allocated some of his best troops, janissaries and elite sipahi cavalry, to a last-ditch assault against Vienna, so that he was already struggling against the Imperial forces when 18,000 Polish horsemen emerged from the forest and smashed into the Turkish lines, threatening to reach the Ottoman camp and capture the vizier himself. Then, at 6pm, the Polish king delivered the final blow – his cavalry, spearheaded by 3,000 "winged hussars" conducted the largest cavalry charge in history, shattering the Turkish resistance. As the remains of Kara Mustafa's army retreated southwards, German cavalry units entered Vienna to inform its citizens that their ordeal was over.

If Vienna was saved, Kara Mustafa decidedly was not. Despite his attempts to blame the failure of the siege on everyone but himself, in December a furious Mehmed IV had his vizier executed by strangulation with a silk rope. Yet the disasters for the Ottomans continued, with the Habsburgs capturing most of the rest of Hungary by 1687 and the Treaty of Karlowitz in 1699 which confirmed this loss merely providing a punctuation point in a long retreat which reached its final conclusion in the Balkan Wars of 1912–13 (see page 156). Vienna, once a longed-for prize, had proved a poisoned chalice.

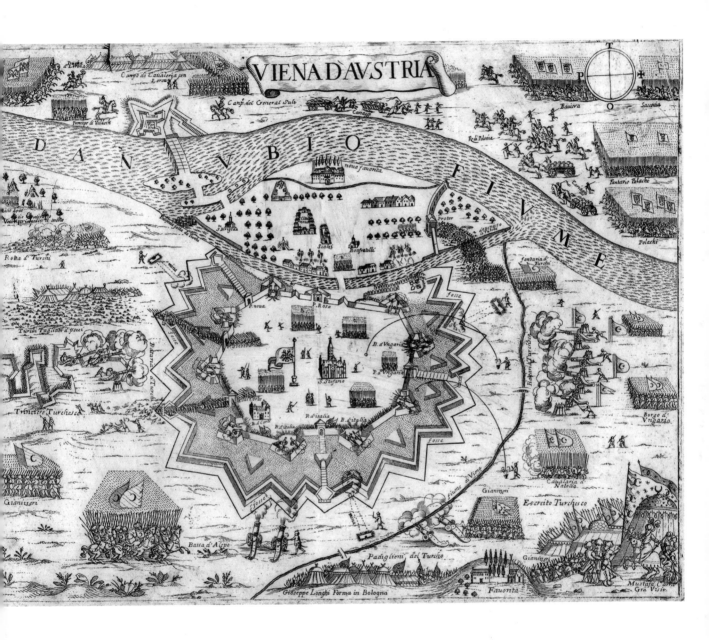

VIENA D'AVSTRIA

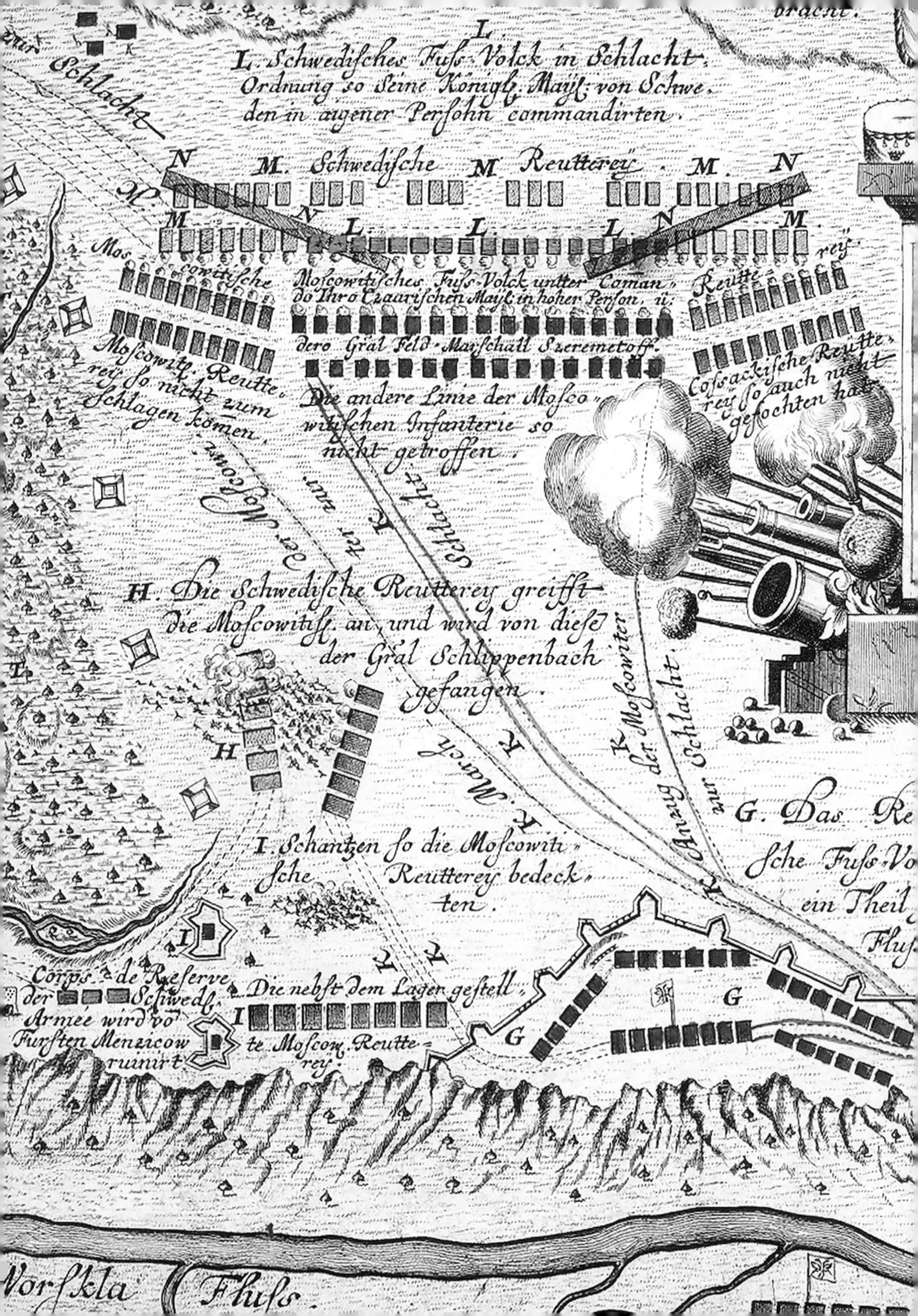

bracht.
zur Schlacht
L
L. Schwedisches Fuss-Volck in Schlacht-Ordnung so Seine Königl. Maijt. von Schweden in aigener Persohn commandirten.
N M. Schwedische M Reutterey. M. N
M M N L L L N M
Moscowitische Reutterey
Moscowitisches Fuss-Volck unter Comando Ihro Czaarischen Maijt. in hoher Person, u. dero Gral Feld-Marschall Szeremetoff.
Moscowitz. Reutterey so nicht zum Schlagen komen.
Die andere Linie der Moscowitischen Infanterie so nicht getroffen.
Cosackische Reutterey so auch nicht gefochten hat.
Der Moscow
zur Schlacht
K
H. Die Schwedische Reutterey greifft die Moscowitisch. an, und wird von diese der Gral Schlippenbach gefangen.
H
K Marsch K
K Anzug der Moscowiter zur Schlacht
G. Das Re
sche Fuss-Vo
ein Theil
Fluss
I. Schantzen so die Moscowitische Reutterey bedeckten.
I
Corps de Reserve der Schwedis. Armée wird vo Fursten Menzicow ruinirt
I
Die nebst dem Lager gestellte Moscow. Reutterey.
G
G
Vorskla Fluss

Battle of Poltava

The map, by Augsburg engraver and publisher Joseph Friedrich Leopold (1668–1726), shows the forces of Sweden (in yellow) locked with those of Peter the Great's Russia (in red) around the Ukrainian town of Poltava. The fine engraving, with its squares of infantry and charging cavalry, gives little inkling of the catastrophe about to befall the Swedish army.

The battle was fought as part of the Great Northern War, a prolonged tussle between Sweden and Russia for control of the south shore of the Baltic Sea that began in 1700 and would only finally end 21 years later. By 1707, King Charles XII of Sweden, then aged just 25 but capable beyond his years, resolved to end the war by invading Russia and seizing Moscow. Stiff Russian resistance, the loss of its supply train and the worst winter in a century – in which flocks of frozen birds fell dead from the trees – gnawed away at Charles's army until only around 25,000 troops remained.

The Swedish king resolved on one last throw of the dice, to take an alternative route through Ukraine and then hook back up northwards to Moscow. In his way stood Poltava on the banks of the Vorskla river, which Charles laid under siege in April. But then, on June 20, a large relieving army under Tsar Peter arrived and set up a fortified camp with its back protected by the river's west bank.

Even though his 49,000-strong army was twice the size of the Swedish force, Peter was conscious that his opponents were better trained. To prevent a direct assault on his camp, he ordered the building of a series of redoubts on the edge of the wooded area between his position and the Swedish siege lines around Poltava. The Swedish side had already suffered a disaster on June 17 when Charles was struck on the foot by a musket ball during a reconnaissance near the Russian camp, which left Field Marshal Carl Gustav Rehnskiöld in overall command of the Swedish army, assisted by General Adam Lewenhaupt, who led the infantry, and severely dented morale.

Rehnskiöld had to act fast, as there were rumours that more than 40,000 Russian reinforcements were approaching. Before dawn on July 8 he unleashed the Swedish infantry against the redoubts, but they were observed and lost the element of surprise. A large detachment under Major General Carl Roos took two redoubts but became bogged down trying to seize a third, while the rest of the infantry under Lewenhaupt pressed ahead. Initially successful attacks by the Russian cavalry had stalled, but equally the momentum of the Swedish advance was lost, as Lewenhaupt paused to wait for Roos, who had been cut off by the Russians and fled into the Yakovetski woods.

At around 6am Peter ordered his men forward from the encampment, and 22,000 Russian infantry and over 80 artillery pieces now faced the Swedes. The stand-off continued for four hours, until Lewenhaupt finally ordered his infantry forward. At 550 yards' range the Russian artillery opened fire; at 55 yards a devastating musket volley scythed into the Swedish lines. Some of Lewenhaupt's troops did reach the Russian battalions, but with their numbers weakened, their left flank buckled and fled, which allowed the Russian cavalry to outflank them and attack from the rear.

The Swedish army disintegrated, and Charles fled with the remaining Swedish troops into the woods, where they hid from roaming Cossacks and Kalmyks for several hours before breaking out to Poltava, collecting the besieging force and beginning a long retreat south. It had been a catastrophe for the Swedes: they lost nearly 7,000 dead and wounded, and Rehnskiöld was captured, while Lewenhaupt surrendered most of the rest of the army at Perevolochna three days later. Only Charles and about 1,500 survivors made it to Moldavia, where the king threw himself under the protection of the Ottoman Turkish sultan Ahmed III.

The "protection" soon became lightly disguised captivity, and Charles only managed to return to Sweden in late 1715, but his attempts to revive Swedish fortunes ended when he was killed while leading an invasion of Norway in 1718. It was left to his sister Ulrika Eleonora to negotiate the Treaty of Nystad, by which Sweden was stripped of its possessions in north Germany and lost all of its holdings on the eastern coast of the Baltic. As Peter the Great himself put it, an invasion that had threatened to destroy his realm had instead achieved the opposite, and "Now with God's help, the last stone has been laid to the foundation of St Petersburg."

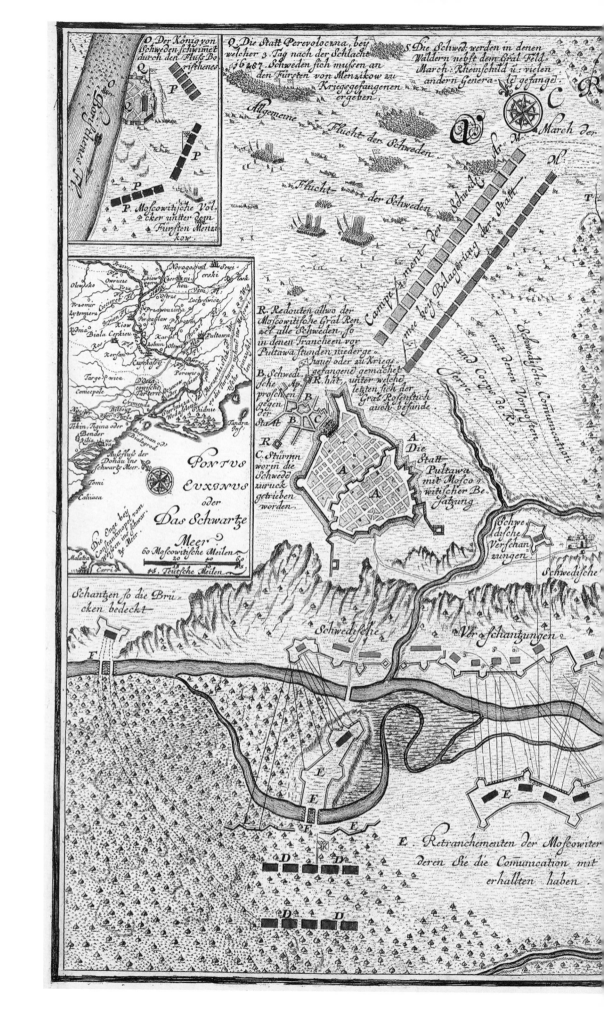

O. Der König von Schweden schwimet durch den Fluss Boristhenes.

Q. Die Statt Perevoloczna, bey welcher 3 Tag nach der Schlacht 1648? Schweden sich mussen an den Fürsten von Menzikow zu Kriegsgefangenen ergeben.

S. Die Schweden werden in denen Wäldern nebst dem Gral Feld March. Rheinschild u: vielen andern General: gefangel:

Allgemeine Flucht der Schweden

Flucht der Schweden

P. Moscowitsche Volcker uniter dem Fürsten Menzikow

Campement der untre der Belagerung der Statt

March der Poll:

Schwedische Comunication mit denen Vompostern mit denen Corpus de Re

R. Redouten allwo der Moscowitsche Gral Ren azl alle Schweden, so in denen Trancheen vor Pultawa stunden niederge: hauel oder zu Kriegs: gefangend gemachet R. hat, unter welchen letzten sich der Gral Rosenstuch auch befande.

B. Schwedische Approschen gegen der Statt

C. Sturm worin die Schwede zurück getrieben worden.

R.

A. Die Statt Pultawa mit Moscowitischer Besatzung

Schwedische Verschanzungen

Schwedische

Pontus Euxinus oder Das Schwartze Meer

60 Moscowitsche Meilen
45 Teutsche Meilen

Schanzen so die Brücken bedeckt

Schwedische Ver schanzungen

E. Retranchementen der Moscowiter deren sie die Comunication mit erhallten haben

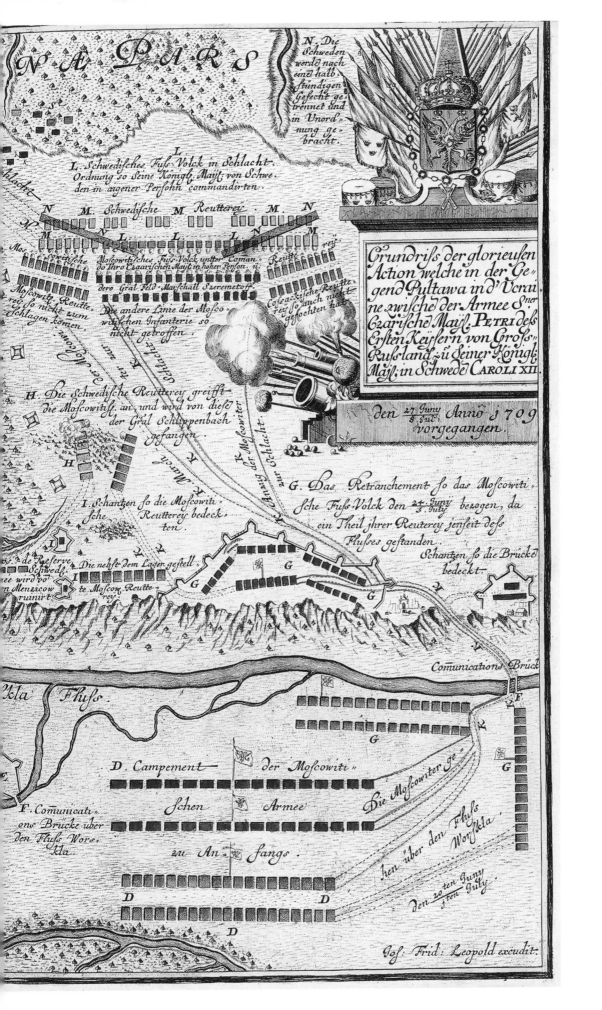

L

L

M

Q

Q

Q

Q

K

K

H

M

P

K

K

H

20. Can:

O

G

R

R

G

G

H

Dixieme Attaque

G

H Can:

G

G

40.

H

N

Bois de Tainiere

p

C

C

M

N

C

p

Deuxieme Attaque

B

N

L

P

B

M

P

B

N

Premiere Attaque

Bo

Bleron

Blarignie
Quartier du Prince
Eugene
et Duc de Marlboroug

Battle of Malplaquet

The plan shows the wooded terrain scored by ravines within which the bloodiest battle of the 18th century and the last major engagement of the War of the Spanish Succession took place. Drawn up by a Captain Brüchmann, an engineer from the Duchy of Hannover who was present at the battle, and published by Elizabeth Verseyl, widow of Nicolaes Visscher, one of Amsterdam's leading printmakers and cartographers, it also maps out the victory which very nearly tarnished the reputation of John Churchill, Duke of Marlborough, who had become one of Britain's military heroes.

Fought on September 11, 1709, near the village of Malplaquet in northeast France, the battle was the culmination of a conflict which broke out when King Louis XIV of France tried to get his grandson Philip of Anjou placed on the Spanish throne. When Charles II of Spain died in November 1700, having bequeathed his crown to Philip, Louis XIV acted swiftly to send French troops into the Spanish Netherlands to secure his position. An alliance of the Netherlands, Britain and Austria was formed to thwart Louis's ambitions, and for eight long years the fortunes of war swung, with Marlborough's victories at Blenheim (1704) and Ramillies (1706) never quite crushing the French capacity to continue the conflict.

Peace negotiations in early 1709 collapsed under the weight of unreasonable Allied demands, which led Louis to resume the war, appointing Claude-Louis-Hector, duc de Villars, to mastermind a French fightback. His army turned out to be in a parlous state, and it soon became clear that the best Villars could hope for was to hold back the Allied army to salvage a position from which a more favourable peace could be negotiated.

Deft manoeuvring directed by Marlborough tricked Villars into weakening the garrison of Tournai, which the Allies promptly captured on September 3. Louis then ordered Villars to prevent at all costs the capture of Mons. As Marlborough was already besieging the town, Villars decided to face him to the south, at Malplaquet, while the British general, keen to crush France's last major field army, was eager to oblige.

Villars's position was in principle very strong; his army, arrayed between the woods of Lagniere and Tainiere, was protected by breastworks built across gaps in the broken terrain and artillery batteries sited on his flanks to provide enfilading fire. Marlborough's plan was a copy of that which had won him his other victories: to mount attacks on the flanks, cause his opponent to send reinforcements to meet these, and then deliver a knockout blow in the weakened centre.

When the attack began around 8am after a desultory exchange of artillery fire, things soon began to diverge from the plan. The first attack on the right flank by the Prussian Marshal Johann von der Schulenburg was met with devastating fire from French troops stationed in the woods, and the Allied advance lost cohesion as hundreds of men fell and others became entangled in the woods. To Schulenburg's left, Marshal Carl Philipp, Graf von Wylich und Lottum fared better, but his men were caught up in bitter hand-to-hand fighting along the French breastworks.

On Marlborough's left flank the Prince of Orange, who had been supposed to mount only a diversionary attack, instead launched a full-scale one, which was met with a cannonade from twenty French guns and furious musket fire. Some 5,000 casualties resulted in minutes, and still Orange did not pull back, incurring thousands more.

By 10am, though, Schulenburg had made his way through the Bois du Sart, and Lottum, reinforced by Lord Orkney, was pushing forwards. As Villars fed in reinforcements to hold back Schulenburg's advance, vicious fighting erupted in the woods: flying splinters of wood pierced men's eyes and branches crushed their limbs. By now Villars's centre too had buckled. Schulenburg had dragged a battery through the woods and was raining down fire on his left. Wounded in the left knee, Villars collapsed from loss of blood, while the death of the comte de Chémerault further undermined the French resistance. Although their cavalry commander Louis-François, duc de Boufflers took over and launched charge after charge, it was not enough, and by 2pm the French were in retreat.

The battlefield was a gruesome sight: the French had lost around 12,000 men and the Allies up to 25,000 from their original force of 110,000. The toll was so horrific that Marlborough was never again permitted to engage the French in a full-scale battle – and so denied the chance to win a final victory. Instead, diplomacy took over, which led to a final series of peace treaties in 1713. As Villars later wrote: "If God will grant us the grace to lose such a battle again, Your Majesty can count on all his enemies being destroyed."

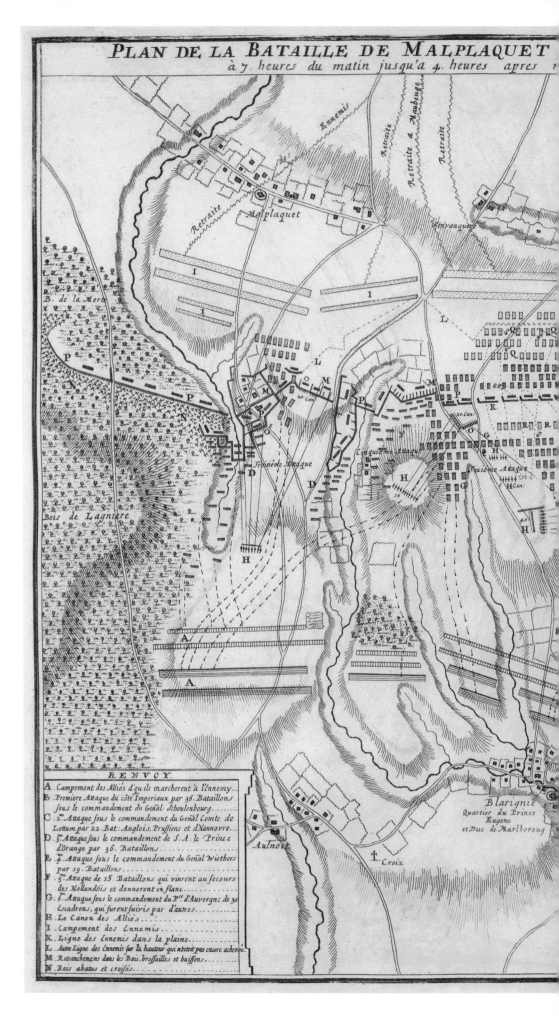

Retraite des Ennemis

Retraite à Maubeuge

Retraite

Malplaquet

Venyanque

B. de la Mert

Tr.ième Attaque

Bois de Laguiere

Cinquième Attaque

Dixieme Attaque

Blarignie
Quartier du Prince
Eugene
et Duc de Marlboroug

Aulnoi

Croix

RENVOY.

A. Campement des Alliés d'qu ils marcherent à l'ennemy.

B. Premiere Attaque du côté Imperiaux par 36. Bataillons
sous le commandement du Genäl. Schoulenbourg.

C. 2.ᵉ Attaque sous le commandement du Genäl Comte de
Lottum par 22. Bat: Anglois, Prussiens et d'Hannovre.

D. 3.ᵉ Attaque sous le commandement de S. A. le Prince
d'Orange par 36. Bataillons.

E. 4.ᵉ Attaque sous le commandement du Genäl Wiethers
par 19. Bataillons.

F. 5.ᵉ Attaque de 15. Bataillons qui vinrent au secours
des Hollandois et donnerent en flanc.

G. 6.ᵉ Attaque sous le commandement du P.ᶜᵉ d'Auvergne de 30.
Escadrons, qui furent suivis par d'autres.

H. Le Canon des Alliés.

I. Campement des Ennemis.

K. Ligne des Ennemis dans la plaine.

L. Autre Ligne des Ennemis sur la hauteur qui n'estoit pas encore achevée.

M. Retranchemens dans les Bois, brossailles et buissons.

N. Bois abatus et croisés.

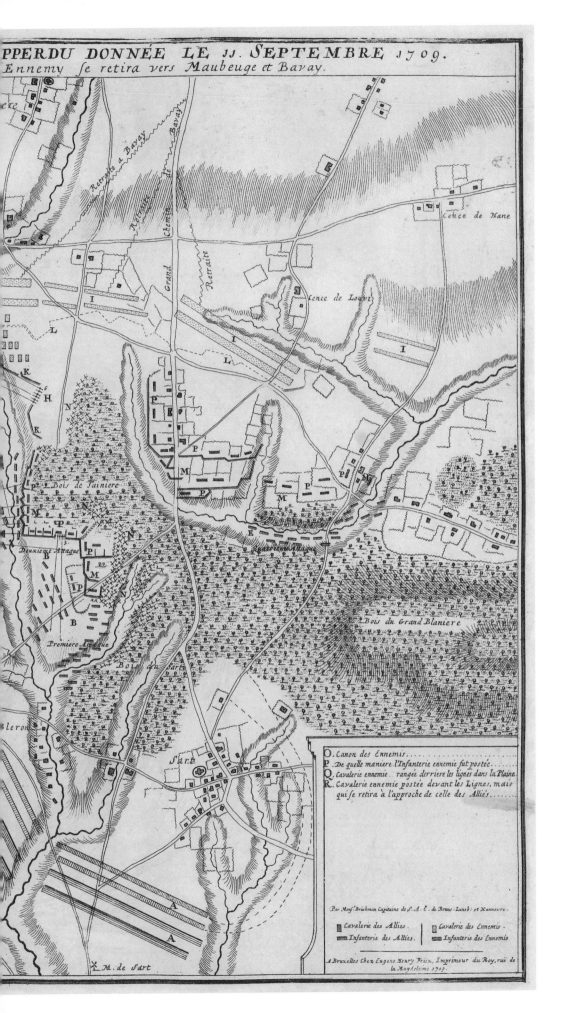

Retraite a Bavay

Retraite a Bavay

Grand Chemin de Bavay

Retraite

Cence de Hane

I

L

I

Cence de Louvi

I

L

H

K

N

K

Bois de Jainiere

P

M

P

M

P

P

M

E

Deuxieme Attaque

Grand Chemin de Mons

N

B

P

M

B

Premiere Attaque

Bois du Grand Blaniere

Bois du Sart

leron

Sart

M. de Sart

O. Canon des Ennemis . . . .
P. De quelle maniere l'Infanterie ennemie fut postée . . . . .
Q. Cavalerie ennemie . rangée derriere les lignes dans la Plaine .
R. Cavalerie ennemie postée devant les Lignes, mais
   qui se retira à l'approche de celle des Alliés . . . .

Par Monſ. Bruchman Capitaine de S. A. E. de Bruns: Luneb: et Hannovre.

Cavalerie des Alliés.   Cavalerie des Ennemis.
Infanterie des Alliés.   Infanterie des Ennemis

A Bruxelles chez Eugene Henry Frix, Imprimeur du Roy, rue de
la Magdeleine 1709.

Battle of Plassey

The engraving, published in the *London Magazine* in 1760, shows the encounter that decided the fate of India. Fought at Plassey, the battle between the East India Company forces of Robert Clive (then a lowly colonel) and Siraj-ud-Daulah, Nawab of Bengal, marked an acceleration in Britain's engagement with India that would result, within a century, in its annexation of almost all of it.

The British had first established a small commercial post at Surat in 1612, gaining the protection of the Mughal emperors in order to enjoy a modest commercial gain. But as the Mughal grip on power weakened, a constellation of former tributaries and upstart powers devoured its former territory, vastly complicating the task of the East India Company's governors and tempting them to turn to force to assert their trading privileges.

Then, in 1756 Aliwardi Khan, the Nawab of Bengal, died, to be succeeded by his young great-nephew Siraj-ud-Daulah, a far more mercurial figure, who decided to dislodge the East India Company from the bridgehead they had held at Kolkata since 1690. On June 19, 1756, the nawab's forces stormed Kolkata, incarcerating 146 European prisoners in a tiny, airless room (later infamous as the "Black Hole"). Most of them suffocated to death. The storm of emotion this aroused and the suspicion that the French, in the shape of General Joseph Dupleix, were egging on the nawab to favour French merchants in place of the British led the East India Company to send Robert Clive with an expeditionary force backed by a flotilla of gunships to seek vengeance and retake Kolkata.

Siraj-ud-Daulah's small garrison soon surrendered to Clive, and by early February 1757 he had stormed the nawab's camp at Cossimbazar and forced him to sign a new treaty confirming the company's privileges. Yet the outbreak in Europe of war between France and Britain led hostilities in India to flare up again, as Clive feared the nawab would make common cause with the French. A British attack on the French settlement at Chandernagore led to a testy series of diplomatic negotiations, and then the nawab moved his army south to Plassey, 23 miles south of Cossimbazar and threateningly close to Kolkata.

Clive took this as tantamount to a declaration of war and moved to intercept the nawab. His complement of 950 European soldiers, 2,100 sepoys (Indian troops in company service) and a battery of 6-pounder guns seemed a paltry force to face Siraj-ud-Daulah's more than 50,000 men. But Clive had prepared his ground well, making contact with dissident factions at the Bengali court, most notably Mir Jafar Khan, to whom he offered the position of nawab if he betrayed the current incumbent. Around 6am on June 22, 1757, Clive's force crossed the Bhagirathi river amid driving monsoon rain and reached Plassey the next night, taking shelter in a mango grove beyond the village.

What Clive knew, but the nawab did not, was that two thirds of the Bengali force, led by Mir Jafar and Rai Durlabh, had pledged to stand aside from the fight. The battle began with an artillery duel between the nawab's gunners, reinforced by a battery of French artillery lent to him by Dupleix, and the East India Company's 6-pounders. The Indian gunners' slower rate of fire and their lack of elevating screws to enable accurate ranging meant the nawab's force came off worse, particularly after Clive withdrew his guns back into the shelter of the mango grove, from where they could still fire. The death in the cannonade of Mir Madan, Siraj-ud-Daulah's only reliable general, and the soaking by a monsoon downpour of most of the Indian gunpowder supply caused a crisis. A section of Clive's army under Major Kilpatrick rushed forwards, sucking the remaining loyal Bengali forces back into battle. The storm of musket fire and the lethal rain of artillery shells took their toll on the Bengalis, and with the French contingent dislodged from a protective redoubt by 5pm and the nawab's cavalry refusing to engage, Siraj-ud-Daulah had little choice but to retreat.

The East India Company had lost just 22 dead and 50 wounded against over 500 casualties in the nawab's army. Siraj-ud-Daulah was captured ten days later and executed as he tried to escape north. Mir Jafar proved less pliable than hoped, so did not enjoy his position as the new nawab for long, being deposed by the British East India Company three years later. Clive was lionised as a hero, though later accused of corruption on a grand scale and the subject of a two-year inquiry in parliament, after which he killed himself by slitting his throat with a paperknife. Plassey showed the huge advantage modern, well-drilled artillery gave, but Siraj-ud-Daulah, ultimately, had a revenge of sorts.

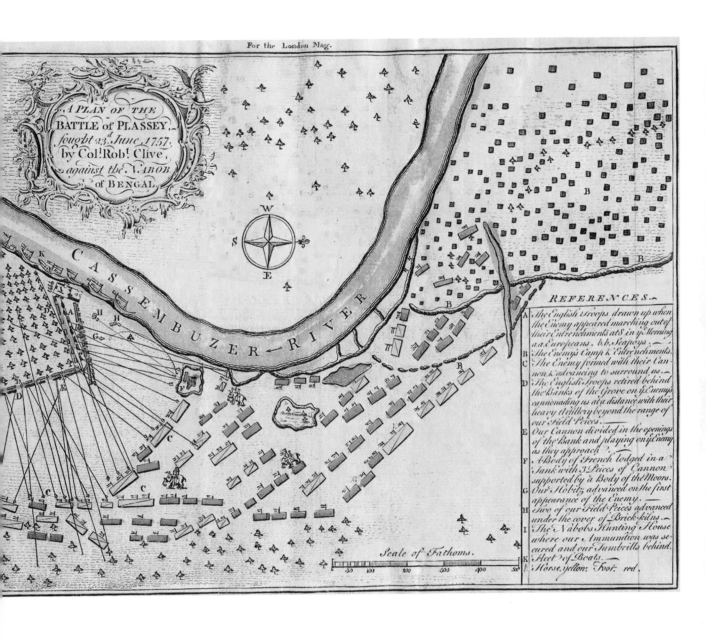

A PLAN OF THE
BATTLE of PLASSEY,
fought 23d June 1757,
by Col. Robt. Clive,
against the NABOB
of BENGAL.

CASSEMBUZER RIVER

W
S   E

Scale of Fathoms.

50   100   200   300   400   500

REFERENCES.

A | The English Troops drawn up when the Enemy appeared marching out of their Entrenchments at 8 in ye Morning a.a. Europeans. b.b. Seapoys.
B | The Enemy's Camp & Entrenchments.
C | The Enemy formed with their Cannon & advancing to surround us.
D | The English Troops retired behind the Banks of the Grove on ye Enemy's cannonading us at a distance with their heavy Artillery beyond the range of our Field Peices.
E | Our Cannon divided in the openings of the Bank and playing on ye Enemy as they approach.
F | A Body of French lodged in a Tank with 3 Peices of Cannon supported by a Body of the Moors.
G | Our Hobitz advanced on the first appearance of the Enemy.
H | Two of our Field Peices advanced under the cover of Brick-kilns.
I | The Nabobs Hunting House where our Ammunition was secured and our Tumbrills behind.
K | Fleet of Boats.
L | Horse, yellow. Foot, red.

Battle of Leuthen

The fine lines in this plan by the Dutch engraver Jakob van der Schley show one of the decisive battles in the Seven Years' War, which originally erupted between Frederick the Great's Prussia and Maria Theresa's Austria over the latter's desire to regain Silesia, lost to Prussia in a previous conflict in the 1740s. The war spread to become a global struggle, sucking in France and Britain, and involving campaigning in North America and even India (see page 78).

Everything, though, became focused on the small town of Leuthen (now Lutynia, near Wrocław in Poland) on a bitter December day in 1757. The road there had been long, and Frederick had already displayed his tactical astuteness and reaped the rewards of his reforms of the Prussian army which enabled it to perform complex manoeuvres flawlessly even at the height of battle. In August 1756 Frederick pre-empted an expected Austrian attempt to recover Silesia, striking first south into Saxony, where he sought to make further gains. By May 1757 he was besieging Prague, but then turned back towards Prussia to deflect an Austrian move against Berlin. At Rossbach, near Leipzig in Saxony, his army of 20,000 beat a Franco-German force twice that size on November 5, but Frederick's delight was tempered by the news that the main Prussian force in Silesia had been scattered by a huge Austrian army led by Charles of Lorraine.

Frederick hurried east to rescue the situation, on the evening of 4 December finding the Austrians encamped to the west of the Schweidnitz river, arrayed along a four-mile-long ridge close to Leuthen. Charles commanded 65,000 men with 235 artillery pieces, but Frederick benefited from the fact that the Austrians had chosen to fight in the area where the Prussian army held its regular autumn training manoeuvres, and so he and his generals knew every inch of it intimately.

Frederick's plan was audacious, exploiting this knowledge of the terrain to maximum effect. At 5am the following day, the king deployed a forward guard of cavalry supported by a small number of infantry on Frederick's right flank before beginning an advance against the numerically far superior Austrian left. It was a trap and one into which Charles duly fell as he moved battalions from his own right to meet this perceived threat. All the while, the rest of the Prussian army was marching to the northwest, shielded by gullies and hillocks which blocked the Austrian commanders'

view of their movement (their advance shown by "C" on the plan). By 1pm they had passed Sagschütz, when General Franz Nádasti on the Austrian left caught sight of them and frantically called for help, but so convinced was Charles that the main attack was still against his right, that he ignored the general.

The Prussians, in perfect formation, passed beyond the Austrian left flank. Then, the full might of Frederick's attack fell on the rear of inexperienced battalions of Württembergers, who quickly broke, allowing the Prussian line to advance towards Leuthen. Nádasti tried to throw his horsemen against him, but Frederick's cavalry commander Hans Joachim von Zieten countered with his own charge which threw back the Austrians. Although Charles belatedly shifted his battalions to the left, it was too late, and he was forced to wheel his entire army to face south, which created further disorder and confusion. By 3pm bitter fighting had erupted around Leuthen, where the Austrians used the stone churchyard walls as barricades and shot from behind the pews of the church itself. Salvation seemed to appear in the shape of Joseph, Count Lucchesi d'Averna, commanding the bulk of the surviving Austrian cavalry. Unfortunately, his own flank was struck by 40 squadrons of von Zieten's horse, while General Georg von Driesen charged him head-on with 30 squadrons more. The Austrian attack dissipated, while the unfortunate Lucchesi was decapitated by a cannon ball.

By now the light was failing, and the Austrians were in full retreat towards Lissa, with the Prussians in pursuit. Frederick's infantry broke into a chorus of *Nun danket alle Gott* ("Now Thank We All Our God") as they took the bridge there, forestalling any Austrian attempt to make a further stand. Frederick must have thanked God too, for, despite the ingenuity of his plan, had Charles not taken the bait, the Prussians would have fared far worse than the 1,175 dead they suffered against 10,000 Austrian dead and wounded and 12,000 captured.

The battle cemented Frederick's reputation as a military genius, but it neither ended the war, which had a further six years to run, nor in the end delivered the hoped-for gains. The Prussians kept Silesia, and Frederick was denied possession of Saxony. A great victory, as Frederick learnt, does not always lead to a great peace.

PLAN DE LA BATAILLE,

gagnée par Sa Majesté le Roi de Prusse, sur l'Armée Autrichienne, aux ordres de S. A. R. le Duc Charles de Lorraine, près de LEUTHEN, ou LISSA, en Silesie; le 5 Decembre 1757.

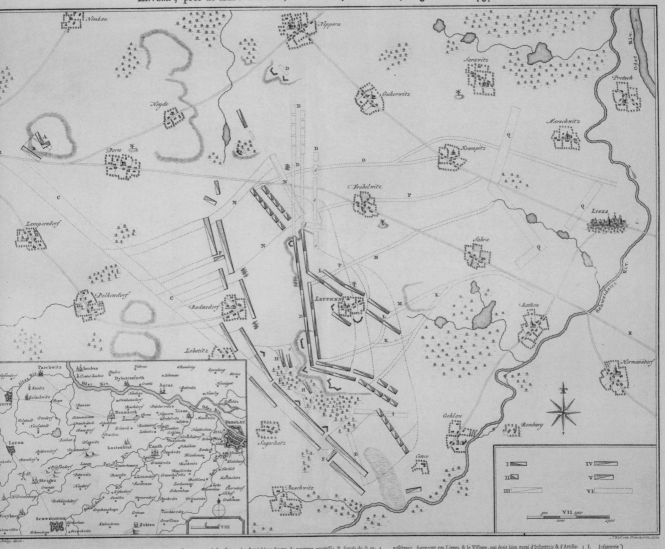

A LA HAYE, Chez PIERRE DE HONDT, 1758.

sur laquelle le Corps du Général Nadasti étoit posté, pour observer les mou-
 de l'Armée Prussienne; mais qui se retira à l'approche de l'Avant-Garde des
.

 de l'Avant-Garde Prussienne contre une partie de ce Corps, composée de 2
 ns de Chevaux legers Saxons, & de 2 Régimens de Hussars Autrichiens, com-
 par le Comte de Nostitz, Lieutenant Général Saxon, lesquels furent desaits &
 fuite vers leur Camp, avec perte de quelques Etendarts. Les Prussiens furent,
 occasion, 700 Prisonniers sur les Ennemis.

 de l'Armée Prussienne contre l'Aile gauche des Autrichiens.
 ere Disposition de l'Armée Autrichienne, qui, à l'approche de toute l'Armée
 nne contre son Aile gauche, fut obligée de la changer, & d'employer une gran-
 tie de l'Infanterie de son Aile droite, avec le Corps de reserve 1.) pour renforcer
 gauche.

 ue de la Cavalerie Autrichienne de l'Aile gauche contre la droite des Prussiens,
 quelque Cavalerie fut obligée de plier; mais, par le feu vif des Bataillons de Gre-
 , postés entre la première & la seconde Ligne, à

F. pour couvrir les flancs, les Autrichiens furent de nouveau repoussés & forcés de se retirer en confusion; cependant ils se remirent à la faveur d'une vive Canonnade.
G. Bois où les Autrichiens avoient posté diverses Brigades d'Infanterie de Wurtemberg &
 de Baviere, qui, à l'approche de l'Infanterie Prussienne, furent attaquées par le Géné-
2.) ral Major Wedel, avec quelques Bataillons, près de 2.) délogées & obligées de se retirer en
 confusion sur la Coline derriere le Bois, où elles se rallièrent.
H. Seconde Attaque de l'Infanterie Prussienne, qui suivit immediatement la première, pour
 la soutenir, avec l'effet, que l'Infanterie de l'Aile gauche Ennemie, postée sur une hauteur, fut forcée, après un combat opiniâtre, à plier & à abandonner ses pièces de canon;
 ce qui occasionna une grosse Ouverture dans les Lignes Autrichiennes; Surquoi
I. la Cavalerie Prussienne de cette Aile attaqua de nouveau celle des Ennemis, qu'elle
 renversa, après un combat des plus vifs; de sorte que toute cette Aile fut mise en fuite
 vers
K. & les Prussiens firent, à la même occasion, quantité de Prisonniers sur les Autrichiens.
L. Nouvelles Lignes que formèrent les Autrichiens, près du Village de Leuthen, par les
 Troupes qu'ils y avoient tiré de leur Aile droite; Les Prussiens, après une vigoureuse

 resistance, forcerent ces Lignes & le Village, qui étoit bien garni d'Infanterie & d'Artille-
 rie, & mirent les Ennemis en fuite vers
M. où ils tâchèrent bien de se rétablir & de faire encore quelques efforts; mais ils furent
 de nouveau repoussés.
N. Attaque de la Cavalerie Prussienne de l'Aile gauche contre la droite des Ennemis, qui fut
 renversée & mise en fuite vers
O. Surquoi quelques Escadrons de Dragons Prussiens 3.) tombèrent en flanc & à dos sur l'In-
3.) fanterie, qui se trouvoit par là à découvert; ce qui la mit dans le plus grand desordre,
 & deux de ses Régimens furent faits prisonniers; après quoi son centre se vit aussi en-
 fin réduit à prendre la fuite vers
P. & de cette façon les Autrichiens, fuyant de toutes parts, furent poursuivis par les Prussiens
 victorieux, à l'entrée de la nuit, jusqu'auprès de Lissa, où l'Armée Prussienne s'arrêta
 la nuit à
Q. occupa encore Lissa, &, le 6 au matin, passa la Rivière Schweidnitz, pour continuer
 de poursuivre les Ennemis.
R. Grand Chemin de Neumarck à Breslau.

I. Infanterie
II. Cavalerie des Autrichiens.
III. Attaques

IV. Infanterie
V. Cavalerie des Prussiens.
VI. Attaques

VII. Echelle de 2500 Pas, ou $\frac{1}{4}$ de mile d'Allemagne.

VIII. Echelle d'un mile d'Allemagne.

WARFARE
IN THE AGE OF
REVOLUTIONS

1775–1855

Battle of Saratoga

The plan shows the position of Lieutenant "Gentleman Johnny" Burgoyne's British Army at Saratoga (around 30 miles north of Albany in what is now New York State). Drawn by Isaac A Chapman, it is based on a sketch by an officer on the American side in the battle fought there in mid-October 1777 which denied the British control of New England and an early end to the Revolutionary War. The map was published in 1818 in the Philadelphia-based *Analectic* magazine, whose influence on the narrative of early United States history is demonstrated by Thomas Jefferson having been one of its subscribers and its publication, in 1814, of the poem *The Defence of Fort M'Henry* by Francis Scott Key, which became the basis of *The Star-Spangled Banner*, the American national anthem.

Burgoyne's command of the high ground, anchored around a series of redoubts and dominating the approaches from Albany and across the Hudson River, should have guaranteed him victory. The campaign which brought him to Saratoga aimed at dividing the New England colonies from those in the south, cutting the territory controlled by the Continental Army in two and throttling the revolution. Burgoyne departed in June from St Johns in Canada with around 9,000 men (half of whom were actually German, from Brunswick and Hesse). If he could join with General William Howe, who was advancing from the south, and a smaller detachment under Colonel Barry St Leger, their combined forces would be irresistible.

Having occupied Fort Ticonderoga (which the American commander, General Philip Schuyler, wisely evacuated) on July 6, Burgoyne was held up by the need to forage for supplies and build bridges across the many waterways that lay between him and Albany. By the time he crossed the Hudson and camped around Saratoga on September 13, he was down to around 7,000 men and had learnt that Howe had abandoned the campaign in favour of an attack on Philadelphia.

As a result, Burgoyne was outnumbered when General Horatio Gates, who had replaced Schuyler, arrived with 12,000 Continental troops and set up camp about 4 miles away on Bemis Heights. Understanding the danger, on September 19 Burgoyne moved south to dislodge the Continental forces before they could receive any further reinforcements. At Freeman's Farm, he found himself on the wrong end of irregular warfare, as Colonel Daniel Morgan's sharpshooters operating from dense woods took a terrible toll on the British (and in particular the officers). Although they were forced to withdraw, the Americans had inflicted 440 dead on the British for the loss of only 90 from their ranks.

As Burgoyne fretted from his vantage point on Breymann's Redoubt (to the left of the plan), Gates's strength only grew. On October 7 he finally renewed his attack on the Americans at Bemis Heights, but the element of surprise was lost and the British retreated, pursued by General Benedict Arnold. They rapidly swept aside the 200 German defenders of Breymann's Redoubt, and though Arnold was seriously wounded, the remaining British troops found themselves unable to escape further north and surrounded at the Balcarres Redoubt.

Although Burgoyne dug in, his position was hopeless. Inadequate supplies and the loss of any prospect of serious reinforcements forced him into a fruitless week of trying to negotiate terms, after which he capitulated and suffered the humiliation of an unconditional surrender. Worse than the loss of a whole army was the effect it had on Britain's European rivals, as France now became convinced that the revolution in America was a cause worth backing and negotiated a formal alliance with the colonists. Directing a war across the huge logistical barrier of the Atlantic Ocean was one thing; facing an enemy that knew its home territory and played to the strengths of militia adept at skirmishing and guerrilla tactics was another. But it was the entry of France into the war, enticed by Burgoyne's loss at Saratoga, that would ultimately prove fatal to Britain's cause. Six years later, the last major British force was surrounded by the Americans at Yorktown. His supplies and retreat denied by a blockading French fleet, its commander General Charles Cornwallis was forced to surrender and march out of the town to the sound of drummers beating out *The World Turned Upside Down*.

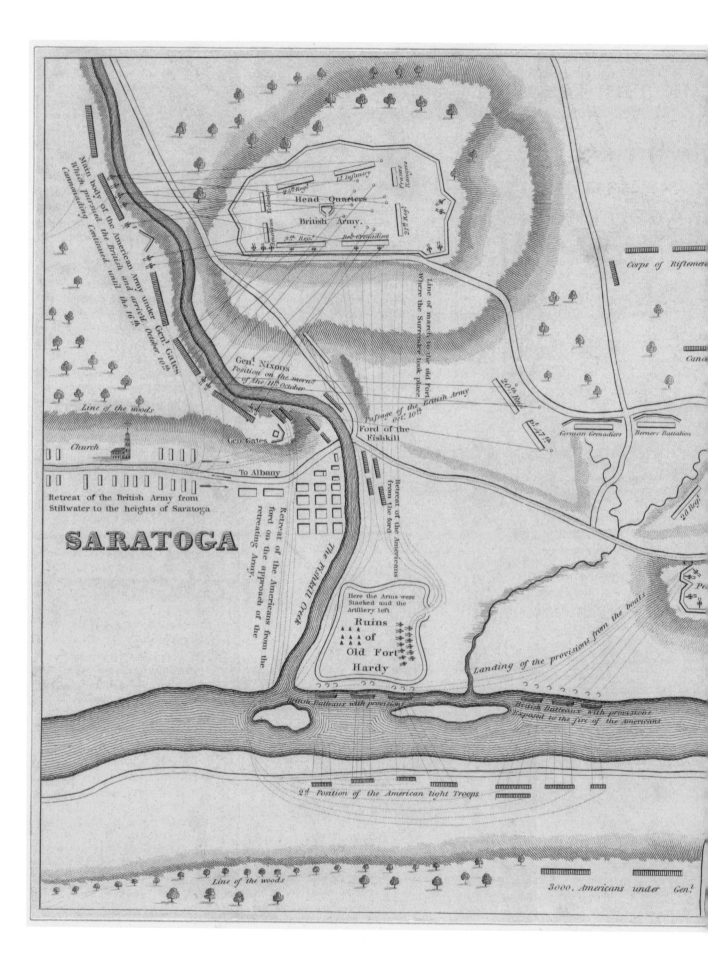

Main body of the American Army under Genl. Gates
which pursued the British and arrivd. October 10th
Commanding Continued until the 16th

Corps of Riflemen

Head Quarters
British Army.

24th Regt.   L.t Infantry

9th Regt.   Brk Grenadiers

Line of march to the old Fort
where the Surrender took place

21 Reg.

20th Reg.

Canc

Genl. Nixons
Position on the morng.
of the 11th October

Line of the woods

Line of the British Army

20th Reg.

German Grenadiers   Berners Battalion

Church

Genl. Gates

Pafsage of the
Ford of the
Fishkill
Octr. 10th

To Albany

Retreat of the British Army from
Stillwater to the heights of Saratoga

SARATOGA

Retreat of the Americans
from the ford

Retreat of the Americans from the
ford on the approach of the
retreating Army.

The Fishkill Creek

Pe

Here the Arms were
Stacked and the
Artillery left

Ruins
of
Old Fort
Hardy

Landing of the provisions from the boats

British Batteaux with provisions

British Batteaux with provisions
exposed to the fire of the Americans

2d. Position of the American light Troops

Line of the woods

3000. Americans under Genl.

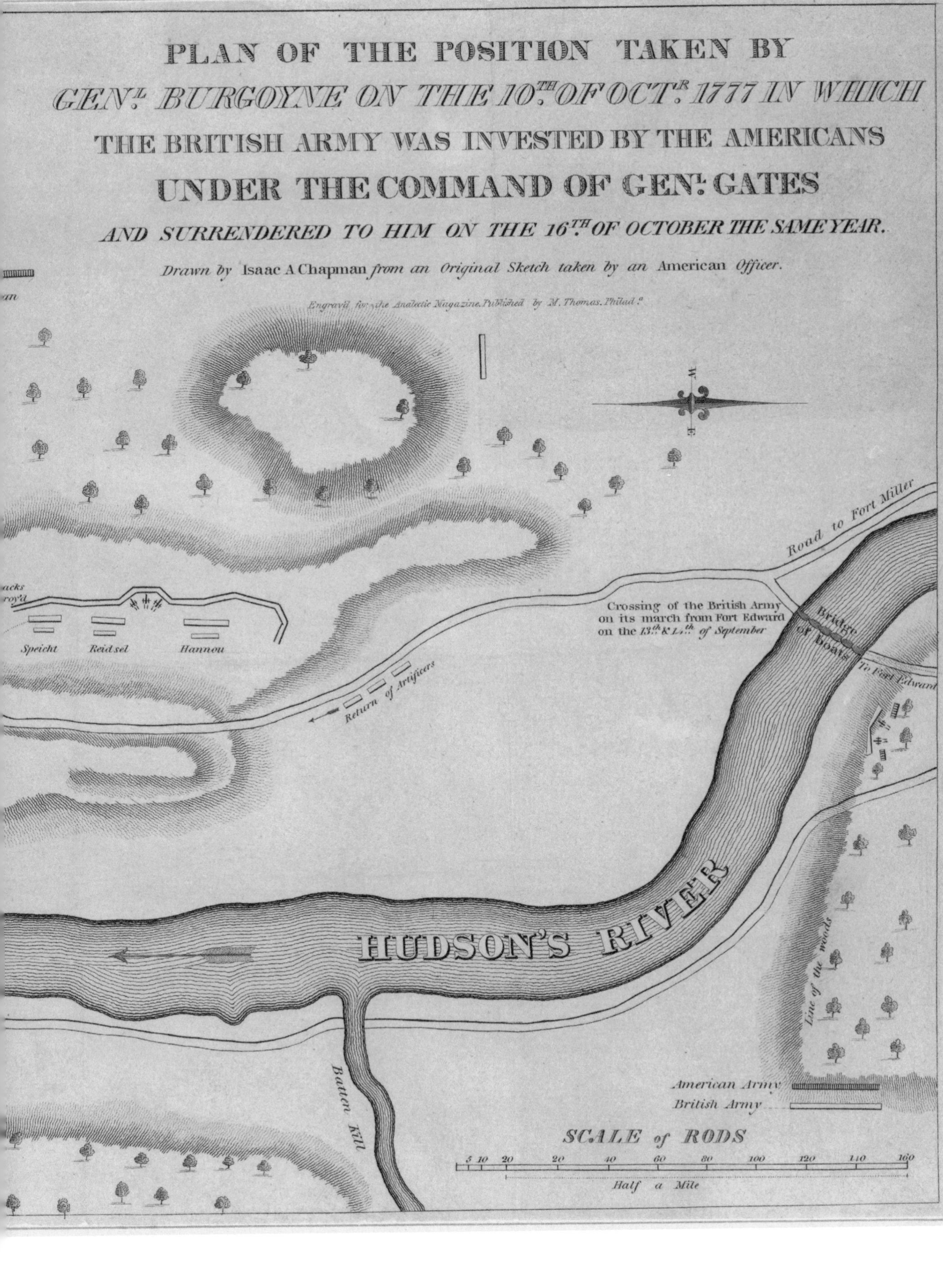

PLAN OF THE POSITION TAKEN BY
GENL. BURGOYNE ON THE 10TH. OF OCTR. 1777 IN WHICH
THE BRITISH ARMY WAS INVESTED BY THE AMERICANS
UNDER THE COMMAND OF GENL. GATES
AND SURRENDERED TO HIM ON THE 16TH. OF OCTOBER THE SAME YEAR.

Drawn by Isaac A Chapman *from an* Original Sketch *taken by an* American *Officer.*

Engraved for the Analectic Magazine. Published by M. Thomas. Philad.a

Road to Fort Miller

Crossing of the British Army
on its march from Fort Edward
on the 13th. & 14th. of September

Bridge of boats

To Fort Edward

Speicht   Reidsel   Hannou

Return of Artificers

HUDSON'S RIVER

Line of the woods

Batten Kill

American Army
British Army

SCALE of RODS

5 10 20   20   40   60   80   100   120   140   160

Half a Mile

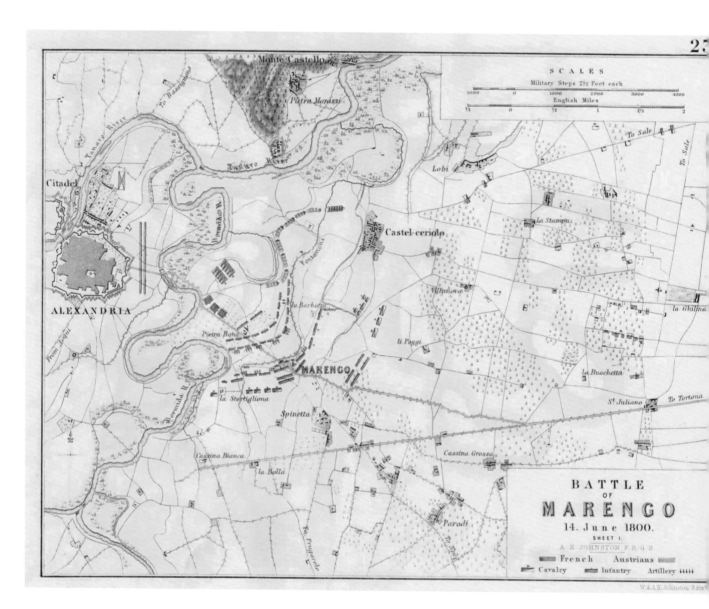

BATTLE
OF
MARENGO
14. June 1800.
SHEET I.
A.K.JOHNSTON F.R.G.S
French   Austrians
Cavalry   Infantry   Artillery

Battle of Marengo

The engraving, published by W & A K Johnston of Edinburgh, shows Austrian and French forces tightly clustered around the small town of Marengo in Lombardy. The battle fought there on June 14, 1800, decided not only the outcome of the War of the Second Coalition – pitting France against a broad alliance that encompassed Austria, Britain, Russia, Naples and Portugal – but also the fate of Napoleon Bonaparte himself. Victory here sealed the Corsican general's military reputation, an image enhanced by his own inflation of his performance there: the battle plan was reproduced in the report that Napoleon commissioned from his chief of staff and minister of war, Louis-Alexandre Berthier, and when the first versions of this hinted that it was not quite the glorious victory that the French commander had made it out to be, they were simply destroyed and replaced by a sequence of ever more rose-tinted accounts.

Having secured power as First Consul in November 1799, Napoleon resolved to lead an army over the Alps to restore the parlous French position there; the only remaining toehold was Genoa, whose garrison was under siege by the Austrians. Napoleon was too late to save it, and the city fell on June 4, but he was now blocking the lines of communication of another Austrian army under General Michael von Melas, which had invaded southern France. Von Melas turned back, hoping to escape to Austria or at least to rendezvous with General Karl Peter Ott, Freiherr von Bartokez, who commanded the Austrian forces which had captured Genoa.

The two Austrian armies concentrated at Alessandria on June 13, wrong-footing Napoleon, who believed his adversary was still at Turin. Unsure which way von Melas would turn, he detached several units to stop the Austrians slipping past, so that when on June 14 advance elements of the French army encountered the combined Austrian force outside Marengo, Napoleon's 18,000 men were outnumbered more than two to one by von Melas's 40,000.

The Austrian commander's three columns surged forward just after dawn, with von Melas leading the centre and Ott and Andreas O'Reilly on the flanks. Yet he sent too many men north towards Castelceriolo, where he believed Napoleon to have a strong contingent. The attack was blunted by the narrowness of the lodgement he gained on the right bank of the River Bormida, and he then withdrew 2,000 cavalry and sent them on a wild goose chase to attack a French unit he wrongly thought was near Cantalupo.

For several hours the French line in front of Marengo was held by General Claude Victor-Perrin with just five guns, but even with the addition of reinforcements under Jean Lannes and Joachim Murat, the French were hard-pressed and Ott's corps threatened to turn their right flank at Castelceriolo. With Victor's corps short of ammunition, the crisis of the battle seemed to have come. Napoleon threw his last reserve, 900 men of the Consular Guard, at Castelceriolo, where they fended off the Austrian envelopment under heavy fire, but in the south Marengo village was lost. A French defeat seemed inevitable.

Just then von Melas, who had suffered a minor wound, withdrew from the battle to seek treatment and, believing he had already won, handed over command to his chief of staff, General Anton Zach. At that moment, General Louis Desaix arrived at Napoleon's command post and announced that his two divisions were about to reach Marengo. Reputedly, when Napoleon asked him if there was still a chance of victory, Desaix pulled out his watch and declared that "This battle is completely lost, but it is only two o'clock, and there is time to win another."

Desaix's divisions, supported by newly arrived artillery batteries which bombarded the weary Austrians and heavy cavalry under General François Kellermann which slammed into Zach's left flank, turned the tide. Soon the Austrians were fleeing towards the safety of Alessandria. The French had lost a quarter of their total force, among them Desaix, who was shot at the moment of victory, but the Austrian casualties were far heavier at 6,000 dead and 8,000 taken prisoner. More importantly, their position in Italy was shattered. Next day von Melas signed the Convention of Alessandria, turning over their remaining fortresses in Piedmont and Lombardy to the French and agreeing not to conduct further operations there.

"The day of Marengo will remain famous throughout history", Napoleon declared after the battle, and his manipulation of the official reports ensured that it became so. His position as First Consul and his reputation for military genius now secured – helped by the collapse of the Second Coalition early the next year – Napoleon enjoyed 14 years as undisputed political master of France and over a decade of unbroken military success. Without Marengo, that would not have been possible.

Battle of Austerlitz

The map, from Marie-Joseph Adolphe Thiers's *Histoire du Consulat et de l'Empire* ("History of the Consulate and Empire") shows the field of one of Napoleon Bonaparte's greatest triumphs, which shattered the Third Coalition against him and established once and for all his reputation as one of history's greatest military geniuses. Beautifully engraved by the military specialist Charles Dyonnet, it appeared in a book by a man with a deep understanding of French political history. Thiers had been a key figure in both the July Revolution of 1830 and that of 1848 which established the Second French Republic, and then, from 1871 to 1873 was the first president of the Third Republic, tasked with bringing together the nation after its disastrous defeat in the Franco–Prussian War.

After the breakdown of the Peace of Amiens in 1803, Napoleon faced a new alliance that ranged Britain, Sweden, Russia, Austria and Prussia against him. Although his canvas of operations to escape destruction by this formidable coalition was Europe-wide, his fate would be decided on the Pratzen Heights outside Austerlitz in Moravia, the raised plateau that runs liked a jagged slash across the centre of Thiers's map.

The key to Napoleon's success, both strategic and tactical, was to prevent his opponents combining their forces, while making maximum use of his own to defeat them piecemeal or to expose localised weaknesses on the battlefield. His priority in 1805 was to stop the Austrian and Russian armies coalescing into an irresistible force. The dispatch of a large Austrian force under Archduke Charles to Italy gave him his chance, and so he struck out into Bavaria, where he smashed another Austrian army under General Karl Mack von Leiberich at Ulm between October 16 and 19. This then allowed him to advance east, occupy Vienna and then turn to face the Russians, who were moving ponderously forwards under General Mikhail Kutuzov. If he could defeat them, then Europe was his.

Although Kutuzov joined forces with the remnants of Mack's army and reinforcements under Tsar Alexander, he made the mistake of fighting on a battlefield which Napoleon had practically hand-picked for its tactical opportunities, dominated by the valley of the Goldbach stream and the Pratzen Heights. Napoleon had hoped to use his 60,000 men to conduct a grand envelopment of the Russian army by enticing them forwards against a weakened centre and then slipping round and crushing them from the rear, but Kutuzov did not quite take the bait.

Even so, the Russian general's combined 73,000 soldiers, with tens of thousands more soon to arrive as Archduke Charles advanced over the Alps from Italy, meant that had Kutuzov been more patient, he should have had enough to defeat Napoleon. Instead, the Russians attacked prematurely on December 1 after Napoleon ordered Marshals Jean de Dieu Soult and Jean Lannes to occupy Austerlitz village and the heights and then retreat, sucking in the Russian forces. Using every fold of the ground, and every building in Sokolnitz and Telnitz villages, the French then held up the Austrians for several hours, while Soult's corps climbed back up to the Pratzen Heights and swept the Russians off. Frantic efforts in the late morning to retake it failed, and by mid-afternoon the French were bombarding Kutuzov's lines from the high ground and sweeping south to envelop them.

Thousands of Russian soldiers were killed as they fled in panic, overtaking a planned withdrawal the Russian general Prince Pyotr Bagration was trying to implement (Kutuzov, cut off, could no longer direct his army). By 4pm the battle was over, with the coalition forces having suffered 29,000 casualties and lost most of their artillery. Napoleon's losses, in contrast, were a third of that number.

Two days later, the Austrian ruler Francis II signed an armistice with France, withdrawing from the Third Coalition, which promptly collapsed. It allowed Napoleon to abolish the Holy Roman Empire (whose last emperor Francis was) and to reshape the German states into the Confederation of the Rhine, a body much more accommodating to his ambitions. Economy of force, able subordinates, effective training and the élan of troops inspired by revolutionary ideals had all played a role in his victory, but it was Napoleon's genius in responding to the fluid events of the battlefield that now made him master of Europe.

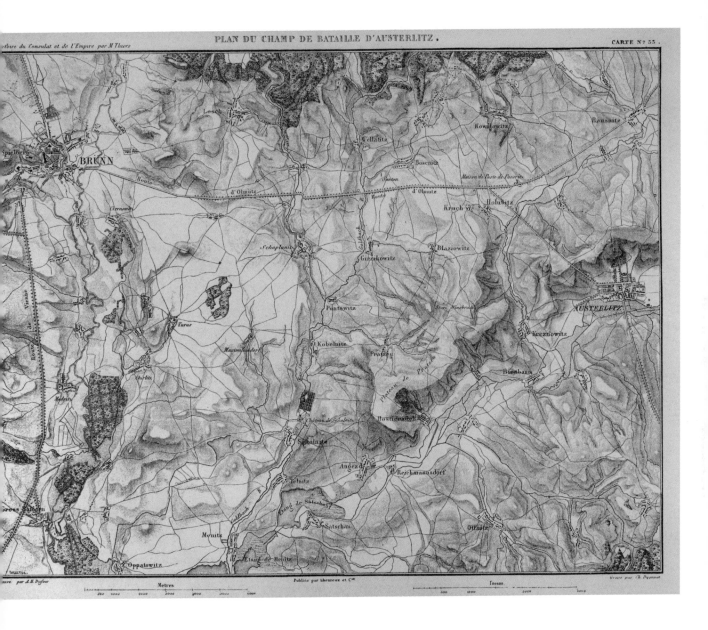

Brünn
Spielberg
Losch
Wellatitz
Kowalowitz
Rausnitz
Bosenitz
Sinton
Maison de Poste de Posoritz
Route d'Olmütz
Route d'Olmütz
Kruch vitz
Holubitz
Czernowitz
Schlapanitz
Girzikowitz
Blaziowitz
Turas
Puntowitz
Stari Winohrady
AUSTERLITZ
Maximsdorf
Kobelnitz
Pratzen
Kreznowitz
Chirlitz
Plateau de Pratzen
Biesbaum
Modreit
Chateau de Sokolnitz
Hostieradek
Sokolnitz
Augezd
Reichmannsdorf
Gross Raborn
Telnitz
Goldbach
Etang de Satschan
Satschau
Ottnitz
Menitz
Oppatowitz
Etang de Menitz

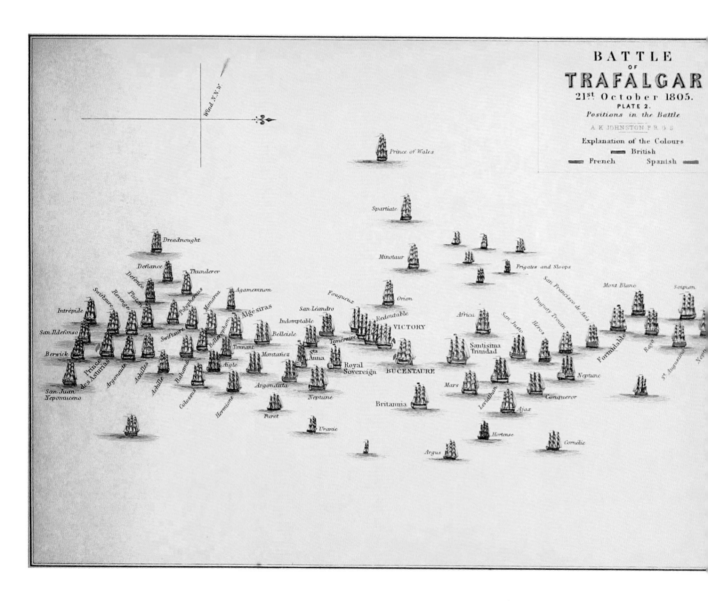

BATTLE
OF
TRAFALGAR
21st October 1805.
PLATE 2.
Positions in the Battle

A. K. JOHNSTON F.R.G.S.

Explanation of the Colours ▬ British
▬ French   Spanish ▬

Battle of Trafalgar

The plan shows a critical moment in one of Britain's greatest naval victories, as the *Victory*, flagship of Admiral Horatio Nelson, tussles with the French *Redoutable* at the height of the Battle of Trafalgar on October 21, 1805 (the French ships are lined in blue, their Spanish allies in green and the British vessels in red). It was drawn up by the eminent Scottish cartographer Alexander Keith Johnston (who was appointed Geographer Royal in 1843) as part of the atlas volume accompanying Archibald Alison's 1848 *History of Europe*, which covered the course of the French Revolution and the subsequent Revolutionary and Napoleonic Wars.

Trafalgar was one of the flex points in that long period of conflict, a victory which probably would not have been won without the genius of Horatio Nelson, Britain's most talented naval commander. Throughout the summer of 1805, he had been hunting down the main French naval squadron under Admiral Pierre-Charles Villeneuve and finally, in mid-September, managed to bottle it up in the Spanish port of Cadiz. The British 27-strong flotilla led by Nelson and his second-in-command Vice-Admiral Cuthbert Collingwood tried to entice Villeneuve out, confident that the superior British guns would decimate the Franco-Spanish fleet. The wait was long, but unexpectedly on October 19, Villeneuve sallied forth, having heard Napoleon intended to replace him, and resolved to make a break for the Mediterranean.

It took more than a day for the 33 battleships of Villeneuve's fleet to reach open water, and by then Nelson had devised a dramatic plan. Rather than approach the enemy in a long line and exchange broadsides, as was the customary naval tactic, he organised his ships into two columns – one headed by *Victory*, the other by Collingwood in the *Royal Sovereign* – which would puncture holes in the French line and then turn about to attack Villeneuve from behind.

Having issued a morale-raising signal, "England expects that every man will do his duty", Nelson ordered the attack.

Collingwood's column impacted the startled French line first, smashing into it around midday near the Spanish *Santa Ana*. This precipitated a sharp exchange of fire that became a general mêlée as more of Collingwood's ships moved forward and a cluster of French and Spanish vessels rushed to reinforce their line. Nelson's column hit the French about 20 minutes after Collingwood, with the *Victory* becoming rapidly embroiled in a duel with the *Redoutable*.

Early 19th-century naval warfare was a savage affair, with cannon balls splintering timbers and musket fire raking the decks as each side tried to disable the enemy's ability to fire, kill as many of their crew as possible and then board and capture their ships to take as prizes. Around 1.15pm Nelson fell victim to these tactics, when a French sharpshooter on the *Redoutable*, probably spotting his admiral's uniform, mortally wounded him in the chest. By the time he died three hours later, though, the French had been beaten, with 17 of their 33 ships captured, one destroyed and nearly 7,000 of their sailors and marines killed or wounded. Thousands more were captured (with 3,000 French prisoners beings shipped back to England and nearly 5,000 Spanish seamen being released on parole in Gibraltar). The British victory, though, was somewhat marred by the escape of ten ships under the Spanish commander Federico Gravina and a subsequent storm that scattered the Franco-Spanish vessels they had captured and allowed others to escape, so that in the end Collingwood came away with only five prize vessels.

British maritime supremacy in the eastern Atlantic and the Mediterranean had, however, been assured and, though Napoleon might win battles on land, at sea the Royal Navy suffered no serious challenges, hampering the French emperor's attempts to blockade the ports of the countries arrayed in coalitions against him and beginning a period of British naval dominance that would last for a century.

PLAN OF THE BATTLE
OF
WATERLOO
or Mount St. John,

reduced from the large Plan of the same
Battle, made up and published in 1816,

BY W. B. CRAAN,

Engineer-Examiner of the Register of lands of Braband,

Published

by H. Gerard, rue de la Bergere, 6, at Brussels.

CONVENTIONAL SIGNS

FIRST POSITIONS at 12 o'clock.   GENERAL SIGNS

English and Hanovrians
Prussians
Belgians and Dutch
of Brunswyck
of Nassau
French

ULTERIOR POSITIONS

Signs and less deep Colours

N.B. In the retreat which was made
greatest disorder the mass flew away by the right
left side of the King's house to reach Genap

Battle of Waterloo

The map shows the Anglo-Dutch army of the Duke of Wellington arrayed against the French force of Napoleon at the height of one of history's most decisive battles. Waterloo was Napoleon's last gasp, a "damn near-run thing", as Wellington afterwards put it, in which the offensive tactical genius of the French emperor ran up against the defensive brilliance of the British general, losing him the one battle he absolutely had to win.

The plan, by the Dutch-Belgian cartographer Willem Craan, benefited from his ability to interview many of the wounded soldiers when they were taken back to Brussels. The British line (in red) is drawn up behind a sheltering ridge, anchored in the centre and west on the strongpoints of La Haye Sainte farmhouse (labelled as "Holy Haye"), the inn of La Belle Alliance and the chateau of Goumont (now known as Hougoumont).

Napoleon's path to the battlefield had not been smooth. Having slipped away from exile on the Italian island of Elba on February 26, 1815, he was back in Paris three weeks later. Loyalists flocked to him and royalists fled. Although conscription had been abolished by the restored monarchy, denying Napoleon many experienced troops, he still had a solid core of veterans, including his elite Imperial Guard, and he scrambled to raise a new army, aware that over 600,000 Prussian, Dutch and British troops would soon be arrayed against him.

By June 15, the French force was across the Dutch frontier. Striking fast and decisively and preventing enemy concentrations had been hallmarks of his military career, and now he hoped to defeat the Prussians under Marshal Gebhard von Blücher before they could join up with Wellington. The key engagements took place south of Waterloo: on June 16 Napoleon defeated Blücher at Ligny, but failed to prevent his adversary's retreat and so most of the Prussian army remained intact and ominously close to Wellington, who fought an indecisive draw with Marshal Michel Ney at Quatre Bras.

Nonetheless, Wellington withdrew north to a ridge near Mont Saint Jean. He knew this would protect his men from the worst of the inevitable French artillery barrage and obscure Napoleon's view of his true strength. To shield his main line, he posted a garrison to Goumont on his right and La Haye Sainte. While Napoleon detached 33,000 men to pursue Blücher, the remaining two thirds of his army formed up, with the village of Planchenois to the right and the Imperial Guard stationed in reserve near La Belle Alliance.

It was critical to defeat Wellington before Blücher's Prussians could reach the battlefield. The British commander, whose 67,000 troops were fewer than the French, resolved to absorb Napoleon's attacks and wait until Blücher tipped the scales in his favour. The main engagement began around noon, with waves of infantry attacks on Goumont and La Haye Sainte, where an increasingly beleaguered British garrison held off determined attacks by the Comte d'Erlon's corps. A counterattack by British heavy cavalry smashed against the French artillery batteries but was beaten back. It seemed like stalemate, but the Prussians were drawing ever closer and Napoleon needed to force the issue. About 4pm, Marshal Ney, believing the allies were retreating, sent 9,000 cavalry crashing into Wellington's lines west of La Haye Sainte. But the British infantry formed into squares, a formation cavalry found it almost impossible to break, and the attacks simply absorbed more time.

Although Ney's move had allowed d'Erlon finally to take La Haye Sainte, by now General Friedrich Wilhelm von Bülow's IV Prussian Corps had begun to arrive east of Planchenois, which he attacked, forcing Napoleon to reinforce that flank. More reinforcements reached Wellington's left, permitting him to strengthen his centre around La Haye Sainte, which had been under severe pressure after the loss of the farmhouse. With little other option, Napoleon threw in the Imperial Guard. It was a unit which had never known defeat, but the stubborn Allied resistance first stemmed their advance and then forced them to retreat. The effect on the morale of the rest of the French army was devastating and, as Wellington ordered his men to advance from the ridge line, surging past d'Erlon's corps, only a brief rally near La Belle Alliance interrupted what had become a rout.

Napoleon had lost around 25,000 dead and wounded, but he had also lost any chance of reconstructing his empire. He fled back to Paris, soon realised there was little hope of salvaging his cause and on July 15 surrendered himself and was exiled to the Indian Ocean island of St Helena, too distant for any prospect of escape. In the six years of life left to him, he may often have wondered what would have occurred had this "close-run thing" turned out differently.

First Anglo–Afghan War

Two red-coated British soldiers survey the forbiddingly mountainous terrain of Afghanistan from a vantage point on the North-West Frontier. The map, created around 1900 by WH Payne for the London stationery publisher Letts, artfully suggests that buyers might like to outlay a further sixpence for flags "for sticking in the view".

It was precisely such flag-sticking that brought the British ruin in Afghanistan, an invasion in 1839–42 ending in one of the country's worst-ever military disasters (although that did not deter them from ignoring its lessons and becoming embroiled in a further Afghan war). The First Anglo–Afghan War had begun when the British invaded to place their favoured candidate, the already deposed Shah Shujah Durrani, on the Afghan throne. Initial successes by their 39,000-strong force, with the capture of Kandahar in April 1839, contributed to British overconfidence, which was further inflated by the routing of the army of Shah Shujah's rival, Dost Mohammed. By August, the British were in Kabul (Cabul on the map), but the two brigades they left behind – and William Macnaghten and Alexander Burnes, the envoys appointed to ensure Shah Shujah remained compliant – seemed blithely unaware that, far from it having been a triumph, they had walked into a trap.

Shah Shujah's popularity soon plummeted, his extreme corruption contributing to the resentment against the British troops who had installed him. Violence against the British mounted, and in November 1841 Burnes was murdered by a mob, to be followed almost two months later by Macnaghten.

Far from taking firm action against the perpetrators, General William Elphinstone, the senior British officer, ordered the evacuation of Kabul, hoping to reach the safety of Jalalabad (Jelalabad on the map). He thought he had secured safe passage by agreeing to leave most of their artillery behind, and on the morning of January 6, 1842, a column of 4,500 soldiers (mostly British Indian army sepoys) and 12,000 families and servants snaked out of Kabul. Yet, despite the assurances, they were soon subjected to harassing fire by Afghans, whose long *jezail* rifles began to pick off stragglers, while the British, with their shorter-range muskets, were unable to reply. As discipline broke down, the column only made 6 miles of progress, and a freezing cold night without any tents was followed by two further days of attacks.

By the time the column entered the Khurd Kabul Pass, a narrow 5-mile stretch in which they were sitting ducks for ambushes from the heights above, many of the sepoys had deserted and the Afghan emir Akbar Khan, who was leading the attacks, demanded an assurance Jalalabad would be handed over to him, as well as most of the surviving senior British officers as hostages, as the price of desisting. Despite Elphinstone's agreement, next day the attacks renewed, leaving over 3,000 dead, including many women and children. The carnage continued, as Afghan marksmen shot down would-be deserters, and camp-followers trying to escape froze to death in the bitter cold.

By January 11 only 200 British troops remained, and they had managed only half the distance to Jalalabad. Two days later they were down to 60, who halted to make a last stand at Gandamak (Gundamuk on the map), where they were cut to pieces by the Afghans, now outnumbering them a hundred to one.

A few officers were taken prisoner, including Captain Thomas Souter, whom the Afghans mistook for a person of high rank when the regimental colours which he wrapped around himself seemed like a precious robe. Half a dozen made a last-minute dash for freedom, but five were killed on the road to Jalalabad. Only Assistant Surgeon William Brydon made it through, and when, dusty, bloodied and exhausted, he reached Jalalabad that afternoon, he had to inform the garrison that of the 16,500 who had left Kabul a week earlier, he was the sole survivor.

Although a few dozen hostages and prisoners from the Gandamak engagement had also survived, the shock of the news was profound; Lord Auckland, the Viceroy of India, is said to have had a heart attack when he heard it. Although an "Army of Retribution" under Generals William Nott and George Pollock entered Afghanistan again in March, relieved an Afghan siege of Jalalabad, levelled any settlement considered to have helped Emir Khan and burnt the Kabul bazaar to the ground in September, it then withdrew. With Dost Mohammed now on the throne, and the British reputation for military prowess shattered, the whole war had been a disaster. Not, of course, that it stopped the British trying again in 1878, in a war which, though it did not result in a disaster on the scale of 1842, signally failed to achieve any lasting domination over that impossibly mountainous terrain.

▶

LETTS'S BIRD'S EYE VIEW

THE APPROACHES TO INDIA.

The Capture of Canton

The map shows a key moment in the First Opium War between Britain and China, as a British expeditionary force storms the Chinese-held forts which formed the main defensive perimeter of Canton. It appeared in the *Narrative of the Second Campaign in China* by Keith Stewart Mackenzie, who was Military Secretary to Commodore Gordon Bremer, commander of the British forces in China.

Canton was where the war began. The British East India Company had long chafed at the problem that, while there was an insatiable appetite for Chinese porcelain, tea and silk in Europe, there was little that China wished to buy from the company in return, which led to a constant drain of silver to pay the Chinese. Its solution, to export Indian-grown opium to China (as much as 1,400 tons a year by 1838), solved its trade deficit but created tens of thousands of opium addicts. Concerned at the devastating social consequences of this, the Qing emperor Daoguang sent Lin Zexu as special Imperial Commissioner to Canton, the sole legal conduit port of entry into China, with orders to stamp out the opium trade.

Lin acted decisively, seizing and burning the British merchants' stocks of opium. A fragile calm then prevailed until a skirmish between Chinese war junks and British naval vessels off Kowloon in September 1839 and the breaching by several ships of the blockade the British Superintendent of Trade, Charles Elliot, had imposed on the Pearl River escalated into war. Although Britain had a number of naval vessels in the region, it took time to assemble a larger expeditionary force, with Bremer in charge of the fleet and the Royal Marines, and Major General Sir Hugh Gough as commander of land forces. They planned to seize a number of Chinese ports, hoping to force the Qing court to permit the opium trade's resumption. The first elements of the force arrived in June 1840, and after capturing Dinghai as a base of operations, began months of alternating negotiations and small-scale military clashes as the Chinese sought to regroup and the British received a steady stream of reinforcements.

By January 1841, the British were ready to push up the Pearl River towards Canton, but this had been reinforced by the Qing admiral Guan Tianpei and now had a formidable garrison of 10,000 troops. It looked for a moment as if a clash might be avoided, as Elliot negotiated a settlement with his Chinese counterpart under which Britain would receive the island of Hong Kong and an indemnity of six million silver ars. However, both the British government and the g court swiftly repudiated the agreement – with Lord nerston, foreign secretary at the time, accusing Elliot of ting his instruction as "so much wastepaper".

British fleet then fought its way methodically up Pearl River, reducing fort after fort, until in March a ingent of troops reoccupied the British commercial ter south of Canton. A truce was declared and Elliot red the withdrawal of most of the Royal Navy's ships, but an, the new Qing commander in the region, continued uild up forces, and on May 21 ordered an attack on the ish factories. The British defenders held out for four until a hastily assembled relief force, comprising the Cameronians, 49th Foot, 18th Royal Irish, 37th Madras ments and the Royal Marines, reached the vicinity of ton aboard the steamers *Atalanta* and *Nemesis*. Gough's rapidly secured the factories, outflanked the Chinese seized four forts on the heights overlooking Canton to north. With the British now able to bombard them at the Qing garrison panicked and fled, leaving crowds antonese villagers to mount a last-ditch defence before gh took possession of the city.

Although the British withdrew on payment of the "Ransom of Canton", a hefty indemnity of £60,000, and the war dragged on for a further 13 months until the capture of Shanghai in June 1842, the taking of Canton, for the loss of just two officers and 15 men killed, exposed the huge fragility of the Qing government. Dispirited and defeated, in August it signed the Treaty of Nanking, which ceded Hong Kong to Britain, permitted the resumption of the opium trade and opened five more ports (including Shanghai) to European traders. The Chinese attempt to reverse this humiliation led to a further Opium War in 1856–60, which ended with an even more disadvantageous treaty. Ironically, by then, the East India Company, whose exploitation of the opium trade had caused the war, had itself suffered utter ruin, removed from its commercial monopoly in the East and deprived of its political authority after the Indian Mutiny in 1857 (see page 112) convinced the British government to impose direct rule on India.

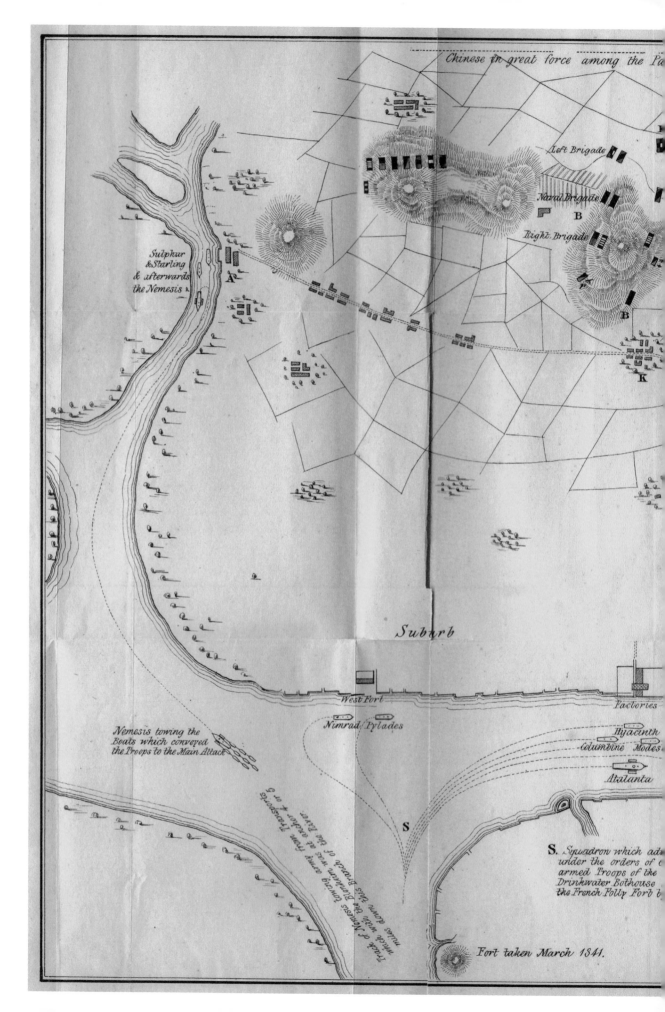

Chinese in great force among the Pa[...]

Left Brigade

Naval Brigade

B

Right Brigade

B

K

Sulphur
& Starling
& afterwards
the Nemesis

A

Suburb

West Fort

Factories

Nimrod Pylades

Hyacinth
Columbine Modeste

Atalanta

Nemesis towing the
Boats which conveyed
the Troops to the Main Attack

Track of Nemesis Blenheim this
which with the Boats, up or
miles down the River

S

S. Squadron which adv[...]
under the orders of [...]
armed Troops of the [...]
Drinkwater Bothouse [...]
the French Folly Fort b[...]

Fort taken March 1841.

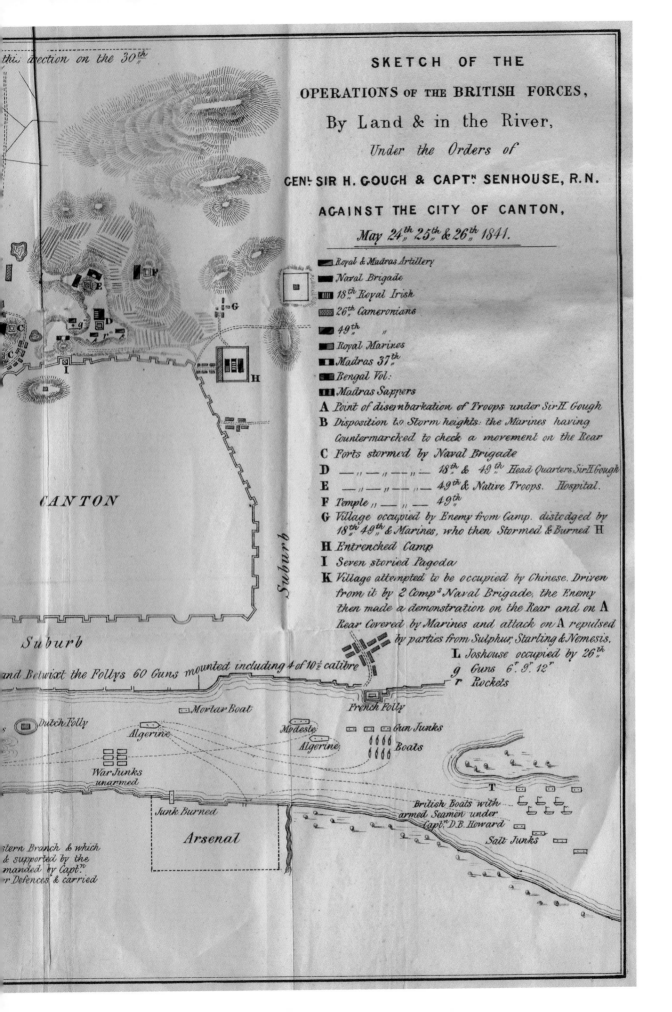

SKETCH OF THE

OPERATIONS OF THE BRITISH FORCES,

By Land & in the River,

Under the Orders of

GENL. SIR H. GOUGH & CAPTN. SENHOUSE, R.N.

AGAINST THE CITY OF CANTON,

May 24th, 25th, & 26th, 1841.

Royal & Madras Artillery
Naval Brigade
18th Royal Irish
26th Cameronians
49th "
Royal Marines
Madras 37th
Bengal Vol:
Madras Sappers

A Point of disembarkation of Troops under Sir H. Gough
B Disposition to Storm heights: the Marines having Countermarched to check a movement on the Rear
C Forts stormed by Naval Brigade
D —"——"——"— 18th & 49th Head Quarters Sir H. Gough
E —"——"——"— 49th & Native Troops. Hospital.
F Temple —"——"— 49th
G Village occupied by Enemy from Camp. dislodged by 18th 49th & Marines, who then Stormed & Burned H
H Entrenched Camp
I Seven storied Pagoda
K Village attempted to be occupied by Chinese. Driven from it by 2 Comps Naval Brigade, the Enemy then made a demonstration on the Rear and on **A** Rear Covered by Marines and attack on **A** repulsed by parties from Sulphur, Starling & Nemesis.
L Joshouse occupied by 26th
g Guns 6". 9". 12"
r Rockets

thi direction on the 30th

CANTON

Suburb

Suburb

and Betwixt the Follys 60 Guns mounted including 4 of 10½ calibre

Mortar Boat

French Folly

Dutch Folly

Modeste

Gun Junks

Algerine

Algerine

Boats

War Junks unarmed

Junk Burned

Arsenal

T

British Boats with armed Seamen under Capt. D.B. Howard

Salt Junks

stern Branch & which & supported by the manded by Capt.
r Defences & carried

Battle of Buena Vista

The dramatic terrain of Buena Vista, 5 miles south of Saltillo in the northeastern Mexican state of Coahuila, is scored with ravines. The difficulty of traversing them (which gave the area its alternative name of Angostura, "the Narrows") highlights the problem faced by the Mexican army of General Antonio López de Santa Anna in overcoming the much smaller force of General Zachary Taylor that stood in his way during the Mexican–American War of 1846–48. The battle made a number of reputations on the American side. Taylor, who rejoiced in the nickname "Old Rough and Ready" for his willingness to share the hardships of life on the march with his troops, used his victory there to cement his successful bid for the presidency the year after the war ended. Jefferson Davis, who played a prominent role in the battle, was destined to become the Confederacy's first and only president during the US Civil War. One of the surveyors of the map, Lieutenant William B Franklin, rose to high command on the Union side. The map was drawn by Captain Thomas B Linnard of the Corps of Topographical Engineers.

The Mexican–American War began after the United States' annexation of Texas led to a border dispute with Mexico, which claimed that the Nueces River, rather than the Rio Grande, should mark the new frontier between the two countries. President James K Polk ordered troops under General Taylor to move into the disputed territory, but a pre-emptive attack by Mexican troops gave him a pretext for war. His plan was to strike deep into Mexico, while a second force under Stephen Kearny occupied New Mexico and California.

The strength of the plan was diluted by a decision to divert many of Taylor's best troops to assist General Winfield Scott in a new invasion point through Veracruz on the east coast. With only 4,500 soldiers, Taylor was left to cover an extended line reaching nearly 400 miles between Tampico and Saltillo. The Mexicans, marshalled by Santa Anna – who had been in exile in Cuba but had persuaded President Polk to allow him to return on the pretext that he would negotiate a peace – assembled an army of 25,000 soldiers which marched to intercept Taylor.

The Mexicans were determined but ill-equipped and so, despite their overwhelming numerical superiority, their force was weaker than it seemed. Hearing of Santa Anna's approach, Taylor rushed to deploy in the hacienda of Buena Vista, just south of Saltillo. Flanked by a plateau and guarded by ravines, it offered good visibility and an excellent defensive platform. Thinly spread, though, the Americans were vulnerable to any concerted attack. On February 22, Santa Anna sent Taylor a note demanding immediate surrender, eliciting the firm response: "I decline acceding to your request."

After inconclusive fighting that afternoon, Santa Anna attacked the next day. He sent his most effective units along the plateau (marked "T" to the northwest of the plan), while a diversionary attack along the Buena Vista road tried to tie down as much of Taylor's force as possible. By noon the Mexicans had made progress, breaking the defence of the Second Indiana and Second Illinois, opening the flank of the American positions to enfilading fire and partly clearing the road to Buena Vista. Only the marksmanship of the Mississippi Rifles under Jefferson Davis and the devastating fire from an artillery battery led by Braxton Bragg (who would also become a senior Union general during the Civil War) halted Santa Anna's advance.

As dusk descended, Taylor expected that the onslaught would be renewed the next day. Santa Anna, however, having lost 1,800 dead and wounded, concluded that his men were too exhausted to continue and, having expected to loot supplies from a defeated American force, they were now practically starving. He withdrew to San Luis Potosí, declaring in dispatches back to Mexico City that he had won a famous victory. Taylor's report too described his own performance in glowing terms, but with far greater justification.

Buena Vista secured northern Mexico for the invading American forces. It also relieved pressure on Winfield Scott's Veracruz expedition, which ended up taking Mexico City in September, effectively ending the war and forcing on Mexico the Treaty of Guadalupe Hidalgo (1848) by which it ceded northern California and New Mexico to the United States as well as accepting the Rio Grande frontier. It gave the United States army and many of its officers valuable combat experience when they reached more senior ranks at the start of the Civil War. Perhaps, years later, Santa Anna may have consoled himself that his greatest revenge on the United States had been to launch the career of Jefferson Davis.

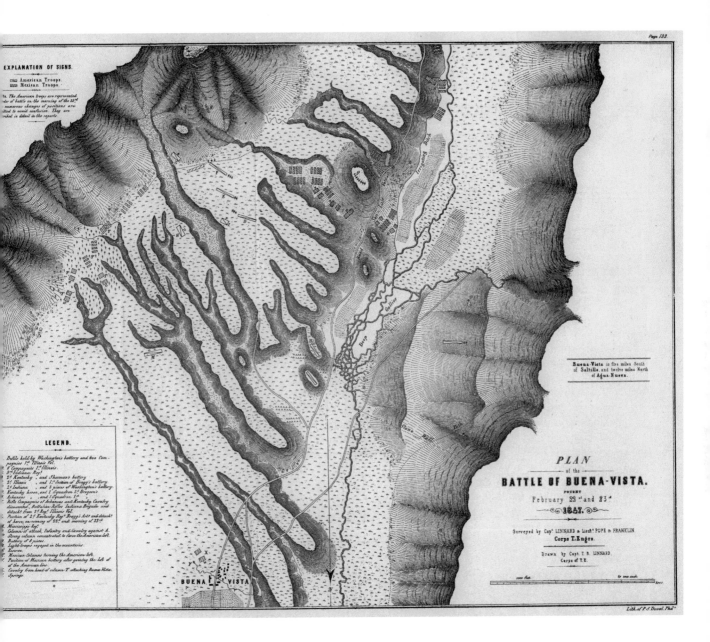

EXPLANATION OF SIGNS.

American Troops.
Mexican Troops.

At. The American troops are represented
order of battle on the morning of the 23rd
numerous changes of position are
mitted to avoid confusion. They are
orded in detail in the reports.

LEGEND.

Defile held by Washington's battery and two Com-
panies 1st Illinois Vol.
B. 6 Companies 1st Illinois.
C. 2d Indiana Reg.
D. 2d Kentucky, and Sherman's battery.
E. 2d Illinois, and 1st Section of Bragg's battery.
F. 2d Indiana, and 3 pieces of Washington's battery.
G. Kentucky horse, and 1 Squadron 2d Dragoon's.
H. Arkansas, and 1 Squadron 1st
I. Rifle Companies of Arkansas and Kentucky Cavalry
dismounted, McKullan Rifles Indiana Brigade and
detached from 3d Reg.t Illinois Vol.
K. Position of 2d Kentucky Reg.t Bragg's Art.t and detach.t
of horse, in evening of 22d and morning of 23d.
L. Mississippi Reg.t
M. Columns of attack, Infantry and Cavalry against A.
N. Strong column concentrated to force the American left.
O. Battery of 8 pieces.
P. Light troops engaged in the mountains.
Q. Reserve.
R. Mexican Columns turning the American left.
S. Position of Mexican battery after gaining the left of
of the American line.
T. Cavalry from head of column T attacking Buena-Vista
Springs.

Buena-Vista is five miles South
of Saltillo, and twelve miles North
of Agua-Nueva.

PLAN
of the
BATTLE OF BUENA-VISTA.
FOUGHT
February 22d and 23d
1847.

Surveyed by Capt.n LINNARD & Lieut.s POPE & FRANKLIN.
Corps T. Engrs.

Drawn by Capt. T. B. LINNARD,
Corps of T.E.

1000 feet. to one inch.

BUENA VISTA

Lith. of P. S. Duval, Phil.a

Battle of Balaklava

The ghostly symbols and lines on the map appropriately mark one of Britain's most infamous military disasters. The Charge of the Light Brigade at the Battle of Balaklava during the Crimean War (1853–56) was a classic example of military muddle and rigid adherence to orders in the face of battlefield reality.

The war broke out over Russian designs in the Balkans. Tsar Nicholas I posed as the protector of Orthodox Christians in the Ottoman Empire, and his interference sparked a conflict which soon spread, as France and Britain came down on the Ottoman side, fearing the empire would collapse and Russian influence in southeastern Europe might grow uncontrollably.

In September 1854, a large Anglo-French expeditionary force landed on the west coast of the Crimean Peninsula, aiming to capture the key port of Sevastopol, throttle Russia's access to the Black Sea and force the tsar into submission. But after an early victory a week later at Alma, the allies did not follow up and attack Sevastopol from its vulnerable north and then failed to intercept the Russian commander Prince Menshikov when he escaped northeast out of the port.

Instead, they moved southeast to Balaklava, where they established a supply base at the harbour for their 70,000 troops and then settled into what would become a protracted siege of Sevastopol, beginning with a massive bombardment on October 17 that failed to dislodge the beleaguered garrison.

Finally, Menshikov was prodded by his superiors in St Petersburg to return and snuff out the allied bridgehead at Balaklava. On October 24 he sent General Pavel Liprandi to capture the four outer redoubts that defended the port and occupy the Fedioukine Hills and other elevations which overlooked it. By the next morning the hills were bristling with Russian artillery, which created a deadly killing zone in the valleys below.

The early stages of the battle went well for the British commander Lord Raglan. As the Russian heavy cavalry thundered towards Balaklava in the early morning, they ran into Major General Sir Colin Campbell's 93rd Highlanders. Rather than forming his men into the traditional infantry square to face mounted opposition, he arranged them in two lines. Against all expectations, volleys from this "thin red line" forced the 3,000-strong Russian cavalry back. As it retreated, it ran into the British Heavy Brigade led by Brigadier General James Scarlett, whose charge further scattered the Russian horsemen.

Raglan, though, was aware that the Russian guns were still in place and, worse still, were being reinforced by British artillery pieces captured at Sevastopol. With few options other than to stand and wait, he ordered the commander of the Cavalry Division, Lord Lucan, to commit his Light Brigade under Lord Cardigan. Probably intending they support an attack on the slopes to neutralise the Russian guns, Raglan instead issued a fatally ambiguous order that "Lord Raglan wishes the cavalry to advance rapidly to the front – follow the enemy and try to prevent the enemy carrying away the guns." This was interpreted to mean an attack on the artillery battery which lay straight ahead of the brigade in the valley, so around 670 men of the Light Brigade were sent on a suicidal charge under the noses of the Russian guns stationed on three sides of them. The few who made it to the Russian battery ran into squadrons of hussars and Cossacks who forced them back, where their retreat was once again blasted by the gauntlet of Russian guns.

Only 200 of those who made it back were unwounded, leaving the bloodied bodies of 113 in the "Valley of Death". The French commander General Pierre Bosquet, who watched the whole debacle from the Sapoune Heights remarked, "C'est magnifique, mais ce n'est pas la guerre" ("It is magnificent, but it is not war"). It cost Raglan his victory, Lucan his reputation and meant that Sevastopol held out for ten more months.

The war itself ended in stalemate in March 1856, with few real gains by either side. Instead, as well as for the Charge of the Light Brigade, it became best known as the first industrial war, with the Minié rifles – which could fire 300 metres (1,000 feet) – adding to the carnage, and the technology of steamships and electric telegraphs making commanders ever more able to deliver troops to the battlefield and governments to direct them from afar.

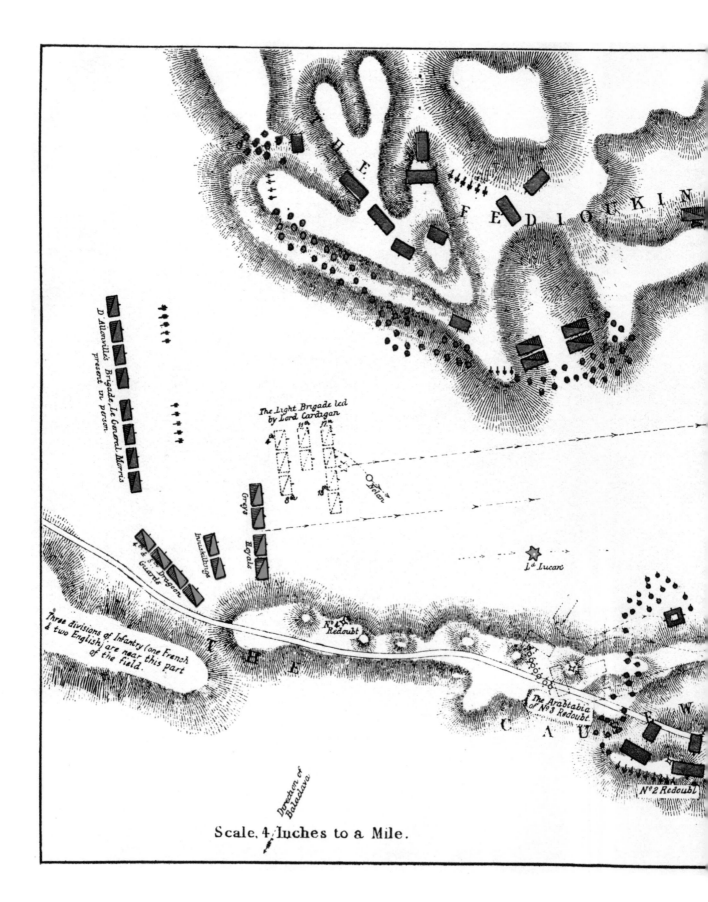

THE FEDIOUKIN

D'Allonville's Brigade, le General Morris present in person.

The Light Brigade led by Lord Cardigan

Greys

Inniskilling

Royals

4 & 5 Dragoon Guards

L'd Lucan

Three divisions of Infantry (one French & two English) are near this part of the field.

THE CAUSEW

N° 4 Redoubt

The Arabtabia of N° 3 Redoubt.

N° 2 Redoubt

Direction of Balaclava.

Scale, 4 Inches to a Mile.

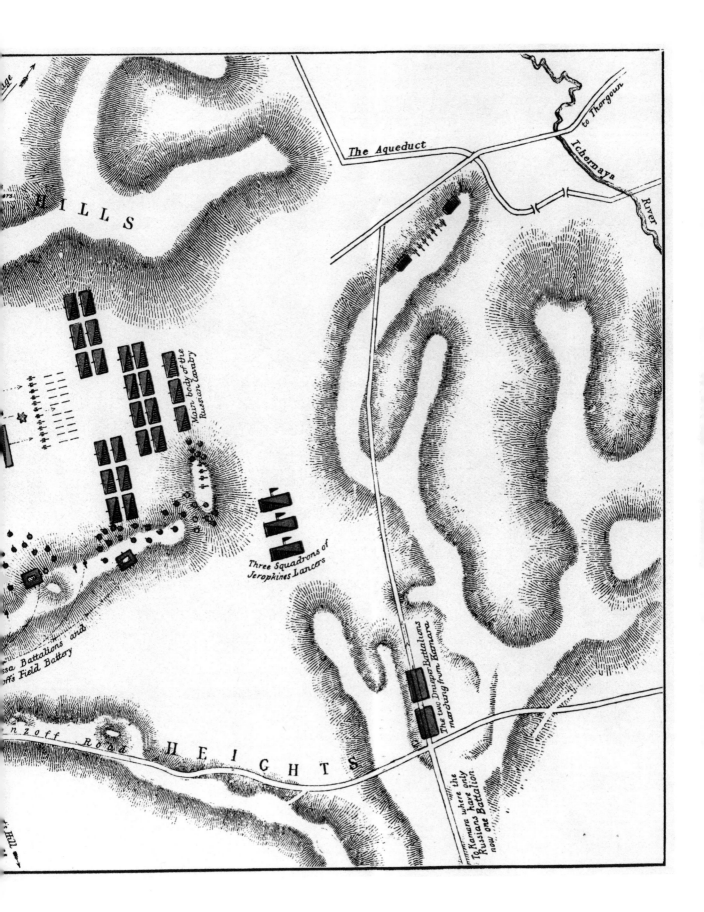

HILLS

The Aqueduct

to Thorgoun

Ichernaya

River

Main body of the Russian Cavalry

Three Squadrons of Jerophines Lancers

...ssa Battalions and ...off's Field Battery

...nzoff Road HEIGHTS

The two Dnieper Battalions marching from Kamara

Kamara where the Russians have only now one Battalion.

WARS

OF

EMPIRE

AND

INDUSTRY

1855–1900

Second Battle of Cawnpoor

The battle plan, published in 1882 in James Taylor's *The Age We Live In: A History of the Nineteenth Century*, shows British troops under Sir Colin Campbell on the point of retaking the key city of Cawnpore (now Kanpur in Uttar Pradesh). Its capture in December 1857 hastened the end of a rebellion which had threatened to destroy Britain's grasp on India altogether.

British rule over the subcontinent had seemed immovable since Robert Clive won the Battle of Plassey exactly a century previously, gaining control over Bengal (see page 78). After it, Britain's East India Company remorselessly swallowed up Indian state after Indian state as the demands of trade, defending existing holdings or simply naked ambition pushed its borders ever further forward.

By 1857 Britain's hold over India was secured by the company's army, largely made up of native-born sepoys, but in May that year simmering discontent burst out into the open when false rumours spread that a new type of rifle cartridge being issued to the sepoys was greased with both pork and beef fat (which made it repugnant on religious grounds to both Hindu and Muslim soldiers). When protesting sepoys were arrested, a full-scale mutiny broke out, which embroiled the faded remnants of the old Mughal Empire (by now confined to a part of Delhi) and soon spread to key northern towns such as Agra and Lucknow.

At Cawnpore, the commander, General Sir Hugh Wheeler, believed the situation was under control and even felt relaxed enough to send troops to support beleaguered Lucknow. But he underestimated the threat and by June 5 found himself under siege in the fortified entrenchment to the south of the city with a small detachment of 250 British troops and a few loyal native sepoys. They held out for three weeks as temperatures mounted and food ran short, but, finally, the suffering of the thousand civilians they were sheltering persuaded Wheeler to surrender under a guarantee of safe conduct from the mutineers' commander, Nana Sahib. But when his force and the accompanying civilians reached the River Ganges to board boats, the men were cut down by rifle fire and the women and children taken back to Cawnpore, where they were held prisoner in a small house named the Bibigarh. Only four men escaped to tell the tale of the slaughter.

When a relieving force under General Henry Havelock, which had arrived too late to save Wheeler, reached the town on July 16, a combination of artillery fire and desperate charges by Scottish Highlander battalions won the day, but the women and children still held by Nana Sahib and his co-commander Tantya Tope were massacred. British vengeance on those mutineers they found was savage (extending to forcing them to lick the blood of the Bibigarh dead from the floor before hanging them).

Within months, it looked as though the city might fall all over again, as the need to relieve Lucknow left Cawnpore exposed and a force under General Charles Ash Windham found itself once again besieged there. Tantya Tope, in command of 15,000 troops, seemed on the point of overwhelming the British defenders in late November but was stopped when General Colin Campbell managed to rush reinforcements from Lucknow to prevent him. This is the situation shown on the map, with Windham's men to the north and west of the city and Campbell's lines anchored around Wheeler's old entrenchment.

Having received further reinforcements, and in particular a battery of 24-pounder naval guns, Campbell now had 10,000 well-trained British troops. At 9am on the morning of December 6 he unleashed a massive bombardment against Tantya Tope's lines. At the same time, a contingent under Brigadier Adrian Hope pushed round the mutineers' right flank to cut them off from the Ganges Canal. Outgunned, with British shells slamming into their lines and fearing becoming trapped, the troops of the Gwalior contingent which formed the main part of Tantya Tope's army retreated, and the rest of the Indian forces followed.

Cawnpore was finally secured for the British and with it access to the River Ganges, which allowed them to pacify Oudh and put an end to the mutiny by early 1858. In its wake British India would be reorganised, with the political authority of the East India Company abolished and direct rule by the British Crown imposed. Yet had Colin Campbell not won the Second Battle of Cawnpore, the British might never have been able to do so.

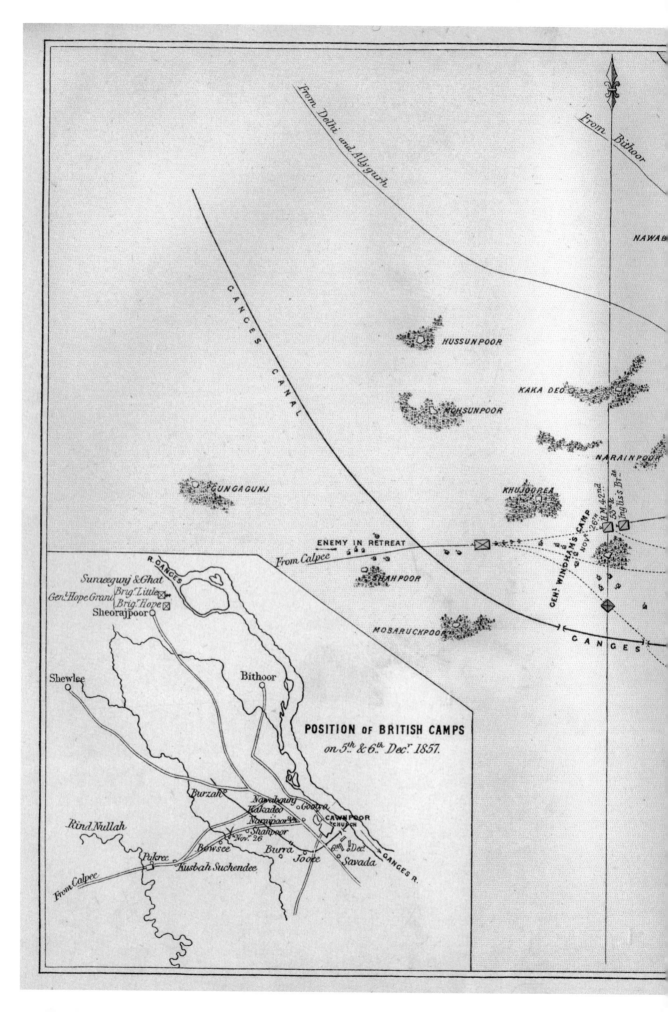

From Delhi and Allygurh

From Bithoor

GANGES CANAL

NAWAB

HUSSUNPOOR

KAKA DEO

NOHSUNPOOR

NARAINPOOR

GUNGAGUNJ

KHUJOOREA

H.M. 42nd

53rd R.

Inglis's Bt.

ENEMY IN RETREAT

GEN.L WINDHAM'S CAMP

Nov.t 26th

From Calpee

R. GANGES

SHAHPOOR

Sursegunj & Ghat

Brig.r Little

Gen.l Hope Grant

Brig.r Hope

Sheorajpoor

MOBARUCKPOOR

GANGES

Shewlee

Bithoor

POSITION OF BRITISH CAMPS

on 5th. & 6th. Dec.r 1857.

Burzah

Nawabgunj

Goolra

CAWNPOOR

Kakadeo

CHURCH

Rind Nullah

Nasripoor

Shahpoor

Nov.r 26

6th Dec.

Bowsee

Burra

Jooee

Savada

Pukree

GANGES R.

From Calpee

Kusbah Suchendee

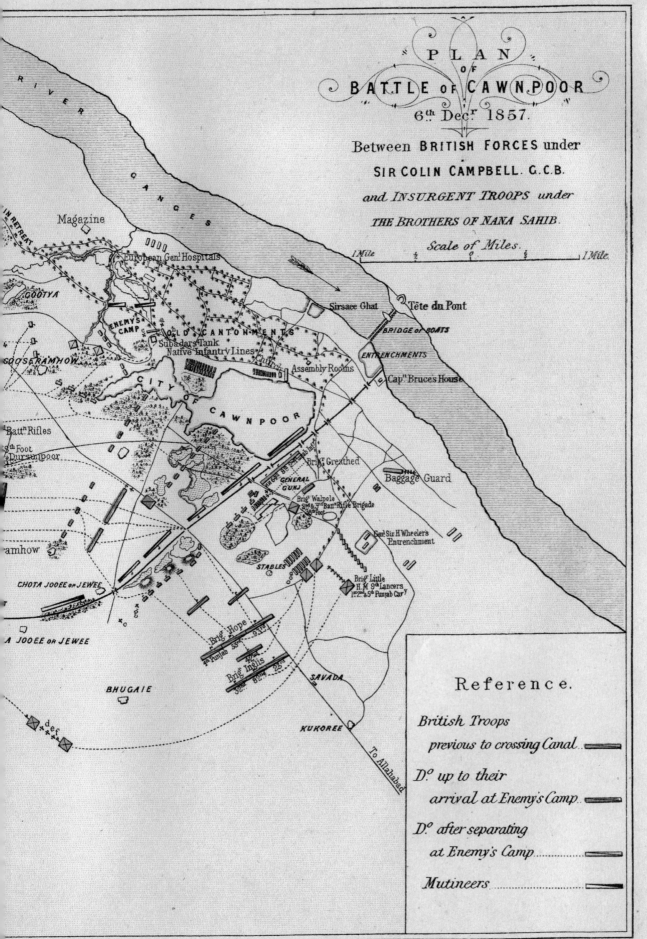

PLAN
OF
BATTLE OF CAWNPOOR

6th Decr 1857.

Between BRITISH FORCES under

SIR COLIN CAMPBELL. G.C.B.

and INSURGENT TROOPS under

THE BROTHERS OF NANA SAHIB.

Scale of Miles.

1 Mile   ½   0   ¼   1 Mile.

RIVER GANGES

Magazine

IN RETREAT

GOOTYA

European Genl Hospitals

ENEMY'S CAMP

OLD CANTONMENTS

Subadars Tank

Native Infantry Lines

GOOSERAMHOW

Sirsaee Ghat

Tête du Pont

BRIDGE OF BOATS

ENTRENCHMENTS

Assembly Rooms

Capt Bruce's House

CITY OF CAWNPOOR

Battn Rifles

8th Foot

Dursunpoor

Brigr Greathed

Baggage Guard

GENERAL GUNJ

Brigr Walpole

2nd & 3rd Battn Rifle Brigade

Genl Sir H Wheeler's Entrenchment

ramhow

STABLES

Brigr Little

H. M. 9th Lancers

1st 2d & 5th Punjab Carv

CHOTA JOOEE or JEWEE

A JOOEE or JEWEE

Brigr Hope

4th Punjab 53rd 93rd

42nd

Brigr Inglis

32nd 82nd 23rd

SAVADA

BHUGAIE

KUKOREE

def

To Allahabad

Reference.

British Troops
previous to crossing Canal

Do up to their
arrival at Enemy's Camp

Do after separating
at Enemy's Camp

Mutineers

GUYOT & WOOD, EDINR

Battle of Solferino

The map marks a key moment in the struggle for the unification of Italy and the independence of large swathes of the northeast of the peninsula from rule by the Austrian Habsburgs. Drawn by the prominent French mapmaker, Alexandre Vuillemin (whose cartographic spectrum ranged from the small scale, as in this map of the Battle of Solferino, to an Atlas of the Cosmos published in 1867), it appeared in Amédée de Cesena's history of the Second Italian War of Independence, which appeared the year following the battle.

The failure of an earlier attempt in 1848 to expel foreign overlords, such as the branch of the Habsburgs who ruled in Tuscany, had frustrated the growing band of Italian nationalists. By the late 1850s they were instead focusing their efforts on using the Kingdom of Sardinia-Piedmont, ruled by King Vittorio Emanuele II, as the core of a hoped-for pan-Italian state. They were aided in this by Emperor Napoleon III of France, who formed an alliance of convenience with the Italians, which he saw as a way of discomfiting his great Austrian rivals.

At the end of April 1859 the Habsburg army crossed into Lombardy, seizing Turin, but their commander Count Franz Gyulai was soundly defeated by a Franco-Italian force at Magenta near Milan and forced to retreat back towards the Austrian-held provinces in the northeast. Pursued by a Sardinian-Piedmontese force under Vittorio Emanuele and a French army which was led in person by Napoleon III and which had been swiftly transported by rail from France – the first time a rail network had played such a vital military role – the 120,000 Austrians thought they had reached safety. But, now under the direct command of Emperor Franz Josef I, on June 24 they unexpectedly found themselves caught by the Franco-Italian army near Solferino in Lombardy.

Spread out in a large arc from Pozzolengo in the north to Guidizzolo in the south, the Austrians (yellow on the map) came under heavy attack on several fronts. The battle began in the early morning around 5am, with the securely entrenched Austrians fighting off wave after wave of French attacks and inflicting heavy losses, until the arrival of the French artillery finally forced them out of the town around 2.30pm.

Further south, around Medole, the French fared better, as a series of uncoordinated Austrian attacks failed to dent General Adolphe Niel's IV Corps despite it being outnumbered two to one. At San Martino village to the north, they repulsed wave after wave of attacks by the Piedmontese, and to the west of Solferino itself, where they had managed to dig themselves in securely, they inflicted huge losses on General Patrice de MacMahon's French division. Although the fighting in the north, around San Martino and Madonna della Scoperta, favoured the Austrians, as disjointed Italian attacks failed to make an impression, the Austrians had collapsed by mid-afternoon, which threatened Franz Josef's headquarters at Cavriana, and caused the Austrian high command to order a retreat across the Mincio river to the safety of the "Quadrilateral", the network of fortresses which defended the Veneto.

The battle had been hugely costly and bitterly fought with weapons such as the Austrian Lorenz and the French Minié rifles, whose rifled barrels gave them greater range and lethality. The Austrians lost around 22,000 men, and the allies suffered 17,000 casualties. The carnage had such an impact on the Swiss businessman Henri Dunant, who saw the aftermath of the battle, that he began lobbying for better treatment of wounded soldiers, a campaign which eventually resulted in the establishment of the International Red Cross.

The result of the battle was not as decisive as Vittorio Emanuele might have hoped. Although he wished to damage the Habsburgs, Napoleon III had no intention of unleashing the chaos which might result from their complete collapse in Italy, and the Armistice of Villafranca which ended the war in July – although it ceded Lombardy (including Milan) to Sardinia-Piedmont – left the Veneto in Austrian hands. The momentum was with the Italians, however, and popular uprisings and the activities of the Italian patriot army under Giuseppe Garibaldi meant that within a year Tuscany, much of the Papal States, Sicily and Naples had fallen to them, and the whole peninsula was unified under Piedmontese rule in 1870. Without Solferino, none of it would have been possible.

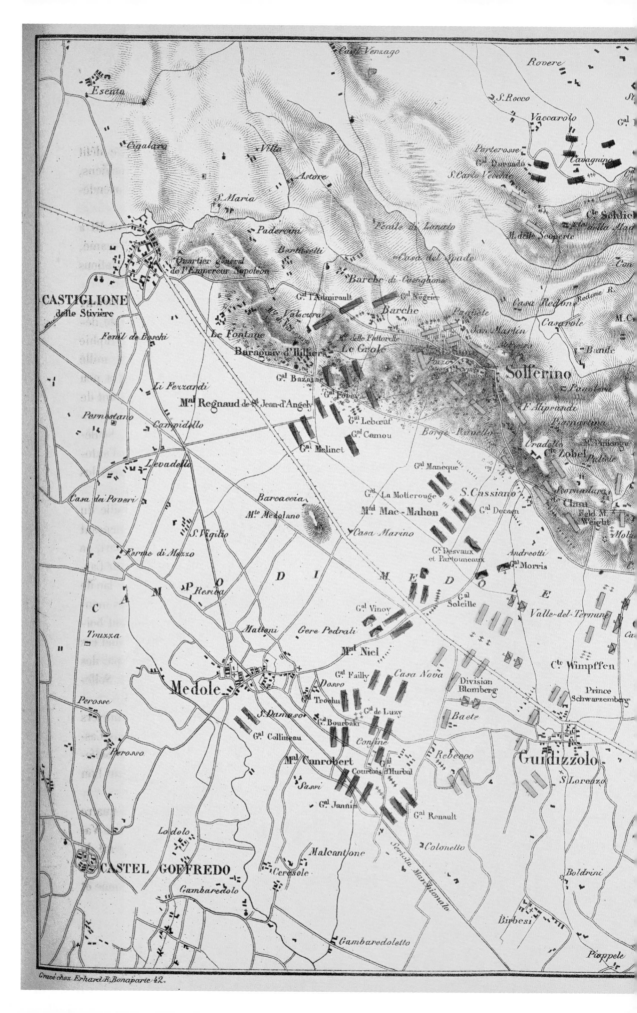

Casa Venzago

Rovere

S. Rocco

Esenta

Vaccarolo

Gal Duvando

Porterosse

Cigalara

Villa

Cavagnino

S. Carlo Vecchio

Astore

S. Maria

M. delle Scoperte

Cte Schlich

Paderani

Fenil di Lonato

Bertivelli

Casa del Spade

Barche di Castiglione

Gal l'Admirault

Gal Negrier

Casa Redon Redon R.

Valscura

Barche

QUARTIER GÉNÉRAL
de l'Empereur Napoléon

Casarole

Pozzo

M. C.

CASTIGLIONE
delle Stiviere

Le Fontane

San Martin

Bande

Fenil de Boschi

Buraguay d'Illiers

Le Grole

Gal Bazaine

Solferino

Li Ferzandi

Mal Regnaud de St Jean-d'Angely

Gal Forey

F. Aliprandi

Pernostano

Gal Leboeuf

Borgo Ronello

Campidello

Gal Camou

Cradello

Cte Zobel

Gal Melinet

Levadello

Gal Maneque

S. Cassiano

Casa dei Poveri

Gal La Motterouge

Barcaccia

Mal Mac-Mahon

Gal Decaen

Field M.
Weight

Mte Medolano

Casa Marino

Gal Desvaux
et Partouneaux

Andreotti

Gal Morris

S. Vigilio

Ferme di Mezzo

Gal Soleille

Valle-del-Termine

CAMPO DI MEDOLE

P. Resica

Gal Vinoy

Truzza

Mattoni

Gere Pedrali

Mal Niel

Cte Wimpffen

Gal Failly

Casa Nova

Dosso

Division
Blomberg

Prince
Schwarzemberg

Perosse

Medole

Gal Trochu

Gal de Luzy

Baete

S. Damaso

Gal Bourbaki

Perosso

Gal Collineau

Confine

Rebecco

Guidizzolo

Mal Canrobert

Courtois d'Hurbal

S. Lorenzo

Sasvi

Gal Jannin

Gal Renault

Lodolo

Malcantone

Colonetto

Boldrini

CASTEL GOFFREDO

Ceresole

Gambaredolo

Birbesi

Gambaredoletto

Pioppele

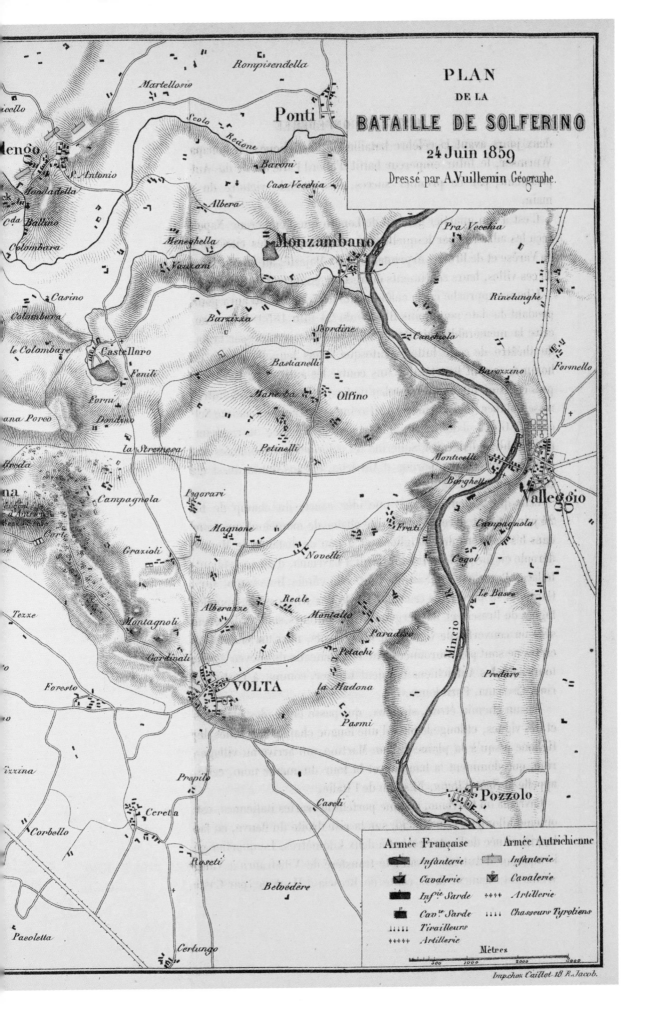

PLAN
DE LA
BATAILLE DE SOLFERINO
24 Juin 1859
Dressé par A. Vuillemin Géographe.

Armée Française	Armée Autrichienne
Infanterie	Infanterie
Cavalerie	Cavalerie
Inf.ie Sarde	Artillerie
Cav.ie Sarde	Chasseurs Tyroliens
Tirailleurs	
Artillerie	

Mètres

500 1000 2000

Imp. chez Caillet 18 R. Jacob.

First Battle of Bull Run

The Union flag flies above Centreville, and that of the Confederate Army led by Pierre Beauregard is planted close to Bull Run in this map drawn by Robert Knox Sneden, a former architect and one of the most talented cartographers on the Union side during the American Civil War. The first major field encounter in the war, the battle was fought on July 21, 1861 after three months of sparring after the Confederate capture of Fort Sumter, near Charleston. This in turn followed years of tension between Northern and Southern states over the issue of whether and where slavery should be permitted, and the secession of what eventually became the eleven states of the Confederacy. Many of those who fought on the Union side at Bull Run (their positions marked in purple) had joined up on a three-month enlistment scheme that brought 75,000 men to swell the comparatively modest pre-war Federal Army.

The three months were about to expire, and President Abraham Lincoln was keen for an early victory. As Confederate forces approached from Virginia, uncomfortably close to the federal capital, Washington DC, it was clear that the railway junction at Bull Run, which gave any army controlling it direct access to the Shenandoah Valley to the south and Washington to the north, would be critical.

Lincoln pushed a rather unwilling General Irvin McDowell to move south with 35,000 troops, but Beauregard was already in place at Bull Run and an inconclusive skirmish at Blackburn's Ford caused McDowell to postpone further attacks for three days. On July 21, he decided to advance up Bull Run Creek and envelope Beauregard's left flank, but his inexperienced troops floundered and allowed Beauregard to detach three brigades to try his own envelopment.

Even so, the Union troops managed to force their way across the Stone Bridge near the centre of the Confederate lines, and they had the best of the fighting all morning, driving Beauregard's men back onto the open hilltop of Henry House. There Brigadier Thomas J Jackson rallied them, gathering shattered units and welding them together into a defensive line that held fast so resolutely that the action gave Jackson his later nickname of "Stonewall".

McDowell's attempts to storm the hill were shattered by the Confederate artillery. Late in the afternoon, reinforcements under General Joseph E Johnston arrived.

They helped push the Federal Line away from Henry Hill, captured a portion of McDowell's artillery and sparked a general Union withdrawal which turned into a near rout once Jeb Stuart's Confederate cavalry arrived on the field and thundered into McDowell's disintegrating force.

The battle ended in chaos. The Confederates were too disorganised to cut off the retreating Union army, while the route off the battlefield was clogged by civilians who had come down from Washington in droves to watch the battle, for all the world as if it were Sunday picnic outing. Jefferson Davis, the Confederate president, though, must have enjoyed a moment of triumph when he arrived shortly after the fighting ended. It had been a bloody affair, the 2,896 Union casualties and the 1,982 suffered by the Confederacy making it the costliest battle thus far in American history. Yet those figures would soon be surpassed, as neither side had realised that Napoleonic-era tactics of massed advances would incur a terrible cost in the face of increasingly industrialised war, with ever more effective artillery and new rifled muskets firing the Minié ball (a hollow bullet that provided greater stability and thus range), which began to appear at Bull Run in the shape of the Model 1855 Springfield rifle.

For the moment, though, it looked as though the war, scarcely begun, was already won. Yet Lincoln managed to stem the panic, dispense with the hapless McDowell and fight on through four gruelling years until final victory in 1865. One person who had the misfortune to see the war from beginning to end was Wilmer McLean, a Virginia grocer whose farmhouse was requisitioned by Beauregard to form his headquarters and was badly damaged by shelling at the start of the battle. Eager to escape the hazards of war (there was a second Battle at Bull Run the following August), McLean moved his family to the apparent safety of an isolated community 125 miles to the south in Appomattox County. It was there, as chance would have it, that the war ended, when the new McLean house became the venue for the negotiations between Union General Ulysses S. Grant and his Confederate counterpart, General Robert E Lee, for the final Confederate surrender. As McLean ruefully put it, "The war began in my front yard and ended in my front parlor."

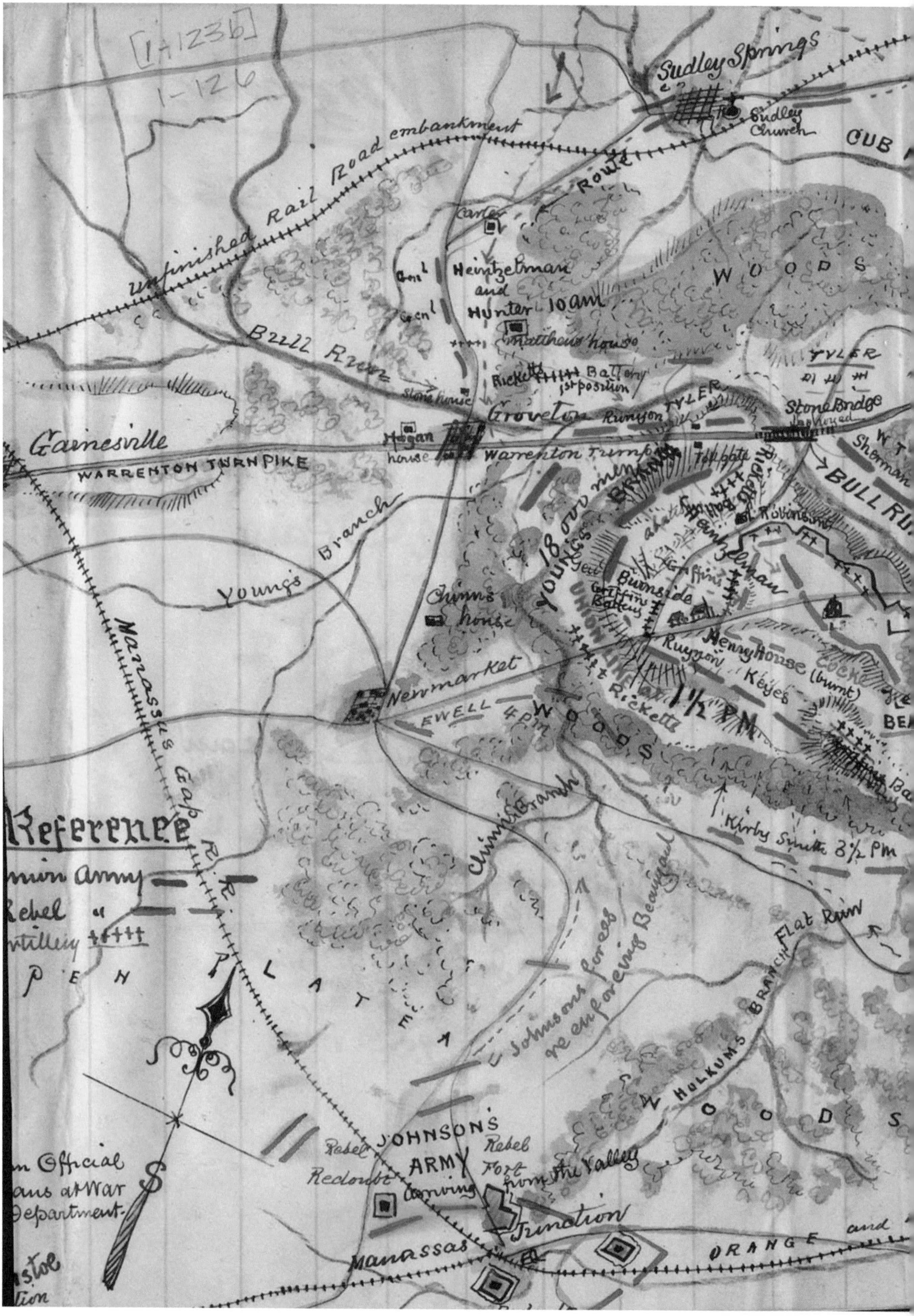

[A1236]
1-126

Sudley Springs
Sudley Church
CUB

unfinished Rail Road embankment
WOODS

Carter
Route
Genl Heintzelman and Genl Hunter 10am
Matthews house

TYLER
21 40 7H

Bull River
Ricketts Battery 1st position
Stone house
Groveton
Runyon TYLER
Stone Bridge

Gainesville
Hogan house
Warrenton Turnpike
WARRENTON TURNPIKE

Togate
Ricketts
abatis
Heintzelman
Robinson's
W.T. SHERMAN
BULL RUN

18 own men
BRANCH
YOUNGS
Young's Branch
Griffin
Burnside
Griffin
Jeff
UNION
Griffin Battery

Chinns house
Henry House
Runyon Keyes
Henry House (burnt)
Ricketts
1½ PM
BEA

Newmarket
EWELL 4PM
WOODS

Manassas Gap R.R.

Chinns Branch

Kirby Smith 8½ PM

Reference
Union Army
Rebel "
Artillery
P E N

Johnsons forces reenforcing Beauregard

Flat Run
BRANCH

HALKUMS
WOODS

PLATE

S

JOHNSONS ARMY
Rebel Redoubt
Rebel Fort
coming
from the Valley

n Official
ans at War
Department

stol
tion

MANASSAS
Junction
ORANGE and

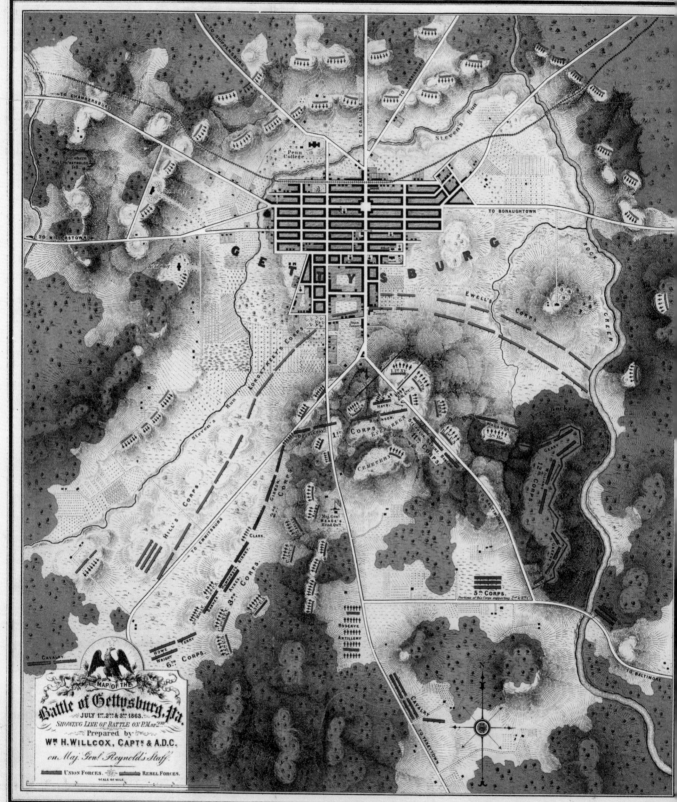

MAP OF THE
Battle of Gettysburg, Pa.
JULY 1st, 2nd & 3rd 1863.
SHOWING LINE OF BATTLE ON P.M. or 2nd
Prepared by
Wm. H. WILLCOX, CAPTn & A.D.C.
on Maj. Genl. Reynolds' Staff

UNION FORCES. REBEL FORCES.
SCALE OF MILE

Lith. of P.S Duval & Son cor. of 5th & Minor Sts. Philada.

J.O.Shoemaker and

19 x 17.

Battle of Gettysburg

The map, by Captain William H Wilcox, shows the positions of the Union (in red) and Confederate (in blue) armies at Gettysburg on July 2, 1863, at the mid-point in the encounter that proved to be the turning point of the American Civil War. For the man who sketched the battle lines around which the future destiny of his nation hung it also proved a personal turning point: Wilcox, who had joined up as a topographical engineer early in the war, resigned from military service just three months after Gettysburg, devoting himself to a more pacific career as a designer of churches and architect of early skyscrapers in Seattle.

The battle came about when Robert E Lee, by then established as the Confederacy's most effective general, decided on a rapid strike on the North to capitalise on his victory at Chancellorsville in May. He hoped to rattle the Union leadership and force them into suing for peace before the North's superior manpower resources and industrial might could outpace and crush the South. By June 28, Lee's Army of Northern Virginia was deep in Pennsylvania when he received intelligence reports that General George G Meade's Union Army of the Potomac was approaching from Frederick, Maryland. His way to Washington DC blocked, Lee turned to face Meade, and the two forces collided at the strategic crossroads of Gettysburg, 35 miles southwest of Harrisburg.

Initial skirmishing broke out on the morning of July 1 as the first Union brigade, armed with Spencer repeating carbines, held off the advancing Confederate units, until John F Reynolds's 1st Corps took up position on Seminary Ridge (though they soon lost their commander, the most senior officer to die at Gettysburg). By early afternoon the Union side had been driven back to Cemetery Hill, having incurred massive casualties, but the decision by General Richard S Ewell, leading one of the three Confederate Corps, to hold back from an attack on the hill in the declining light proved a costly mistake.

The second day saw fighting along virtually the whole of the extended crescent shape of the two sides' lines, with Confederate attacks at Little Round Top, Devil's Den, the Wheat Field and the Peach Orchard all failing to make a breakthrough, as they were uncoordinated and Meade was able to move reserves to face each of them. Around 6pm a final attack by Ewell's troops reached Cemetery Hill and part of Culp's Hill, but it was beaten off. In total, around 20,000 men died, were wounded or captured that day, which made it one of the bloodiest of the entire Civil War.

A frustrated Lee still hoped to make a breakthrough and almost did so without a fight, as Meade was on the point of withdrawing to avoid further losses before his senior officers dissuaded him. The Confederate commander's final throw of the dice was an all-out assault with ten brigades against the Union centre, while Ewell carried out a diversionary attack against Culp's Hill. Although James Longstreet directed the attack, it became immortalised as "Pickett's Charge", as a third of the troops were commanded by General George E Pickett. The 12,000 grey-clad Confederate infantry moved out of the cover of woods to cross the almost three quarters of a mile of open ground in front of Cemetery Ridge. As they closed to 700 yards, the Union artillery opened fire, blasting great holes in the Confederate ranks. Then, as Pickett's men reached within musket range of the stone walls behind which the Union troops had been sheltering, Meade's troops let off devastating volleys. Some Confederates made it onto the ridge, but they were outnumbered, surrounded and soon cut down. Hundreds were taken prisoner and the rest retreated, as the last high tide of the Confederacy ebbed away down the bloodied slopes.

The two sides faced each other for a further day, but the carnage of Pickett's charge had left both commanders wary, and, taking advantage of heavy rain which would hamper any attempt to pursue him, late on July 4 Lee slipped away back towards Virginia. Deprived of most of his cavalry, which had gone on a quixotic raid led by General Jeb Stuart, and suffering from a lack of co-ordination with his subordinates, Lee had taken a fatal risk in gambling all on Pickett's Charge. He had lost 28,000 men (though Meade's losses, at 23,000 were almost as great), and never again would the Confederacy have so good a chance of ending the war. With the news soon emerging that they had lost the key position of Vicksburg on the Mississippi (see page 127), it now became clear that it was now the Union's war to lose, rather than the Confederacy's to win.

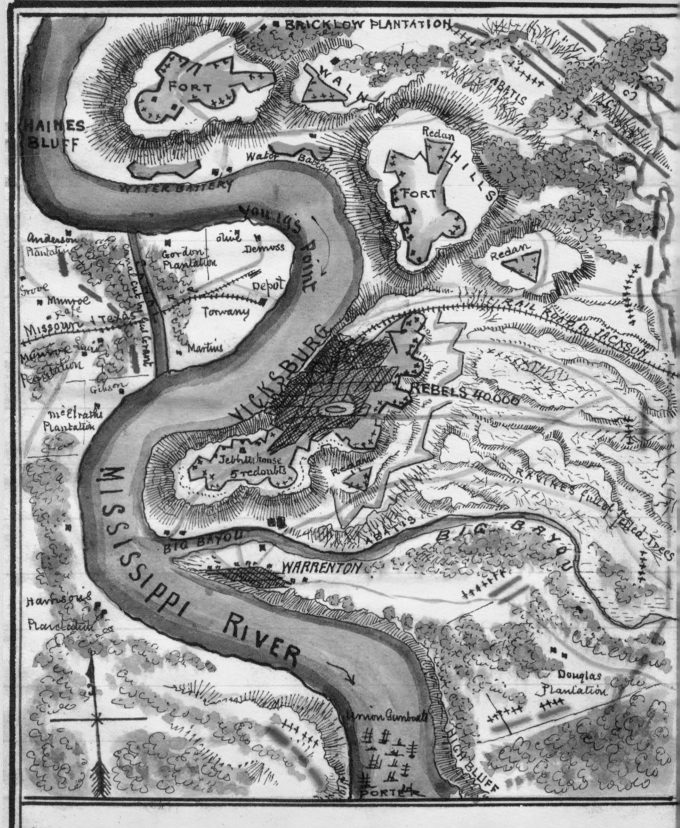

Map of the Rebel Position at VICKSBURG. Miss. May 1863. under Pember[t]
Union Army under Grant 65 000 men

Siege of Vicksburg

The blue arc of the Mississippi, the "father of waters", snakes through this map drawn by Robert Knox Sneden, a former architect and one of the most talented cartographers on the Union side during the American Civil War (until his career was cut short by a year spent in the infamous Confederate prisoner-of-war camp at Andersonville, Georgia).

Sneden highlights the town of Vicksburg, nestled in a bend on the east bank of the river, where high bluffs made it hard to assault from the river and marshy ground hindered the approach of any attackers trying to take it from the east. Yet in 1863, as the Union forces – marked in purple on the map – encircled Vicksburg in a necklace of steel, take it they must. The town dominated the central section of the Mississippi, whose 2,000-mile course made it a vital artery of commerce for the seceded states of the Confederacy and a link between its eastern and western halves. As Abraham Lincoln remarked, "Vicksburg is the key. The war can never be brought to a close until that key is in our pocket."

Early on in the war the Confederate cannon mounted on the bluffs prevented Union shipping and, more importantly, troop transports from passing Vicksburg, but by May 1862, the defensive forts at Island No. 10 and New Orleans had fallen to the Union and a squadron under Flag Officer David G Farragut arrived at Vicksburg to demand its surrender. The curt reply of the post commander, Lieutenant Colonel James L Autry, that "Mississippians don't know, and refuse to learn, how to surrender to an enemy" was the precursor to a prolonged campaign that consumed 14 months and several Union armies.

An attempt by General Ulysses S Grant to approach overland became bogged down at Milliken's Bend, Louisiana, and rather than launch a potentially disastrous direct assault, Grant decided to gamble on pushing a naval force north beyond Vicksburg and using this to land troops and then approach the town from the east. On the dark, moonless night of April 16, 1863, Rear Admiral David Dixon Porter led a flotilla up the river, the boats' engines muffled and their lights dimmed. Even so they were spotted, but by hugging the bank furthest from Vicksburg they suffered little damage from the badly ranged Confederate batteries.

With local naval dominance assured, Grant ordered the destruction of the railway lines by which Vicksburg had been resupplied and forced a crossing at Bruinsburg, landing 22,000 men to launch attacks from the east. At first he tried assault rather than strangulation, following up massive bombardments with a series of attempts to storm Vicksburg, one of which, on May 22, was repulsed with 3,000 casualties. Seeing the futility of further direct attacks, Grant finally decided to besiege the town, and by early June the last routes out had been blocked.

As the summer progressed, the food supply inside Vicksburg dwindled and disease began to claim hundreds of victims, while civilians huddled, terrified in the honeycomb of caves that riddled the bluffs, as Union shells rained down relentlessly. Steadily, the Union lines moved forward and engineers excavated trenches for mines to blow breaches in the town's fortifications. One that detonated on June 25 led to a furious 26-hour battle that almost penetrated Vicksburg's perimeter. A second mine, exploded on July 1, blew up one of the town's defensive redans.

Faced with the prospect of Vicksburg's walls being reduced to rubble and knowing the parlous state of the town's supplies, on July 3 General John C Pemberton, the Confederate garrison commander, sent out a deputation of grey-clad Confederate officers to negotiate a surrender. Grant's terms were generous: the defenders were allowed to leave under parole, as long as they surrendered their arms.

The victorious Union forces acquired 172 artillery pieces, 38,000 shells and 50,000 rifles and muskets. More importantly, Grant had broken the resistance of the "Gibraltar of the Confederacy", making the river a conduit for Union trade and troops, and severely damaging both the morale and economy of a Confederacy already reeling from the defeat at Gettysburg the day before (see page 125). The campaign had been a perfect example of the effective use of combined naval and land forces to achieve an otherwise forbidding objective, all crafted through the tactical genius of Ulysses S Grant.

Battle of Königgrätz

Drawn from Heinrich Friedjung's *Der Kampf um die Vorherrschaft in Deutschland 1859 bis 1866* ("The Struggle for Mastery in Germany 1859–66"), the map shows the final battle in the Seven Weeks' War between Prussia and Austria. Friedjung, who was a strong exponent of a "Greater Germany" solution to German unification which would include Austria within its bounds, must have experienced a twinge of regret that the Austrians' defeat in the battle at Königgrätz (or Sadowa) made it clear that it would be Otto von Bismarck's Prussia that would form the nucleus of a German state and that very probably Austria would be excluded from it.

The pretext for war was the Schleswig-Holstein question – a border dispute between Denmark and Prussia so tangled that the British statesman Lord Palmerston reputedly said that only three people had ever understood it: Prince Albert, who was dead; a German professor who had gone mad; and Palmerston himself, who had forgotten. In 1866 Bismarck used a dispute over the administration of the area, which had been divided between Germany and Austria after they seized it from Denmark two years earlier, to provoke a war, marching 12,000 Prussian troops into Austrian-held Holstein.

Of the other German states, only Saxony provided troops to Austria, which meant that a notionally smaller Prussia could muster 350,000 troops against the Austrians' 320,000, a quarter of whom were needed to defend their territories in northern Italy. The Prussians were also armed with the new breech-loading Dreyse needle gun, whose superior rate of fire and greater accuracy gave its infantry a huge advantage.

Prussia's chief of staff, Helmuth von Moltke, also took advantage of the new railway technology to rapidly mobilise his army, transporting them along a wide arc extending from Silesia to Saxony. The 120,000-strong Second Army under Crown Prince Friedrich Wilhelm at Landshut in Silesia was poised to attack the Austrian heartland. To counter this threat the Austrian emperor Franz Josef chose the ageing Ludwig von Benedek, a veteran of the 1859 Solferino campaign in Italy (see pages 116–17), who did not really want the job. His cautious approach, throwing a defensive ring around Vienna, handed the initiative to the Prussians, who by June 29 had brushed aside a Saxon army at Gitschin, causing Benedek to ask his emperor to sue for peace, a request Franz Josef firmly rejected.

Benedek concentrated his troops near the Bohemian towns of Sadowa and Königgrätz, his centre anchored on the village of Chlum. The Prussians reached the area on July 2, with the First Army under Prince Friedrich Karl arriving ahead of the Crown Prince's Second Army. As a result, the Austrian-Saxon army found itself holding back the Prussians in the early light of July 3, unaware that this was exactly what von Moltke wanted: to pin down Benedek until the bulk of his force arrived. By 8am these reinforcements were trickling onto the battlefield, clearing Sadowa of Austrians, pushing into the Swiep Wald woods and beginning an enveloping attack that threatened to cut off the Austrian army's retreat.

Benedek expended precious regiments in trying to clear the Prussians from the woods, hoping to mount a general counterattack that never proved possible. He ordered his IV and II Corps back towards Chlum, but interpreting it as a retreat, several other Austrian corps fell back. Only a spirited counterattack by the Saxons on the left wing stopped Benedek's army from being completely surrounded.

Nonetheless, the Austrians had lost all the high ground and were now subject to intense Prussian artillery bombardment. Facing the loss of Chlum itself, at 3pm Benedek ordered a general retreat. The VI Corps commander, Field Marshal Wilhelm von Ramming, disobeyed the order and advanced, forcing the Prussians out of Rosberitz and briefly threatening to recapture Chlum and snatch an unlikely victory. Yet the Prussians were now too numerous and the envelopment almost complete. As the Austrian cavalry mounted a rearguard screening action that cost them 2,000 dead, the rest of the army escaped.

Benedek had suffered 45,000 casualties (including 20,000 taken prisoner), more than four times the Prussian losses. Faced with a possible Prussian drive straight at Vienna, five days after the battle von Moltke agreed to an armistice. The Treaty of Prague that formally ended the war on August 23 gave Bismarck everything he could have wanted: Schleswig-Holstein was assigned to Prussia (along with Hanover and Hesse-Cassel), while Austria was forced to cede the Veneto to Italy. Prussia's new status as undisputed arbiter of Germany enabled it to form the North German Confederation, a body firmly under the Prussian thumb, and one which excluded Austria. If no one had understood the Schleswig-Holstein question, the aftermath of Prussia's victory at Königgrätz can have left them in no doubt about the extent of Bismarck's ambitions.

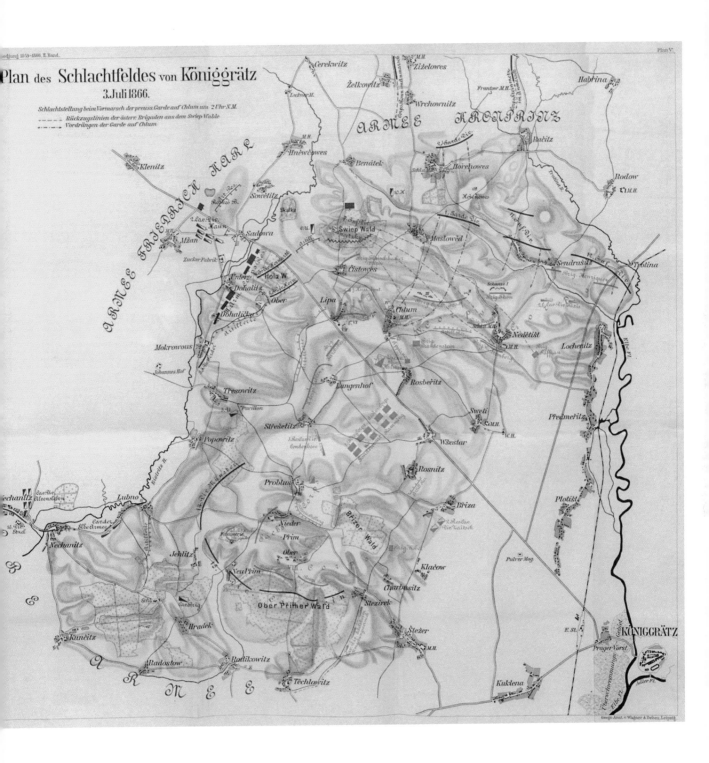

Plan des Schlachtfeldes von Königgrätz.
3. Juli 1866.

Schlachtstellung beim Vormarsch der preuss. Garde auf Chlum um 2 Uhr N.M.
Rückzugslinien der österr. Brigaden aus dem Swiep Walde
Vordrängen der Garde auf Chlum.

ARMEE KRONPRINZ

ARMEE FRIEDRICH KARL

ARMEE

Cerekwitz
Žiželowes
Žělkowitz
Wrchownitz
Habrina
Račitz
Rodow
Horenowes
Benátek
Klenitz
Sowětitz
Skalka
Swiep Wald
Maslowěd
Sendraš
Tyblina
Čistowes
Lipa
Chlum
Nedělišt
Lochenitz
Hněwčowes
Mžan
Sadowa
Zucker-Fabrik
Unter
Hola W.
Dohalitz
Ober
Dohalicko
Mokrowous
Johannes Hof
Tresowitz
Langenhof
Rosbeřitz
Sweti
Předmeřitz
Střesetitz
Popowitz
Wšestar
Rosnitz
Plotišt
Problus
Bříza
Nieder
Prim
Ober
Břízer Wald
Klačow
Nechanitz
Alčeenslěm
Lubno
Jehlitz
Neu Prim
Ober Přiher Wald
Charbusitz
Stezirek
Stežer
Königgrätz
Kunčitz
Hradek
Radostow
Radlikowitz
Techlowitz
Kuklena
Prager Vorst.

Geogr. Anst. v. Wagner & Debes, Leipzig.

Bois de la Gareme

Glaire

480

720

700

780

Cazal
CAV CAV
CAV
CAV

5

Fond de Givonne

Torcy
P.t Torcy

740

20,000
Inhabitants

SEDAN

Swampy
Ground
inundated on the 1st Sept.r 1870

Chateau

Balan

Wadelincourt

Pontoon Bridge
used by 2 B 3 A.

Bazeilles

Chateau

512

R. Maitre Lambert

RAILROAD

2 B 3 A
2 B 3 A

760

1 & S

1 B

12 B
12 B

12 C

1 B Stab
1 B 3 A

1 B 3 A

1 & S

RIVER MEUSE

480

1 B 3 A

Railway bridge used by the
Bavarians in an attack on
Bazeilles the 31st August which was
repulsed.

1 B Stab

2 B 3 A

To Chaumont 1½ Miles

To Noyes ½ Mile

2 B 3 A

To Noyes

2 B 3 A

One Mile

S

F

Pontoon Bridge
used by 1 B C A.S

Battle of Sedan

The map by the London cartographic publisher Stanfords shows the blue of Helmuth von Moltke's Prussian army folded around the red of the French commander Patrice de MacMahon's Army of Châlons. Trapped in the citadel-town of Sedan and hemmed against the River Meuse, the French suffered a disaster which led to the fall of Emperor Napoleon III and a legacy of rancour between Germany and France which contributed in no small part to their subsequent conflict in the First World War. One witness to the battle was Captain George WA FitzGeorge of the Royal Welch Fusiliers, whose first-hand observations helped him draw up what he called a "Short Memoir" (which extended to over 100 pages) giving an account of the fighting, and which included this map.

Napoleon III had been tricked into the war, after an artfully deceptive account of French concessions in negotiations over the succession to the Spanish throne (intended to avert a Prussian Hohenzollern becoming King of Spain) was leaked by Prussian chancellor, Otto von Bismarck, which caused outrage in France. Prussia had prepared well, rapidly mobilising its forces, while the French were disorganised, their army commanded by ageing veterans, and with no clear war aims. A series of reverses on the frontier and a bruising defeat at Gravelotte on August 18, 1870, left a large part of the French army besieged at Metz. In response, Napoleon ordered the formation of a new Army of Châlons and, alongside Marshal MacMahon, set out to rescue them. Yet after a setback at Beaumont on August 30, the French fell back on Sedan, their 120,000-strong army risking the same fate as the defenders of Metz.

A delighted von Moltke remarked, "Now we have them in the mousetrap." Critical to his plan was pinning the French in place while sufficient Prussian troops came up to surround MacMahon's army. Early on September 1, units of Bavarians under General Ludwig von der Tann pushed across the Meuse and began moving towards the village of Bazeilles, where a heroic French resistance in the end only served to give the Prussians time to block off their remaining avenues of retreat. One of these was through La Moncelle, and soon the Bavarians, reinforced by Saxons, had interdicted that route also.

Now, as the morning mist dispersed, the German artillery was able to open fire on Sedan, sending shells crashing into the defenders and increasing the urgency for the French to escape. An order to pull out was given by General Auguste-Alexandre Ducrot, who had taken over from MacMahon after he was wounded early in the battle. Unfortunately, yet another new commander, General Emmanuel de Wimpffen, had not long before arrived in Sedan with orders to replace MacMahon should he ever be incapacitated. Wimpffen promptly countermanded Ducrot's orders to retreat, sowing fatal confusion in the French ranks.

Although Ducrot's I Corps and General Barthélémy Lebrun's XII Corps gained ground in the east, von Moltke saw the danger and reinforced the area, finally forcing the French out of Bazeilles. He then snapped the vice shut by launching an attack through Donchery to the west of the city. Seeing the French army was about to be totally surrounded, General Jean-Auguste Margueritte, commander of the 1st Reserve Cavalry Division, threw his men into a last-ditch charge to try to break out. Margueritte was fatally wounded in the first minutes of the charge, and his troopers were mown down in heaps. From his vantage point above the battlefield, the Prussian king Wilhelm saw the carnage and remarked, "Ah, what brave fellows!"

Many other French units had broken and were flooding into Sedan, which was still under intense Prussian artillery bombardment. As Napoleon III consulted with his generals, new arguments started, with Wimpffen urging a breakout and resolutely refusing, even though he was commander, to capitulate.

By late afternoon, it was clear there was no other option. A surrender was agreed, sealed next day by the French emperor in person. Although the French casualties, at 17,000, were a little over double those of the Prussians, far worse was the more than 100,000 – virtually the entire Army of Châlons – taken prisoner, including their sovereign. Napoleon endured six months' captivity in Germany and died in exile in England two years later. The victorious Prussian army continued its march, placing Paris under siege on September 19. The armistice in January and the final treaty which ended the war on February 26, 1871, were humiliating, above all the loss of Alsace-Lorraine, which the new French Republican government was forced to cede to Prussia. Wilhelm had himself crowned German kaiser (emperor) at the Palace of Versailles, marking the reunification of Germany under Prussian leadership. Sedan had sealed the moment when this new nation replaced France as Europe's principal military power.

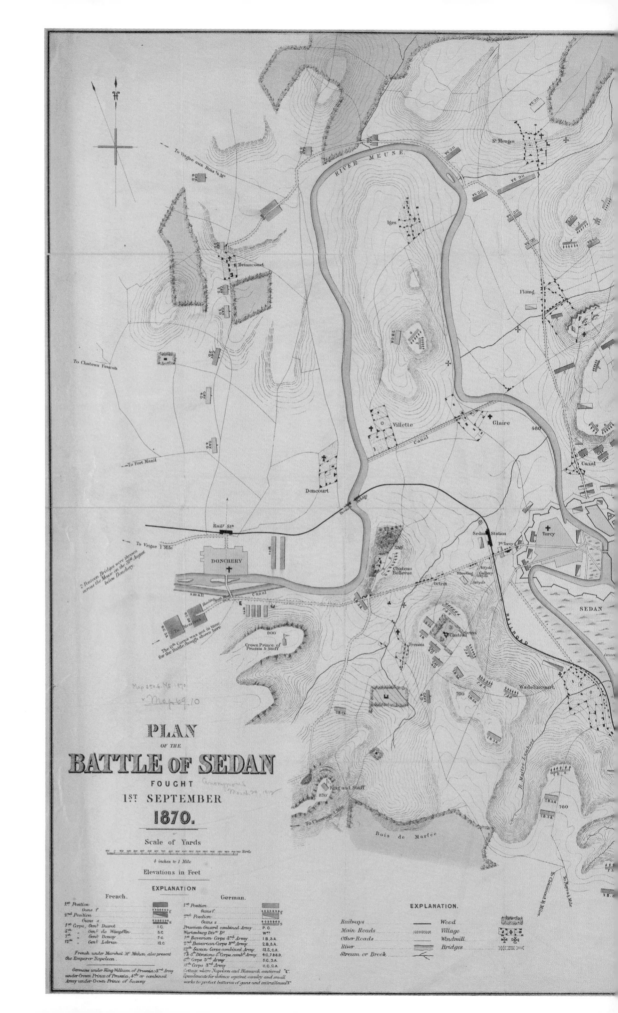

PLAN
OF THE
BATTLE OF SEDAN
FOUGHT
1ST SEPTEMBER
1870.

Scale of Yards

4 inches to 1 Mile

Elevations in Feet

EXPLANATION

French.			German.		
1st Position			1st Position		
Guns f			Guns f		
2nd Position			2nd Position		
Guns x			Guns x		
1st Corps, Genl Ducrot		1.C	Prussian Guard combined Army		P.G.
5th " Genl de Wimpffen		5.C	Wurtemberg Divn Do		W.
7th " Genl Douay		7.C	1st Bavarian Corps 3rd Army		1.B.3.A.
12th " Genl Lebrun		12.C	2nd Bavarian Corps 3rd Army		2.B.3.A.
			12th Saxon Corps combined Army		12.S.C.A.
French under Marshal McMahon, also present			3rd–5th Divisions 5 Corps combd Army		4.C.7&8.D.
the Emperor Napoleon.			5th Corps 3rd Army		5.C.3.A.
			11th Corps 3rd Army		11.C.3.A.
Germans under King William of Prussia (5th Army			Cottage where Napoleon and Bismarck conferred "C"		
under Crown Prince of Prussia, 4th or combined			Emplacements for defence against cavalry and small		
Army under Crown Prince of Saxony.			works to protect batteries of guns and mitrailleuses "F"		

EXPLANATION.

Railways		Wood	
Main Roads		Village	
Other Roads		Windmill	
River		Bridges	
Stream or Brook			

To Vrigne aux Bois ¾ Mr

RIVER MEUSE

St Menges

Iges

Floing

Briancourt

To Chateau Faucon

Villette

Glaire

480

Canal

Cazal

Doncourt

To Fort Manil

Railr Stn

Sedan Station

Torcy

To Vrigne 1 Mile

DONCHERY

Chateau Bellevue

betron

SEDAN

"2 Pontoon Bridges were thrown
across the Meuse on the 31st August
below Donchery."

small

floating Bridge

Chod nl

900

The 6th Corps was not in time
for the Battle though shewn here

Crown Prince of
Prussia & Staff

Fresnois

Chateau Garenne

Wadelincourt

Map 85 + MS 1870

Map 69.10

700

King and Staff

870

To Chevenge 1 Mile

Bois de Marfée

700

Annexgrund
March 29, 1915

Bois de Floing
900'

2 Miles from the Belgian Frontier.

R. Rouillon

Chapelle

870'

Bois de la Garenne

Villers

Cernay

850'

790'

Givonne

Daigny

730'

Bois Chevalier

Fond de Gironne

Lake

Rubecourt

740'

Chateau

Moncelle

Lamecourt

Balan

707'

512'

Chateau Moiville

R. Boulacourt

Bazeilles

Chateau La Rulle

To Carignan 8 Miles

460'

Douzy

RIVER MEUSE

Railway Bridge used by the
Germans on which our attack on
the main bridge was stopped

Pontoon Bridge
used by III C.A.

RIVER CHIERS

455'

To Remilly

To Autrecourt

Allicourt

Stanford's Geograph! Establishm! 6, Charing Cross

Battle of Isandhlwana

The 19th century saw few examples of indigenous troops besting European colonial armies. Only those rulers who possessed forces which were trained, had some element of organisation and possessed an ability to operate for extended periods and across large distances stood any chance of resisting the superior firepower and professional armies of the Europeans.

The Battle of Isandhlwana, shown on the contemporary engraving, was one of the rare victories, won by the African Zulu kingdom against an expeditionary force led by Lord Chelmsford which had invaded their land. He had been instructed to do so by Sir Bartle Frere, the British High Commissioner for Southern Africa, who was keen to annex the Zulu kingdom to Britain's possessions in the region and had issued an ultimatum to dissolve his army, a demand to which the Zulu king, Cetshwayo, could not possibly accede although he attempted to negotiate more lenient terms.

Chelmsford's ultimate objective was the royal kraal at Ulundi. Fatally underestimating the capacity of the Zulu king to mobilise his warriors rapidly, he divided his 17,000-strong force into three columns, leaving a garrison at Rorke's Drift, where he crossed the Buffalo River into Zululand. Chelmsford, in command of the Centre Column, headed towards Ulundi. Progress, with lumbering ox wagons carrying the supplies along tracks rendered treacherous by heavy rain, was painfully slow, and the column covered only about a mile a day.

On January 20, 1879, Chelmsford made camp at Isandhlwana, in what is now the KwaZulu Natal province of South Africa. He did not fortify it by digging entrenchments or using the wagons to form a protective ring around the camp, as would have been normal, believing that the Zulus posed little threat. Then, on January 22 he took two thirds of the force ahead to strike towards Ulundi, leaving just 1,300 men – 600 redcoats of the regular army and 700 from the Natal Native Contingent and irregular units – under the command of Lieutenant Colonel Henry Pulleine. Although the Isandhlwana contingent was further reinforced later that day by 500 Natal Native Contingent troops under Lieutenant-Colonel Anthony Durnford, within hours they found themselves facing 20,000 Zulus who had manoeuvred around Chelmsford's column and concealed themselves around the heights overlooking the British camp.

Under the command of Ntshingwayo kaMahole, the Zulus attacked in a "horns of the buffalo" formation in which the centre sought to hold the enemy in place while the horns flanked and enveloped the British. Although the regular British battalions of the 24th Regiment, which Pulleine sent against the Zulu "chest" held their ground, Durnford's men on the British right flank, armed with inferior rifles and running out of ammunition, were pushed back, while the Zulu right horn also began to make progress. Seeing that he was about to be outflanked, Pulleine ordered a retreat back to the camp, but this turned into a disordered rout with small British units finding themselves surrounded by Zulus and engaged in desperate last stands as they stabbed with bayonets against the mass of Zulu spears. Further chaos was added to the scene by a total eclipse of the sun at 2.30pm which left the battlefield in total darkness for several minutes.

For a while Durnford held a unit of about 150 of his men together between the horns of the Zulu army, defending frantically from within the shelter of several wagons. In the end only a few British soldiers were left, and they were cut down as they tried to flee, one redcoat of the 24th surviving in a nearby cave for a few hours until the Zulus found him. Only a few hundred local auxiliaries and 60 Europeans escaped. Some made it back to Rorke's Drift, where their warning to the 150-strong garrison about the oncoming Zulu host allowed it time to prepare and mount a successful defence of the mission station.

Yet Rorke's Drift did not wipe out the memory of Isandhlwana, the British Army's worst defeat against indigenous forces. For the Zulus, though, the taste of victory was transient. The British were determined to avenge the Isandhlwana humiliation, support for the war mounted and in late March new British columns moved into Zululand, inflicting a final defeat on Cetshwayo at Ulundi in July. Although it was not yet annexed by Britain, the Zulu's power over their kingdom was shattered.

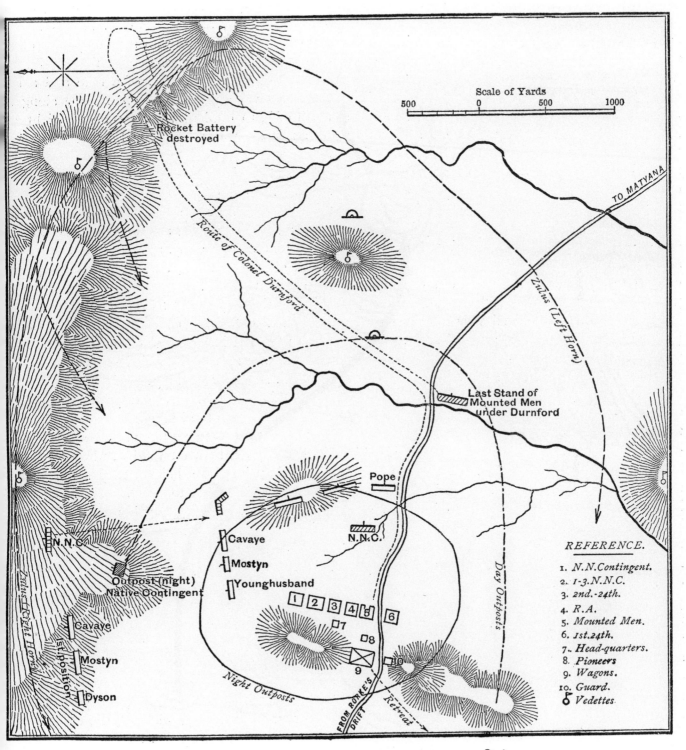

Rocket Battery
destroyed

Scale of Yards
500   0   500   1000

TO MATYANA

Route of Colonel Durnford

Zulus (Left Horn)

Last Stand of
Mounted Men
under Durnford

N.N.C.

Outpost (night)
Native Contingent

Cavaye

Mostyn

Younghusband

Pope

N.N.C.

Cavaye

Mostyn

Dyson

Zulus (Right Horn)

1st position

Night Outposts

Day Outposts

1 2 3 4 5 6
7
8
9   10

FROM RORKE'S DRIFT

Retreat

REFERENCE.
1. N.N.Contingent.
2. 1-3. N.N.C.
3. 2nd.-24th.
4. R.A.
5. Mounted Men.
6. 1st.24th.
7. Head-quarters.
8. Pioneers
9. Wagons.
10. Guard.
ठ Vedettes.

PLAN OF THE BATTLE OF ISANDHLWANA (JAN. 22, 1879).

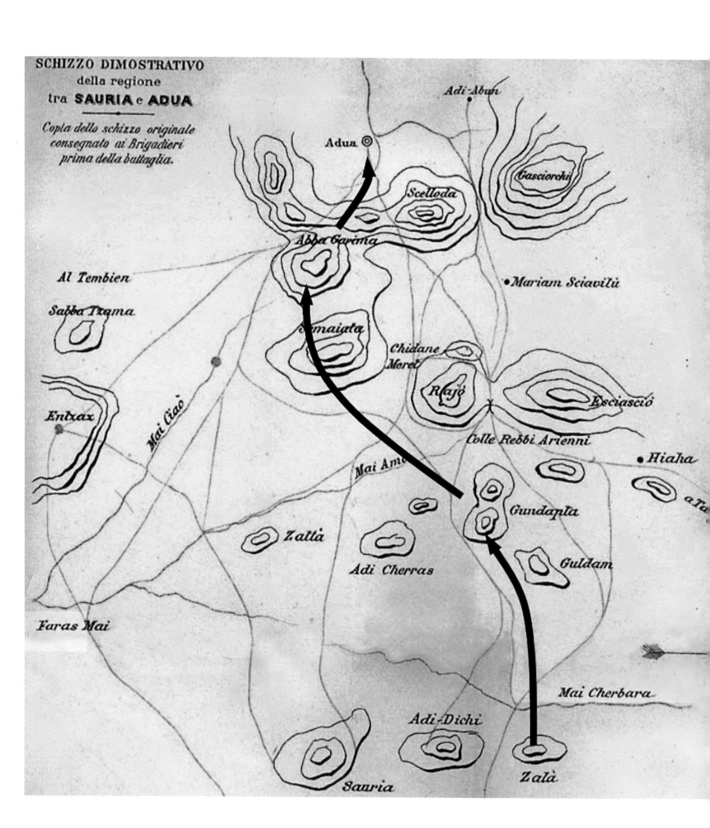

SCHIZZO DIMOSTRATIVO
della regione
tra **SAURIA** e **ADUA**

Copia dello schizzo originale
consegnato ai Brigadieri
prima della battaglia.

Adi-Abun

Adua ◎

Gasciorchi

Scelloda

Abba Garima

Al Tembien

Mariam Sciavilù

Sabba Tzama

Smaigla

Chidane
Meret

Rajò

Esciasciò

Entzax

Mai Ciao

Colle Rebbi Arienni

Hiaha

Mai Amo

Gundapta

Zalà

Guldam

Adi Cherras

Faras Mai

Mai Cherbara

Adi-Dichi

Sauria

Zalà

Battle of Adwa

The sketch of the hilly terrain of northern Ethiopia, made at the end of February 1896 by an Italian military draughtsman, indicates a bold line of advance towards the town of Adwa (formerly Adua). What it could not show was the disaster about to unfold for the expeditionary force of General Oreste Baratieri, one of the worst ever defeats suffered by Europeans at the hands of indigenous African forces.

Italy, like Germany, had been a latecomer to the colonial land grab carried out by the Europeans in the late 19th century, its tardy acquisition of the status of a unified nation state meaning it lacked the lodgements on the African coast from which other more established powers like France and Britain expanded. Italy instead set its sights on Ethiopia, one of the few areas to escape European predation and which, though riven by faction fighting amongst its nobility, possessed a long tradition of independence and a strongly rooted cultural identity centred around its emperor and the Ethiopian Orthodox Church.

The Italians began by acquiring land in Eritrea, starting with the port of Assab in 1869 and expanding gradually until they forced Ethiopian recognition of their holdings by the Treaty of Wuchale twenty years later. The Italian-language version of the treaty also seemed to accept Italy's suzerainty over Ethiopia and its right to mediate in all dealings between the emperor and European powers. Emperor Menelik II and his strong-minded empress Taytu Betul abrogated the treaty when they realised its significance, and this, together with the support they offered to a rebellion in Eritrea in 1895, led the Italian commander there, General Baratieri, to march into Tigray in Ethiopia's northeast that September with a column of 17,000 Italian troops and locally recruited *askaris*.

Baratieri was deceived by the apparently slow pace of Menelik's response into believing he would easily be able to push Italian control further into Tigray and so was wholly unprepared for the massive host of 100,000 soldiers that the Ethiopians had gathered by December, many armed with rifles and supported by modern artillery batteries.

The first ominous signs came at Amba Alagi, where a small Italian force was wiped out, and at the fort of Mekelle, where Empress Taytu forced the Italians to surrender by cutting off their water supply. Menelik pushed on north and made camp on the plateau of Gundapta, hoping that the Italians would take the path of prudence and withdraw back into Eritrea. Baratieri hesitated and took up a position at Sauria, to the east of the plateau. His reluctance, though, evaporated on receiving a telegram from the Italian prime minster Francesco Crispi which threatened to replace him if he did not act swiftly.

By now Menelik had moved his headquarters back to Adwa, and, believing this meant the Ethiopians were retreating, Baratieri ordered an attack. He divided his force into three columns, with two under Generals Matteo Albertone and Vittorio Dabormida sent to seize the passes that gave access from Gundapta to Adwa and a third led by General Giuseppe Arimondi sent to occupy the heights which overlooked them. The plan went disastrously wrong: inadequate scouting meant Albertone overshot and ran straight into Menelik's camp, where his vanguard was wiped out and the rest pinned down by heavy Ethiopian fire. Dabormida, whom Baratieri dispatched to rescue Albertone, got lost and ended up at Mariam Sciavitu surrounded by 15,000 Ethiopians. It was left to Arimondi to try to hold open an escape route for the beleaguered Italian forces, but many of the askaris simply broke and fled, while Albertone was captured, which caused his column to descend further into chaos.

The remaining Italians were hampered by burning heat, thirst and the loss of many of their officers. Any who made a break for it were cut down by the Ethiopians' Oromo cavalry. Towards the end of the afternoon, Dabormida, who had continued to resist, found himself unable to retreat and was killed with most of his force, while the remnant of the Italian army under Baratieri was outflanked and crushed by the jubilant Ethiopians. Of the original force of 17,000, over 6,000 Italians had been killed and 3,000 taken prisoner, the least fortunate being Ethiopian askaris who had fought for Baratieri, who had their right hands amputated.

In the aftermath of the battle, the Italians abandoned their hopes of expanding their Eritrean colony and signed the Treaty of Addis Ababa, which recognised Ethiopia's independence. For the Ethiopians, it was a resounding triumph, proving that European military supremacy was not unassailable, that Africans could resist their encroachment and offering hope for others chafing under colonial rule. It was no accident that when the Organisation of African Unity was established in 1963, it was the Ethiopian capital of Addis Ababa that became its headquarters.

Spanish–American War

The map chronicles a conflict from which a new global military power emerged. The Spanish–American War of 1898 was the first in which the United States confronted a European nation outside North America, and its victory marked the beginning of a shift in geopolitical power away from the old European powers. The map was compiled by Eugenia Wheeler Goff and Henry Slade Goff, a Minnesota husband-and-wife team of cartographic publishers who produced a series of popular historical wall maps, including this one, and a historical atlas of *The United States and her Neighbors*.

The war had its origin in Spain's determination to hang on to its Caribbean colonies, having lost its holdings on the mainland of the Americas over 60 years earlier. An increasingly brutal response to a Cuban revolutionary uprising in the mid-1890s – which involved the herding of anyone with suspected pro-independence tendencies into prison camps where thousands died of disease and hunger – provoked outrage in the United States, marshalled by populist newspapers such as William Randolph Hearst's *New York Journal*.

Throughout 1896 calls grew for United States intervention to stop the activities of the Spanish commander in Cuba, General Valeriano Weyler, aptly nicknamed El Carnicero ("the butcher"). Although President Grover Cleveland fended them off, his successor, William McKinley proved more sympathetic, and when riots broke out in Havana in December 1897, he authorised the dispatch of the USS *Maine* to Cuba to protect US citizens should the situation worsen. But then, on February 15, 1898, the *Maine* sank after a massive explosion whose cause was never established, killing over 260 of the crew. Although the Spanish government offered to submit to the judgment of an arbitration panel, public opinion in the United States was so inflamed and accounts delivered to Congress of the harsh measures still being adopted by the Spanish in Cuba so graphic that on March 26 McKinley delivered an ultimatum to Spain: stop the repression and negotiate with the rebels or suffer the consequences.

When Congress started to press for the granting of Cuban independence, Spain responded on April 24 by declaring war on the United States, a move the Americans reciprocated the following day. The conflict proved absurdly one-sided. Although the United States had not expected war, its navy, including four new battleships – the *Indiana*, *Iowa*, *Massachusetts* and *Oregon* – and a squadron of armoured cruisers under Commodore George Dewey far outmatched

Spain's antiquated fleet, and the Spanish land forces were ill-trained and understrength. The first fighting occurred in the Philippines – the subject of another map by Eugenia Goff – where, by August 13, the United States had crushed the Spanish colonial army and occupied Manila.

The Spanish navy's strongest force, under Admiral Pascual Cervera, had taken refuge in Santiago harbour on Cuba's southern coast, where it remained blockaded by a US flotilla led by Rear Admiral William T Sampson. Destroying Cervera's force might land a decisive blow against the Spanish and so an expeditionary forced led by Major General William R Shafter was landed on June 22 at Baiquiri (now Daiquiri), east of Santiago. Largely composed of "buffalo soldiers", African-American troops of the 8th and 9th cavalry regiments, and the "Rough Riders", volunteer cavalry led by the future president Theodore Roosevelt, the US troops at first laboured against the Spanish infantry, who had been supplied with modern 1893 Mauser rifles. But then on July 1, a charge by the Rough Riders against entrenched Spanish positions at San Juan Hill broke through a key Spanish defensive line, which allowed Shafter's force to come dangerously close to Santiago.

On July 3 Cervera decided to make a run for it from Santiago Harbour, but he was quickly intercepted and all six of his main battleships were grounded, destroyed or scuttled. Santiago now lay wide open to the Americans, and on July 17 the city surrendered. It was fortunate timing, as yellow fever and other diseases had rendered three quarters of Shafter's force unfit for service.

The Treaty of Paris which formally ended the war on December 10, 1898, shattered the remains of Spain's colonial empire. Cuba was granted its independence, while the Spanish were forced to cede Guam and Puerto Rico to the United States and hand over the Philippines to American administration on payment of a $20 million indemnity. In the aftermath of the victory, McKinley easily won a second term in office in the 1900 presidential elections, helped by his vice-presidential candidate, none other than Theodore Roosevelt, whose performance with the "Rough Riders" had established his reputation as a war hero. More than anything though, the war made Americans conscious of their new, enlarged role in world affairs, an awareness which fuelled the demand for publications such as Eugenia Goff's portrayal of their armed forces' recent triumph.

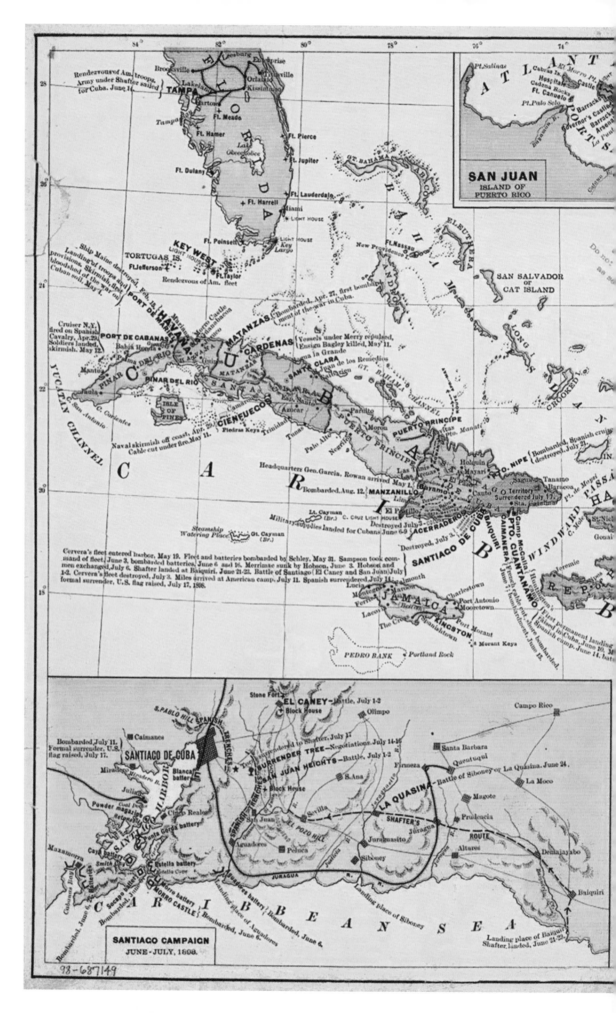

HAVANA

CITY AND HARBOR.

Goff's **Historical** **Map** OF THE

HISH-AMERICAN WAR

IN THE

EST INDIES, 1898

righted, 1899, by EUGENIA WHEELER GOFF, and HENRY SLADE GOFF, authors of
Goff's Historical Maps for Schools and Families.

FORT DEARBORN PUB. CO.

MAP ENGRAVERS AND PUBLISHERS

CHICAGO, ILL.

INDEXED

Battle of Omdurman

The map, showing the closing stages of the battle in which Major General Horatio Herbert Kitchener's Anglo-Egyptian force defeated the Mahdist army of the Khalifah Abdullah, is taken from *The River War* by Winston Churchill, then a junior lieutenant and war correspondent, who wrote a comprehensive two-volume account of the campaign.

Mahdism, an Islamic revivalist movement that arose in reaction to the British political domination of Egypt and the perception that the Egyptian government which acceded to this was un-Islamic, had waned in power since the death of its initial leader, Muhammad Ahmad bin Abdallah (the Mahdi) in 1885. His less charismatic successor, the Khalifah, faced several revolts and imposed a harsh regime to maintain control, all the while awaiting the British revenge for the Mahdist capture of Khartoum in Sudan in January 1885 during which the British administrator Major General Charles Gordon had been killed.

By March 1896, the British were ready and an Anglo-Egyptian column led by Kitchener, the Sirdar (or commander) of the Egyptian army, began a slow advance down the Nile towards the Mahdist capital of Omdurman, just outside Khartoum. It required the building of a new railway through the Nubian Desert to Abu Hamed and the services of several armoured gunboats to push his way through. Alarmed at Kitchener's slow but meticulous progress, in April 1898 the Khalifah sent a force to attack him at Atbara, around 180 miles northeast of Khartoum. Kitchener's comprehensive victory, in which 3,000 Mahdists were killed for the loss of just 80 of his men, cleared the way to Omdurman and showed the devastating power of his artillery and the 20 Maxim machine guns he had brought along.

By September 1, 1898, Kitchener had reached the Nile near Omdurman, where he erected a zeriba (a thorn stockade) at El Egeiga facing a scrubby plain dominated by heights at Jebel Surgham and the Kerreri Hills. His 26,000 troops – roughly two thirds of them Egyptians – included the British 21st Lancers to supplement more irregular cavalry, 46 artillery pieces and four gunboats. These set to shelling Mahdist positions and breached the walls of Omdurman itself, causing huge panic. Although the Mahdist army, some 50,000 strong, advanced to meet Kitchener's force, they then unexpectedly stopped in the early afternoon and settled down for the night.

Around dawn, the expected attack finally came. The Mahdists swarmed up the Jebel Surgham and then launched themselves against the left of the semicircle into which the Anglo-Egyptians had formed up. The Khalifah's plan was simply to overwhelm his opponents, but he underestimated the devastating impact of the British Lee-Metford rifles, the artillery barrage which hit his men at a distance of over 3,000 yards and the Maxim guns which mowed them down far short of the Sirdar's lines.

With the Mahdist attack on the left halted and an attack by Sheikh Osman al-Din in the centre equally faltering in a mire of blood and corpses, the one success for the Mahdists was when the 21st Lancers ran into some of the troops sheltering in a ravine behind Jebel Surgham and mounted a charge with lances couched. The few hundred Mahdists they expected turned out to be over 7,000, and the Lancers only extricated themselves with difficulty, losing a fifth of their number.

As Kitchener took advantage of the growing chaos to move towards Omdurman, the last of the Khalifah's reserves, some 20,000 of his best troops, came rushing forward following a huge black flag, his personal banner. Only quick thinking by Colonel Hector MacDonald of the 1st Egyptian Brigade, the column's rearguard, saved the day for the British. Realising the danger they were in, he formed

his men up and decimated the oncoming Mahdist wave with disciplined volleys. The Mahdists' last charge ebbed, faltered and dissolved, and the Khalifah, realising that the battle was lost, made his escape from Omdurman just before the advance elements of Kitchener's army reached it. By 11am the battle was over.

In the end it was won by technology, training and the disastrous decision of the Khalifah to hurl his troops into the maws of the Maxim guns. The Mahdists lost nearly 10,000 dead, around 13,000 wounded, while about 5,000 were taken prisoner, which meant the Khalifah had suffered more than 50 per cent casualties. In contrast Kitchener's losses were just 47 dead and 340 wounded. The Mahdists were broken as a force (although the Khalifah himself was not captured until 1899). Omdurman and the rest of the Sudan fell under a joint Anglo-Egyptian condominium which lasted until 1956, by which time the career of the young army officer who had written an account of the battle had gone from strength to strength, culminating in Winston Churchill's second stint as British prime minister, which ended just the year before.

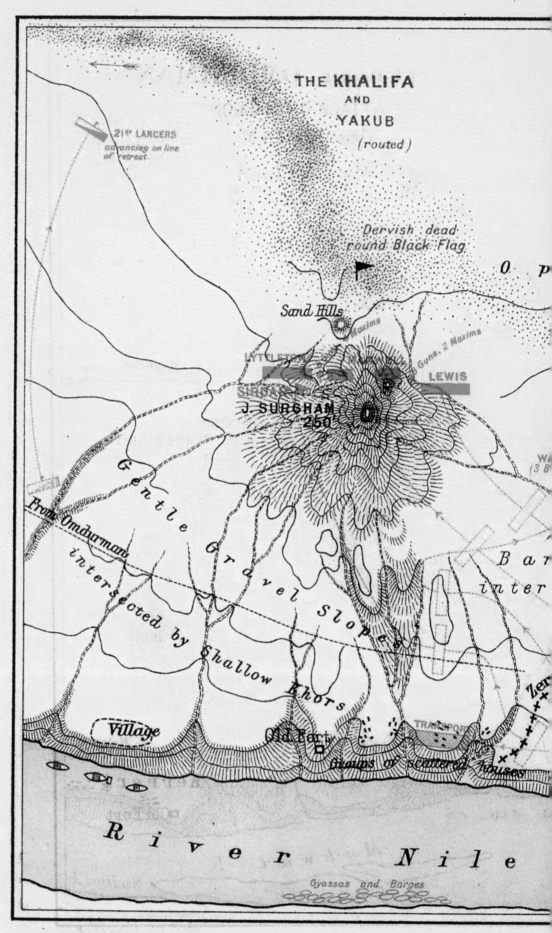

THE **KHALIFA**
AND
YAKUB
(routed)

21ˢᵗ LANCERS
advancing on line
of retreat.

Dervish : dead
round Black Flag

Sand Hills

Maxims

LYTTLETON

6 Guns, 2 Maxims

LEWIS

SIRDAR

J. SURGHAM
250

From Omdurman

Gentle Gravel Slopes

intersected by Shallow Khors

B a r

i n t e r

Zer

Village

Old Fort

TRANSPORT

Groups of scattered houses

R i v e r   N i l e

Gyassas and Barges

Longmans, Green &

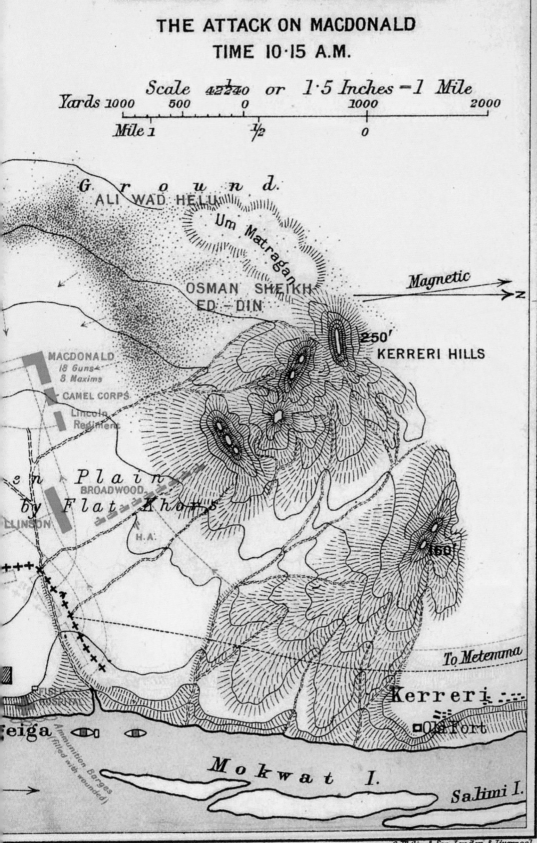

BATTLE OF OMDURMAN

THE ATTACK ON MACDONALD

TIME 10·15 A.M.

Scale 42240 or 1·5 Inches = 1 Mile

Yards 1000   500   0   1000   2000

Mile 1   ½   0

G r o u n d.

ALI WAD HELU

Um Matragan

Magnetic → Z

OSMAN SHEIKH
ED - DIN

250'

KERRERI HILLS

MACDONALD
18 Guns
8 Maxims

CAMEL CORPS

Lincoln
Regiment

en Plain

BROADWOOD

by Flat Khors

LLINSON

H.A.

150'

+++

To Metemma

Kerreri

Fort

eiga

Ammunition Barges
(filled with wounded)

M o k w a t   I.

Salimi I.

G. Philip & Son, London & Liverpool.

New York & Bombay.

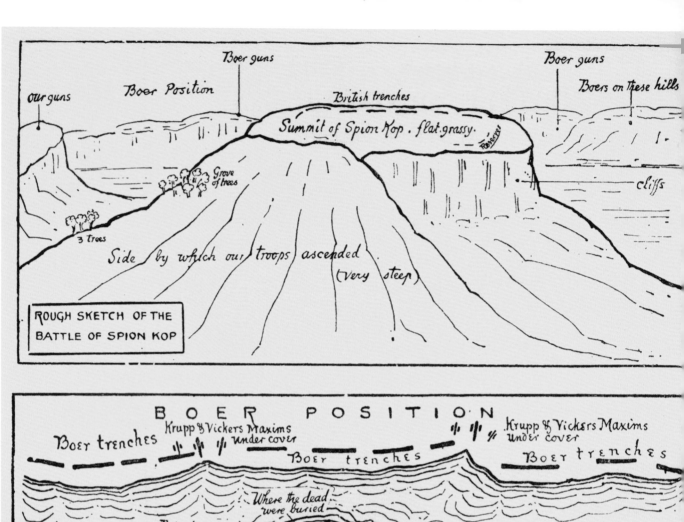

Our guns — Boer Position — Boer guns — British trenches — Boer guns — Boers on these hills

Summit of Spion Kop. flat. grassy.

Grove of trees

3 trees

Side by which our troops ascended. (very steep)

cliffs

ROUGH SKETCH OF THE
BATTLE OF SPION KOP

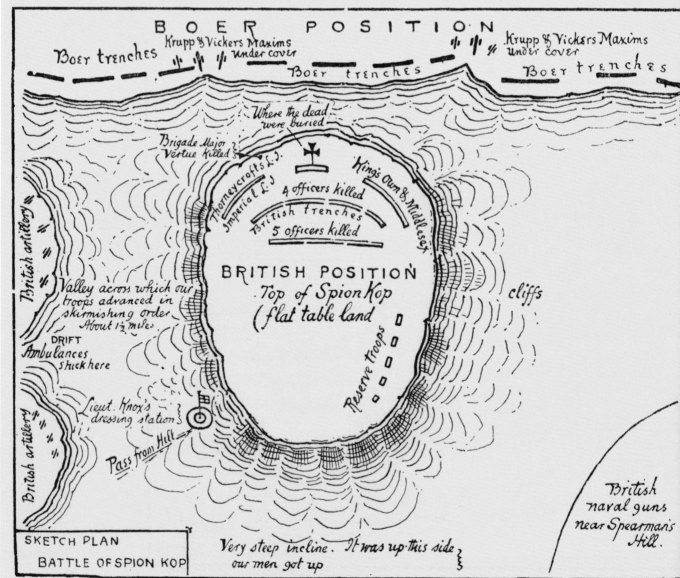

B O E R   P O S I T I O N

Boer trenches — Krupp & Vickers Maxims under cover — Boer trenches — Krupp & Vickers Maxims under cover — Boer trenches

Boer trenches

Where the dead were buried

Brigade Major Vertue Killed

Thorneycrofts (I.)

Imperial (I.)

King's Own & Middlesex

4 officers killed

British trenches

5 officers killed

BRITISH POSITION
Top of Spion Kop
(flat table land

British artillery

Valley across which our troops advanced in skirmishing order. About 1½ miles.

DRIFT
Ambulances stuck here

Lieut. Knox's dressing station

Pass from Hill

British artillery

cliffs

Reserve troops

Very steep incline. It was up this side our men got up

British naval guns near Spearman's Hill.

SKETCH PLAN
BATTLE OF SPION KOP

Battle of Spion Kop

The sketch, published in 1900 in the third volume of Louis Creswicke's *South Africa and the Transvaal War*, illustrates how the high ridge of Spion Kop dominates the battlefield in Natal's Rangeworthy Hills. It was here, in January 1900, that Britain suffered one of a string of ignominious defeats against settler militias from South Africa's Boer republics. The war with the Boers – predominantly farmers of Dutch descent – had broken out after the discovery of gold in the Witswatersrand (Transvaal) in 1886, and the evident designs of the British government to get its hands on this vast new source of mineral wealth led to heightened tensions between the two sides.

The Boers struck pre-emptively in October 1899, sending four columns into British-held Natal, seizing most of the countryside and laying siege to Mafeking, Kimberley and Ladysmith. Caught by surprise at the rapid co-ordinated strikes by what they had dismissed as a rabble of farmers, the British High Command, led by Sir Redvers Buller, was reduced to sending relief columns to the three towns. All ran into stout resistance from the Boers, who were armed with bolt-action Mauser rifles and smokeless powder, which made their sharpshooters hard to spot, and inspired by an almost religious fervour in the righteousness of their cause. The disasters of "Black Week", in which the British suffered losses at Stormberg, Magersfontein and, on December 15, at Colenso, led to the replacement of Buller by Lord Frederick Roberts.

Roberts pioneered a new strategy in which cavalry was used to outflank Boer positions and benefited from huge new reinforcements (to the extent that, by the time the war ended, over 440,000 British and Imperial troops had fought in it). For the moment, though, Buller remained in command in northern Natal, and he determined to rescue his reputation by relieving Ladysmith, setting off on January 16 with 24,000 infantry, 2,500 cavalry and eight artillery batteries. Flanking movements around the Rangeworthy Hills were supposed to circumvent Boer positions, but one column under General Charles Warren found the going too difficult, and so, having halted at the foot of the hills, he resolved to force a route over them by a direct attack on the Boers. He calculated that if he could capture the highest point, the 500-metre high Spion Kop, he could send enfilading fire down on the Boer entrenchments and dislodge them.

The position was only lightly defended by the Boers, and the column which Warren sent up under Lieutenant Colonel Alexander Thorneycroft on the night of January 23 took it easily. They had three hours to dig in before dawn broke and the mists which had enveloped the slopes rose at 7am. But the British found they had made a terrible mistake, having captured only a part of the ridge, which was now exposed to fire from all sides, and in particular from Boer marksmen on the neighbouring Twin Peaks. From there and from Aloe Knoll, the ridge's true (and higher) summit, the Boers poured down withering fire on Thorneycroft's command. A counterattack led by Major General John Talbot Coke only provided more targets for the Boers, and when General Neville Lyttelton's brigade managed to relieve the pressure by capturing Twin Peaks, Buller ordered them to retreat, adding to the chaos.

The Boers too had begun to disperse, moving off Spion Kop as they became aware of Lyttelton's advance. But they were rallied by their commander Louis Botha, and it was instead the exhausted British, led by Thorneycroft, who pulled back from the ridge, leaving the Boers in total control.

The battle had been a fiasco for the British, characterised by inferior intelligence, muddled tactics and poor communications between commanders. It cost the British forces 1,100 dead, almost four times their opponent's losses, though it did not deter Buller from yet another attack to relieve Ladysmith in early February, which failed after days of desultory skirmishing. Eventually, though, Roberts's new tactics and weight of numbers prevailed, as the independent-minded Boer militias found it difficult to co-ordinate or follow up victories. By September 1900 all three besieged cities had been relieved and the main stage of the war was over. Yet fighting dragged on for another year in the form of guerrilla actions which were only ended when the British erected blockhouses and fences to cut off the Boers' supply and communication, and rounded up 120,000 Boer women and children and put them into camps. By the time the Peace Treaty of Vereeniging was signed in May 1902, formally ending the conflict, it had cost Britain 22,000 dead and £200 million in yet another example of European powers' chronic propensity to underestimate the ability of irregular forces to oppose them.

Siege of the Legations

The map shows a small quarter of Beijing's Imperial City, where the legations of the foreign powers which had established a presence there since the Opium Wars (see pages 100–01) clustered. The lines of defence, barricades and ditches marked in on Major EWM Norie's map seem unlikely features of a diplomatic district, but they were all part of the desperate defence of the Legations in 1900 detailed in his official account of the campaigns of the British Contingent of the China Field Force during the Boxer Rebellion.

The very presence of foreigners and the legal privileges, not least in trade, which they enjoyed raised great resentment in China, particularly in the countryside. In 1899, one secret group, the Society of the Righteous and Harmonious Fists, colloquially known as the Boxers, began to attack foreign missionaries and Chinese Christians. The redoubtable Dowager Empress Cixi, the real power behind the Qing throne, decided to harness the Boxers to try to curb the power of the foreigners, but the increasing violence caused the British minister to the Chinese court, Sir Claude MacDonald, to issue an ultimatum to Cixi: rein in the Boxers or risk the wrath of the British Navy.

By now, though, the situation was spiralling out of control. In early 1900, Boxers flooded into Beijing (then Romanised as Peking) to escape a drought in the surrounding region and began attacking churches and missions. The alarmed foreign diplomats, MacDonald included, issued a plea for aid, and the first hastily assembled reinforcements, comprising over 409 troops from eight nations, arrived on May 31. A larger force of 2,000 men under Admiral Edward Seymour was stalled by the Boxers' cutting of the train line to Tientsin.

In Beijing, the situation was deteriorating. Marauding Boxers murdered a Japanese diplomat, and when the German ambassador Baron von Ketteler went for a meeting with Chinese officials to negotiate safe passage out of Beijing for the foreign diplomatic community, he too was killed. War between the foreign powers and China now seemed inevitable, and, in anticipation of an attack, the foreign legations summoned their citizens to take refuge in the embassy district, much of which was sheltered by the high "Tartar Wall". The outlying Austrian and Italian Legations were soon evacuated when a skirmish with the Boxers made it clear they were indefensible, but the "Fu", the palace of Prince Su, just northeast of the legation district was taken over to house Chinese Christian refugees. Most of the non-combatants took refuge in the British Mission which was furthest away from the Tartar Wall (whose ramparts offered ample firing positions if the Boxers took them).

The garrison had just four pieces of light artillery and little ammunition: the Japanese had only 2,500 rounds between their 25 soldiers. The Legations did though have a good water supply and a large quantity of grain. On June 22 the storm broke when the first Boxer attack almost overran the district, as panicked foreign troops pulled back to the British Legation. But the Boxers failed to exploit the opening, and even though outlying buildings were burnt the next day, the defenders weathered the crisis.

Barricades of sandbags were built and sorties mounted to harass the Chinese attackers, but the hold of the defenders on the Tartar Wall was tenuous, and by July 13 three quarters of the Fu had been lost. They were also hampered by communications problems and arguments over which of the foreign diplomats had seniority of command, while, as the Legation perimeter shrank and supplies dwindled, conditions grew intolerable. Worryingly, there were 40 cases of dysentery.

Unbeknown to the defenders, though, help was on its way. An International Relief force of 20,000 men was making its slow way up the Pei Ho river from Tientsin, and, in expectation of its arrival, the Qing authorities declared a truce in the hope of dissuading it from retaliation. The pause was just in the nick of time, as on July 13 the French Embassy had been destroyed by a mine and the Legations' defence seemed doomed. Yet the very next day, the Chinese sent supplies into the Legations, including to the Beijing North Cathedral, where a small contingent of French and a large number of Christian refugees had held out against all the odds.

The Relief force finally arrived on August 13. Despite Cixi's hopes of avoiding an attack, it broke into Beijing, with the Russians in the vanguard, and 24 hours later a contingent of British Indian Army sepoys entered the British Legation. Amid the chaos that ensued, the Qing court, including Cixi, fled. Sixty-eight foreigners, and thousands of Chinese, most of them Boxers, had been killed, and the authority of the Qing was fatally damaged. It had been a very costly diplomatic gesture.

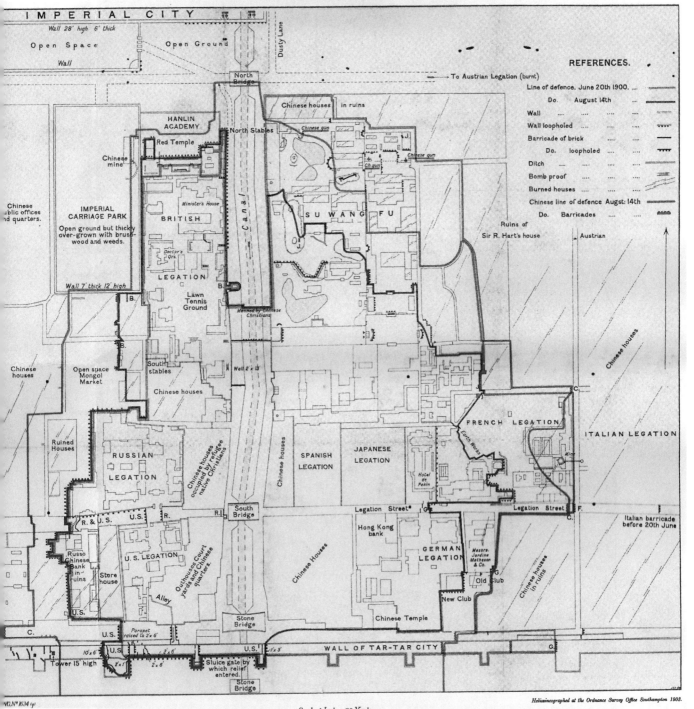

DEFENCE OF ·LEGATIONS

PEKING,

June 20th to August 14th 1900.

IMPERIAL CITY

Wall 28' high 6' thick

Open Space

Open Ground

Wall

Dusty Lane

North Bridge

→ To Austrian Legation (burnt)

REFERENCES.

Line of defence, June 20th 1900. ....

Do.   August 14th   ....

Wall   ....

Wall loopholed   ....

Barricade of brick   ....

Do.   loopholed   ....

Ditch   ....

Bomb proof   ....

Burned houses   ....

Chinese line of defence Augst: 14th

Do.   Barricades   ....

HANLIN ACADEMY

Red Temple

North Stables

Chinese houses   in ruins

Chinese gun

Chinese mine

Chinese gun

Ch gun

Chinese gun

J

SU WANG FU

Ruins of Sir R. Hart's house

Austrian

Chinese public offices and quarters.

IMPERIAL CARRIAGE PARK

Open ground but thickly over-grown with brush-wood and weeds.

Minister's House

BRITISH

Doctor's Qrs.

LEGATION

Canal

J

Wall 7' thick 12' high

B.

Lawn Tennis Ground

B.

Manned by Chinese Christians

B.

Chinese houses

Chinese houses

South stables

Wall 2' x 13'

Chinese houses

FRENCH LEGATION

Earth Works

ITALIAN LEGATION

Chinese houses

Chinese houses

Open space Mongol Market

Ruined Houses

RUSSIAN LEGATION

Chinese houses occupied by refugee native Christians

Chinese houses

SPANISH LEGATION

JAPANESE LEGATION

Hotel de Pekin

Mine

Italian barricade before 20th June

R. & U.S.

U.S.

R.

R.

South Bridge

Legation Street

G

Legation Street

F

C.

Russo Chinese Bank in ruins

Store house

U.S. LEGATION

Outhouses Court yards and Chinese quarters.

Hong Kong bank

Chinese Houses

GERMAN LEGATION

Messrs. Jardine Matheson & Co.

G

Old Club

Chinese houses in ruins

U.S.

Alley

New Club

Chinese Temple

Stone Bridge

C.

U.S.

Parapet raised to 2 x 6'

Stone Bridge

WALL OF TAR-TAR CITY

G.

10' x 6'

U.S.

2' x 6'

U.S.

1' x 3'

Tower 15' high

2' x 1'

2' x 6'

Sluice gate by which relief entered.

Stone Bridge

MLN° 1534 (1)

Heliozincographed at the Ordnance Survey Office Southampton 1903.

Scale 1 Inch = 80 Yards

GLOBAL WAR

1900–1950

Ubin linsa
Hau siën tun
tschun
Sy dia sa 3
Ku tsy yan 100
Kun dia tun 40
San si cau tun
Bhf. Wu sy tai
Siao dsia ho
50
Hu schi tai
Pan dia tai 2
Huan men kou
Sië siu tun
San tai tsy
Schou kou tsu
Pin lua pu 200
Ta wi tun
Siao go sa
Liu kwan tun
Hao san dia sa 15
Tiong schang-tschang
Sian wa
Si ta tschö
Sio tschön tsy
Lian san dia sa 30
Un guan tun
Wu ni tun
ön sin tai sa
Kau si tun
H.
Wan di
a tsy
Wu tai tsy
Tian dsia tun
Ta wa 30
Tsau ho tun
Sy tai tsy
Syl
iao san dia sa 6
Kau li tun
Wan tschön tun
Liu dia kou
Ta schi tschao
Pa dia sa
Yu lin pu 5
Liu diao tun
Tschuan wan tiao 30
San tai tsy 20
Liu dia kiu
San a sy sa
Si ta hun tun
Schak dia sa
Siao han tun 100
Tun örr tai sa
Ta fan sy tun
Grab des Kaisers
Tai tsung
Örr tai tsy 40
Tin dia tun
au dia sa
Siu tschai tsa
Pei ling
Siao fan syn tun
Turm
Ta kwan tun
Mou dia tun
Tin sin tun
Yin sun tai
Fu the 100
Yu huan
Kou nan tai
Yau dia tun
Kulian tun
Tai yin tsuan 10
Lao gu
Ma yi ta
Ma kua tscheu
Niu sian tun
Ma kiu ansa 20
Ta wan
Hou kin dia wasa
Kan dia wasa 10
Schi tiao sa
Pa dia sa
Yu schu
Huan gua tun 50
Bhf.
Pa li pa 10
Esche guan tun
Sy dou yu
Wo fu
Ma tschan
Wan
Li gun pu
Yu ho ün tun
Sau da tsy
Mukden
dia sa
Lin gan tun
Sy wan tun
Fan dia
Liu gun tun
Lgl.
Hca guan tun
syn tun
Tscha tsia yin tsy
Ti dia gia sa
San dia tsy
Yan sy tun 200
Ya fen tun
Sin wan fut
Lun hun tun
Ft.
Liu pu miao
gya tun 120
Ta pu 40
Tschan da ya wasa 40
Wo tau dian tsu
U li ho tsy
Sin tle la
Pu sin tun
Li kwan pu
Furt
Sua fu tu
Kun dia tun 15
Tia ho
Huan myn kan
schu pu
Sa to sa 100
Lan wa 10
Han ho pu 100
Lo go tun
Su
schu
Kaserne
Yan schu dian sa 60
Ti dia wan
Tö yan tun
Gu tsun tsy
Yin tsia tsy
Ma dia pu 100
Tso tsuan tun 100
Sia che tun
San dia fan
Yin tan 20
brücke
Hia gun tun 50
Wan sy tun 50
Tschan sa mu tun 30
Kin bo tai 30
Schan tun 30
Tschen gou su
San lin tsy
Kau lou tsy 125
Bai ta pu 150

Battle of Mukden

The Russian lines in green are in a state of collapse, while the red Japanese front lines move inexorably forward in this map of the Battle of Mukden, a momentous conflict which saw the first major defeat of a European army (in this case the Russian) by a non-European force (the Japanese) equipped with modern weaponry. Taken from an account of the battle by Karl von Donat, a military historian from Germany, where interest in the reshaping of the battlefield by the machine gun and the trench was acute, it shows the final stages, on March 10, 1905, of what was, up until that date, the largest ever battle fought on land, involving more than half a million men.

The battle took place in Manchuria, where Japanese and Russian ambition collided with Chinese weakness. Japan's success in industrialising following the Meiji Restoration in 1868 allowed it to build a well-trained and well-equipped army and navy which showed their mettle in a successful war with China in 1894–95, following which the Japanese occupied Taiwan and the Liaodong Peninsula to the south of Manchuria. Russia's intervention in favour of the restoration of Liaodong to the Chinese (for the price of permitting Russia to build a section of the Trans-Siberian Railway across Manchuria) left the Japanese nursing a grievance and concerned that Russia might pre-empt it in Liaodong.

These fears seemed confirmed in 1898 when the Chinese government signed over the strategic Manchurian city of Port Arthur (now Lüshun) to the Tsarist government under a 25-year lease. Japan steadily built up its armed forces and on February 8, 1904, sent a torpedo squadron to strike at the Russian fleet stationed at Port Arthur. The attack, though, was far less successful than its counterpart against Pearl Harbor 37 years later, and only three Russian ships were damaged. The Japanese now landed troops on the mainland near Chemulpo, breaking through Russian defences on the Yalu river and beginning a prolonged siege of Port Arthur. The Russians held on grimly as reinforcements came painfully slowly up the single-track line of the Trans-Siberian Railway and the Russian Baltic Fleet made its tortuous way around Africa (as the British had denied access to the far shorter route via the Suez Canal) and across the Indian Ocean to the East China Sea.

Russian relief forces were pushed away from Port Arthur, which finally fell to the Japanese in January 1905 (though the assault on a single position, 203 Metre Hill, had cost them 11,000 casualties). The Russian commander, Alexei Kuropatkin, who was stationed near Mukden (now Shenyang), found himself about to be outnumbered by the impending arrival of the Japanese 3rd Army now released from the Siege of Port Arthur. With around 310,000 men by mid-February, he planned to outflank the Japanese commander Field Marshal Oyama Iwao to the west and then roll up the Japanese line from the rear. Instead of the swift victory the Russian commander envisaged, the battle devolved into a three-week-long slog along a 95-mile front, as the Japanese outpaced Kuropatkin, and their 5th Army punched first on the Russian left and the 4th Army to its right. By the time Oyama sent the 3rd Army northwest of Mukden, he had already lured Kuropatkin into sending his reserves to the east.

Kuropatkin realised his error too late. When he shifted his forces west, the movement was uncoordinated, the Russian units became disordered and when the Japanese succeeded in crossing the frozen Hun river on the left flank in the face of a vigorous artillery barrage, the Russian line collapsed. Almost totally encircled, by March 9 Kuropatkin had little choice but to order a general withdrawal north. Although the bulk of the Russian army escaped, it had suffered 90,000 casualties (including 20,000 captured by the Japanese). The humiliation was wholesale: the Russians had been outfought, outmanoeuvered and outgunned by the Japanese, and after their long-awaited Baltic Fleet suffered an equally crushing defeat at Tsushima in May 1905, they were forced to the negotiating table. The Treaty of Portsmouth that ended the war in September 1905 confirmed Japan's dominant position in Korea and its occupation of much of Manchuria, including Port Arthur, and the southern part of Sakhalin island. The war itself signalled to students of strategy that a new age of mass warfare (and casualties) had arrived and that it would be one in which the western monopoly of modern military power would not go unchallenged.

Explanation:

- □□□□ Positions in the Morning.
- ➡ Advance of the Japanese.
- ▪▬▬▬ Positions in the Evening.

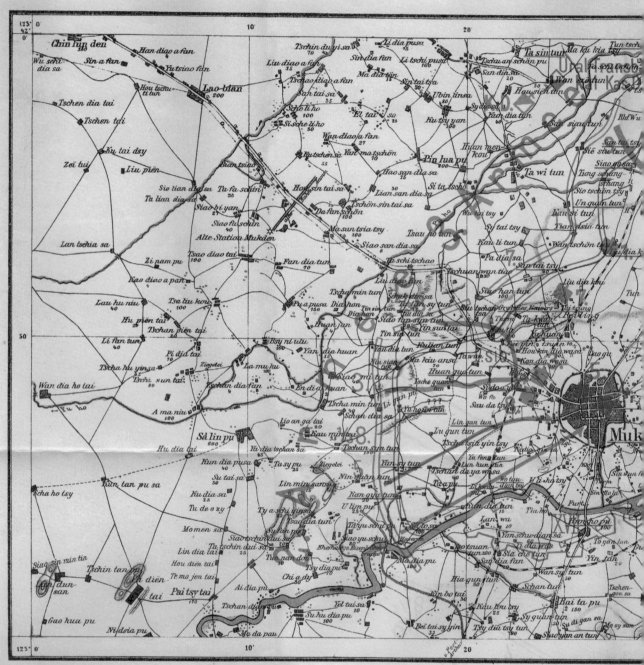

Map Deprtmt. of the Ryl. Prussian Ordnance Survey.

Photolithography from material of the Russian Gen. Staff of 19⁰⁴/₆₂.
Country supplemented from sketches and older russian sources.

Meter 1000
Sashen 500

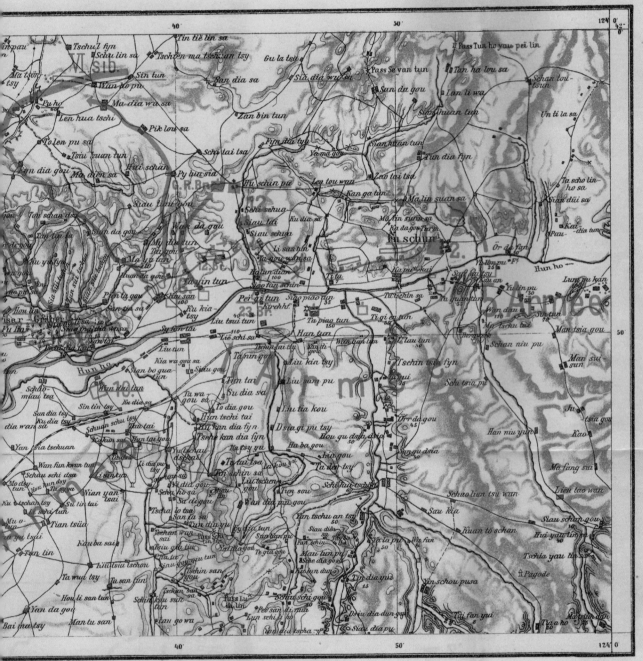

Sept. 1905.

The names are given phonetically from the Russian.

The numbers in connection with the names of the places indicate the number of families in the localities.

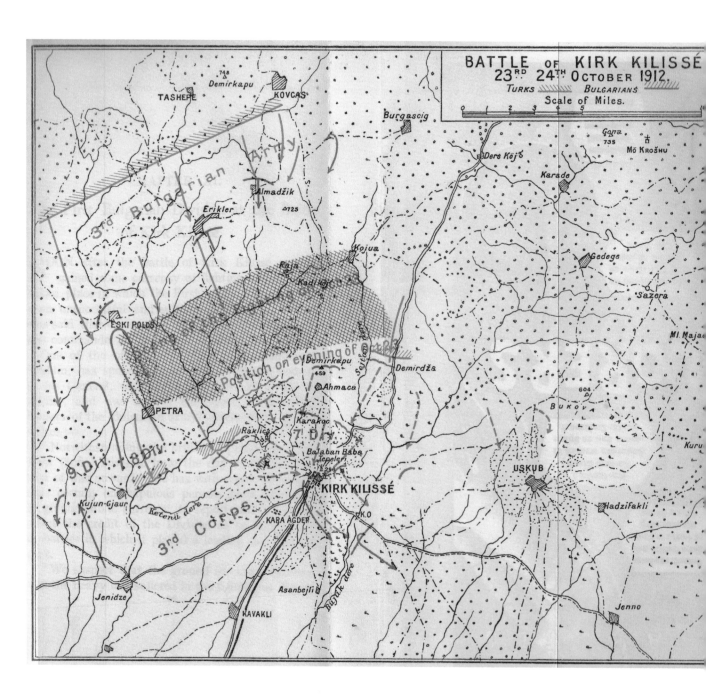

BATTLE OF KIRK KILISSÉ
23RD 24TH OCTOBER 1912.

TURKS ▨▨▨▨ BULGARIANS ▨▨▨▨
Scale of Miles.
0 1 2 3 4 5

Battle of Kirk Kilissé

The map shows the opening stages of the conflict which would itself act as the prelude to the First World War just two years later. The battle at Kirk Kilissé (now Kırklareli) in Ottoman Turkish-controlled Thrace formed the opening salvo of the First Balkan War and was witnessed by Lieutenant Hermenegild Wagner, war correspondent of the Vienna *Reichspost* newspaper, who accompanied the Bulgarian army and included this map in *With the Victorious Bulgarians*, his account of the conflict.

The Austrians remained neutral in the war, although their annexation of Bosnia in 1908 had weakened the Ottoman grip on the Balkans (and the Italian seizure of the Dodecanese islands in 1911 loosened it still further). After that, the other Balkan powers – Serbia, Bulgaria, Greece and Montenegro – looked greedily on Ottoman territory they regarded as rightfully theirs, especially the Bulgarians, who had long smarted at the settlement of the 1878 Treaty of San Stefano which established their state but left it with no access to the Aegean Sea.

The Bulgarians and Serbs began negotiating a military pact aimed at dismembering Macedonia and Thrace, which led to the formation of the Balkan League in March 1912. The joining of the alliance by Greece and Montenegro during that summer added to the forces opposing the Ottomans, though the two new members' own ambitions for expansion complicated the diplomatic politics of the alliance, with ultimately disastrous results.

Both Serbia and Bulgaria mobilised rapidly, the Bulgarian army reaching 350,000 men, while that of Serbia approached 230,000. The allies faced 115,000 Ottoman troops in Thrace and 175,000 in Macedonia, but although the Ottomans could ultimately rely on their far larger population and military forces stationed in Turkey, Syria and North Africa, their army was ill-equipped and trained. In contrast, the Bulgarian infantry divisions each had machine-gun sections with 8mm Maxim guns and field artillery regiments armed with modern 75mm Schneider-Creusot guns, while the Serbian army was similarly equipped and the Greek navy was far superior to anything the Ottomans could deploy.

After a peremptory ultimatum to the Ottomans to cede territory was refused, Bulgarian forces crossed the frontier on October 17, aiming to hold Ottoman forces in place around Adrianople while the 3rd Army flanked the Turks and forced a decisive battle around Lyule Burgas. The Bulgarian plan soon fell apart in the face of a far more rapid Ottoman mobilisation than expected and the attempt by the Bulgarian government – against the wishes of Tsar Ferdinand and the Bulgarian High Command – to open peace negotiations with the Turks resulted in damaging delays in the critical early hours of the attack.

The Bulgarians found themselves moving forward just as the Ottomans did, their opposing advances colliding in a three-day battle between October 22 and 24 along a 40-mile front between Kirk Kilissé and Adrianople, where the Ottoman left flank was anchored. The Ottoman cavalry dashed forward, driving a gap in the Bulgarian line, but then ran straight into the enemy's 1st Army, while, as General Ivan Fichev's 2nd Army prevented the Turkish garrison in Adrianople from advancing to help, the Bulgarian 3rd Army launched an attack on Kirk Kilissé.

The town's fortifications were old and weak and the Bulgarian artillery bombardment relentless, and so after two days of increasingly desperate resistance the Ottoman troops fled, precipitating a general retreat from the Kirk Kilissé–Adrianople line. Mired in mud caused by heavy rain and lacking their baggage (which the Bulgarians had captured), the Turks were sitting ducks, but Fichev's hesitation in pursuing allowed most of the Ottoman army to escape. Their losses were not enormous, but they had seen the effect of modern machine guns and artillery, and their morale was shattered. Another Bulgarian victory at Lyule Burgas followed in late November, and Adrianople finally fell to its Bulgarian-Serb besiegers in March 1913, which left the Ottomans little choice but to sign a peace treaty that gave great swathes of Macedonia, Epirus and Thrace to the Balkan League allies.

The Ottomans might, though, have allowed themselves a warworn smile as the erstwhile allies squabbled over Macedonia, and the granting of independence to Albania threatened Serb and Greek gains in Epirus. By June 1913 the former members of the Balkan League were violently at odds, with Greece and Serbia declaring war on Bulgaria (and Romania joining in). This Second Balkan War ended with Bulgaria losing most of its gains and, wounded, falling into the diplomatic orbit of Austria-Hungary, as it sought new friends to bring down the Serbs. It was thus not only in the realm of military hardware that the Balkan War prefigured the First World War, but in the establishment of an unstable conflict of diplomatic interests that threatened to spiral into conflict at the slightest spark.

First Battle of the Marne

The map, with its deep blue marking German units and fainter grey for the French, shows the positions of the two sides during the Battle of Ourcq in early September 1914, part of the wider First Battle of the Marne, during which French troops fought off a German thrust against Paris that threatened to bring an early end to the First World War. Engraved by the East Prussian lithographer Bogdan Gisevius, it appeared in *Die Schlacht vor Paris: Das Marnedrama 1914* ("The Battle for Paris: The Marne Drama, 1914"), part of a 26-volume history of the war, which was published by Reinhold Dahlmann in 1926, then a lowly captain, but who, after service in the Berlin police and re-enlistment in the army, rose to be a general and chief supply officer to the German forces in the Netherlands, before being abducted by Red Army troops in April 1945, never to be seen again.

At the outbreak of the conflict, the Germans had implemented a version of the prewar Schlieffen Plan, which involved circumventing French defences by invading Belgium and thrusting rapidly west in a great envelopment which would encircle Paris and force a rapid French surrender. Things soon went awry, as the French commander-in-chief, General Joseph Joffre, managed to preserve a large part of his army after a series of holding actions and then took up a position screening Paris from behind the River Marne. The German army had advanced more rapidly than expected, and instead of enveloping Paris from the west as their commander Helmuth von Moltke had ordered, the First and Second Armies under Generals Alexander von Kluck and Karl von Bülow swooped southeast to approach Paris from the east.

This extreme right flank of the German advance offered a chance for Joffre to counterattack and pinch it out, blunting the whole German assault against Paris. He deployed General Michel-Joseph Maunoury's newly raised Sixth Army northeast of Paris, planning to launch an assault on September 6 near Meaux (not far from the Ourcq, a tributary of the Marne). Von Kluck received intelligence of the enemy approach and angled his army to prevent any major French gains. While at first the Sixth Army was facing the German IV Reserve Corps, von Kluck's successful delaying action allowed him to move the more experienced II Corps north to the Marne to push west and threaten to outflank and surround Maunoury.

In the moment of crisis, General Joseph Gallieni, the military governor of Paris, rounded up reinforcements and dispatched them in a fleet of hundreds of taxis from the centre of Paris (the first recorded use of motor vehicles for large-scale troop movements). Stiffened by these new troops, Maunoury was able to hold out and the movement of further elements of the German First Army into the Ourcq front meant that a 30-mile gap had opened up between it and the Second Army. This was spotted by Allied reconnaissance planes (in another military first), and Joffre sent General Louis Franchet d'Espèrey's Fifth Army, together with elements of the British Expeditionary Force, into the Gap. Now it was the Germans who found themselves in danger of encirclement, and on September 9 von Bülow's Second Army began to retreat behind the Marne and von Kluck, finding himself dangerously exposed, ordered his First Army to do likewise.

Less than a week later, realising that the Schlieffen Plan had failed and that Germany now faced a much longer war than anticipated, von Moltke suffered a breakdown with his health, and he was replaced as German commander by Erich von Falkenhayn. He was not the only casualty of the battle. The French and Germans had suffered roughly a quarter of a million killed and wounded each, and though the "Miracle on the Marne" had saved Paris, and very likely France, from German conquest, it was followed by the "Race to the Sea" as the two sides tried to turn each other's flank, ending up facing each other in a 500-mile line of trenches that ran from the Swiss Alps to the English Channel. The Marne may have been a costly victory, but the stalemate that followed it would be infinitely more so.

Karte 2.

Ourcq=Front am 6.9.1914.

Die Stellungen der Truppen des Obersten v. Buttlar
um Varreddes am Morgen sind nicht eingezeichnet.
U. a. waren Züge des II./Res. 27 als Vorposten auf
Barcy u. Chambry vorgeschoben.

━━━━ Deutsche Stellungen u. Beweg. am Morgen beim IV.Res.K.

0   1   2   3   4   5 km

German War Aims Map

The lurid splashes of red on the 1915 map of "What Germany Wants" create a vivid impression that German war aims focused on global domination. Spiced by selective quotes from German nationalist political analysts, it was published by the London-based Stanfords map company (and translated into a number of other languages including Dutch, Swedish and Portuguese) and was part of a vast effort on the part of the British authorities to boost support for the Allies worldwide and to undermine those who championed Germany's cause.

The compilers of the map let no opportunity slip to paint German objectives in the worst possible and most inflammatory light. Pan-Germanism, it is said, "absorbs also the Scandinavians", Belgium "must be struck off the map", Argentina and Brazil are described as "decrepit states", while British possessions in Africa and Southeast Asia and much of Ottoman Turkey's empires also, allegedly, fall within the ambit of German ambition. Much of this was a distortion of a much narrower plan sketched out for the German chancellor Theobald von Bethmann-Hollweg in September 1914, just as German armies were crossing into Belgium. Although it did call for the reduction of Belgium to a vassal state and the annexation of part of France, the main scope of this *Septemberprogramm* was the crippling of France economically by forcing it to pay a vast war indemnity and the creation of a Central European Customs League under German domination.

This, though, was enough for the propagandists of Wellington House, the unit established by the British at the outset of the war to counter Germany's own information effort. Headed by the Liberal politician Charles Masterman, it spent the next three years – until its replacement in 1917 by a section of the Department of Information (part of which would become MI5) – pumping out posters, postcards (100,000 were sent to Russia at Easter 1916) and even cigarette cards, and feeding stories to friendly press outlets, none of which was supposed to be identifiable as official propaganda. By February 1916, over seven million books and pamphlets had been produced, using the network of British-owned shipping companies such as Cunard and P&O to aid their distribution. Illustrated newspapers were produced in local languages, such as the Portuguese *O Espelho*, 15,000 copies of which were dispatched to Brazil each fortnight and *Satya Vani*, aimed at the Indian market, which was issued in Bengali, Hindi, Gujarati and Tamil editions.

Particular attention was paid to the North American market, as the British government mounted assiduous attempts on the political level to woo the American government into joining the war on the Allied side. Early in the conflict the German underwater telegraph cables across the Atlantic had been cut, which stifled the Berlin government's efforts to disseminate its point of view, while a new, even glossier publication, *War Pictorial*, first issued in 1916, was adorned with images taken by the new official photographer appointed by the War Office and widely circulated in North America.

Such subtle efforts were supplemented by official reports including the 1915 *Report of the Committee on Alleged German Outrages*, known as the Bryce Report after the committee's chairman Viscount James Bryce, which uncritically assembled the testimonies of Belgian and French refugees and shaped them into a damning portrait of a pitiless German invader whose troops hacked off the hands of helpless children, violating all international norms for the conduct of war. Germany responded with a "White Book" accusing the Belgians themselves of war atrocities, which prompted the Belgians in turn to issue a counter-refutation in the form of a "Grey Book".

No piece of propaganda, however, was more effective than the Zimmermann Telegram, a message sent in January 1917 from the German Foreign Ministry to Heinrich von Eckardt, its ambassador to Mexico, proposing that he should offer an alliance (and copious funds) to the Mexicans if the United States entered the war on Britain's side. The telegram was intercepted by British intelligence, decrypted and then leaked to the Americans. Claims that it was a forgery were rather torpedoed by its sender, Arthur Zimmermann, admitting during a speech to the German Reichstag that it was genuine. By then German submarines had begun attacking neutral shipping (including American) in the Atlantic and, with anti-German feeling in the United States already stoked by the Zimmermann Telegram, on April 6 Congress voted to declare war on Germany.

Sometimes, the unvarnished truth was the best propaganda. At others, the selective highlighting of opponents' own words to use against them (as on the map), the repetition of half-truths wrapped in a glossy package or the suborning of sympathetic journalists or politicians with funding or outright bribes proved effective. In all these fields the 1914–18 conflict proved a testing ground for the far grander propaganda efforts of the Second World War.

NY WANTS.
ERS OF GERMAN THOUGHT.

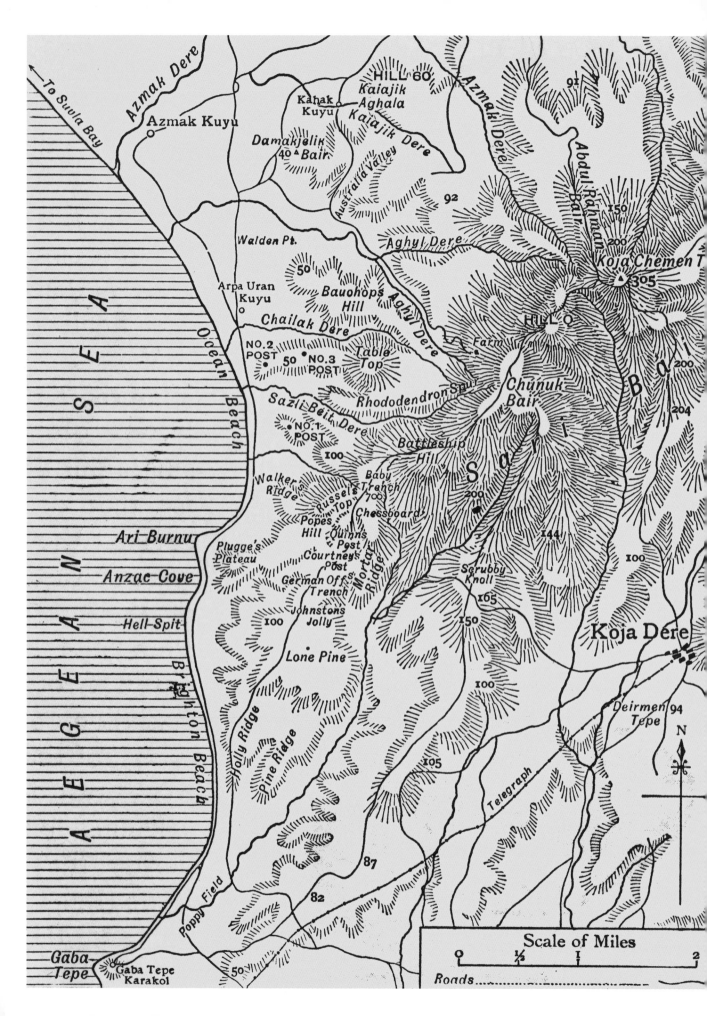

Gallipoli Campaign

The Gallipoli Peninsula juts out like a sentinel, guarding the entrance from the Aegean to the Black Sea. The capture of this narrow stretch of ground was supposed to deliver a rapid knockout blow to an empire or at least to push Ottoman Turkey out of the First World War. Instead, the Allied campaign in Gallipoli became bogged down in a pointless war of attrition, just as it had on the Western Front, costing over 200,000 casualties and achieving little but tarnishing the reputation of the then First Lord of the Admiralty, Winston Churchill.

When Turkey attacked Russian positions along the Black Sea on October 29, 1914, effectively joining the war on Germany's side, the threat to a key eastern ally and the prospect that the Ottomans might block off access through the Dardanelles strait to the Black Sea convinced Churchill that swift action was needed. He ordered a Franco-British flotilla to force its way through and to insert an expeditionary force close to Constantinople, the Ottoman capital – actions he hoped would then provoke a quick Turkish capitulation.

An extensive naval bombardment was hampered by bad weather, and it failed to neutralise Turkish batteries onshore. More damaging, though, were the mines with which the Turks had seeded the Dardanelles, which sank three Allied battleships and damaged several others when they tried to force the strait on March 18. The operation had to be abandoned and was instead replaced by an amphibious landing on the west side of the Gallipoli Peninsula. From there, troops, including a large contingent from the Australian and New Zealand Army Corps (ANZACs), were supposed to battle their way up towards Constantinople.

On April 25 waves of Allied landing craft approached Gaba Tepe, the headland shown in the bottom left of this map from Frank A Mumby's *The Great World War – A History*. Adverse currents drove them too far north, so that they landed at what would become known as Anzac Cove, where a steep rise prevented easy exit from the beaches. Early objectives were not met, and even once the cliffs had been surmounted, the troops were confused by the maze of ravines and gullies inland and thwarted by Ottoman resistance that had begun to stiffen (in part because of the actions of a junior Ottoman officer, Mustafa Kemal – later, as Atatürk, to become Turkey's first president). Amid appalling losses, the Anzacs were penned into the beaches. Landings further south at Cape Helles were more successful, but the next six months saw fruitless attempts to break out of the bridgeheads and to seize and hold positions such as Lone Pine and Chunuk Bair that should have been taken on the first day, with the result of ever mounting casualties for precious little gain.

In one last roll of the dice, the British commander, General Sir Ian Hamilton, ordered a new landing on August 6 at Suvla Bay, just to the north of Anzac Cove, together with an offensive from the original landing beach towards the Sari Bair heights. Indecision, muddle and the difficult terrain once again allowed the Ottomans to reinforce their positions and throw back the attacks. With casualties now surging again, the Allies were faced with the choice of doubling down, throwing in even more troops, or withdrawing altogether. Hamilton argued that 100,000 more soldiers could finish the task, but his political master Lord Kitchener replaced him and ordered a pull-out.

The evacuations, which began at Suvla Bay in mid-December, were about the only part of the whole Gallipoli Campaign that went flawlessly. Casualties were very light, and by the night of January 8, 1916, only 19,000 troops (of the original 140,000 at the start of the evacuations) were left at Cape Helles. Traffic on the military roads was kept going and fires burning to fool the Turks that nothing untoward was occurring. Rifles were rigged up in trenches to fire automatically even after the soldiers had abandoned their positions.

The whole fruitless operation had cost over 187,000 Allied casualties (though the Turks too suffered 160,000 losses). It seared itself into the Allied military consciousness, and particularly that of the Australian and New Zealand troops, playing a key role in forging a distinctive national identity in those two countries. Churchill's political career went into temporary eclipse (though a later evacuation at Dunkirk in 1940 would revive it). Above all, though, Gallipoli proved the dangers of underestimating the tactical abilities of non-European armed forces and the folly of assuming that difficult terrain could be traversed easily by large numbers of troops against stubborn resistance and while relying on tenuous lines of supply.

Battle of Jutland

The plan shows the height of the action between the German and British fleets off the coast of the Danish peninsula of Jutland on the night of May 31, 1916. It is drawn from the *Official History of the Great War*, an enterprise undertaken by the Committee of Imperial Defence, whose Naval Operations volumes were edited by Julian S Corbett, an eminent naval historian and strategist. His championing of the theory of limited warfare at sea, by concentrating on the control of supply lines and conserving precious resources (such as warships), would win him many admirers.

In the first phase of the war, Germany and Britain had conserved their naval fleets, reluctant to risk their dreadnoughts, the latest generation of battleships, whose loss might fatally expose their coastlines to enemy attacks. The German High Seas Fleet remained bottled up in Kiel, while its British equivalent, the Grand Fleet, based at Scapa Flow in the Orkney Islands, was content to let it stay there.

In January 1916, the new German navy commander, Admiral Reinhard Scheer, resolved on a more aggressive posture. On April 25, he ordered a naval bombardment of the East Anglian ports of Lowestoft and Great Yarmouth, which lured a section of the British Grand Fleet southwards to Rosyth, where it joined up with the battle cruiser squadrons of Vice Admiral Sir David Beatty. Scheer hoped to destroy this force before the rest of the Grand Fleet could join it. As a further ruse, he sent out a scouting group of cruisers under Vice Admiral Franz von Hipper, hoping to tempt the British into pursuing it, so that they would run into the main section of the German fleet following 50 miles behind Hipper.

The plan might have worked had not the British intercepted crucial German naval signals which gave the game away. So, when Scheer put to sea in the early morning of May 31, the whole Grand Fleet led by Admiral Sir John Jellicoe was waiting for him off the Jutland coast. Between them, the two fleets had 250 ships and over 100,000 officers and men, which made the clash that followed the largest in naval history.

The two sides met almost by accident the same afternoon, after the German light cruiser *Elbing* spotted a Danish civilian vessel and, when it approached to investigate, encountered a British light cruiser on a similar mission. By 3.20pm Hipper's cruiser squadron was exchanging fire with its British equivalent under Beatty, inflicting serious damage, including the sinking of the *Queen Mary*, which exploded when its main magazine was struck. Beatty withdrew, hoping to turn the tables by sucking the German fleet towards the main British force. Visibility was poor and Beatty's signals unclear, but still Jellicoe managed to deploy to "cross the T" of Scheer, with his vessels in a line able to open fire simultaneously on the advancing column of German ships.

Naval warfare in the dreadnought was merciless, but Scheer, despite his lead vessels, the *Lützow*, *König* and *Kaiser* being under fire, fought back. One 12-inch shell fired from the *Derfflinger* scythed through a gun turret on the *Invincible*, the British flagship, and then ignited the ammunition magazine far below. The massive explosion caused the ship to sink in just 15 seconds, and of the crew of 1,032, only six men survived.

The engagement had lasted barely 15 minutes, but now Scheer could see that the odds were stacked too heavily against him and ordered his ships to turn 180 degrees and retreat. Yet Jellicoe's deployment barred Scheer's way back to port, and so the German commander ordered another about-turn, hoping to bypass the edge of the British line. He was wrong and ran straight back into Jellicoe's massed guns. In a bid to escape, Scheer ordered his battle cruisers and torpedo boats to sail directly at the British, sacrificing them in order to slip away.

It worked: Scheer was able to open up distance between him and the Grand Fleet, and then cross past the British line under cover of darkness. By 3am he had reached safety behind the Horns Reef minefield, which the British, lacking a map, could not cross.

The British had lost three battle cruisers, three cruisers and eight destroyers against the one battleship, one battle cruiser and five light cruisers of the Germans, while they suffered 6,768 seamen killed and wounded, more than twice the number of Germans. Still, the British trumpeted Jutland as a success. In a sense they were right: the Germans had failed to break the British blockade and, save for the odd small-scale sortie, remained bottled up in port for the rest of the war. It was, in the end, an endorsement of Corbett's theory that total warfare was not necessary to win a war.

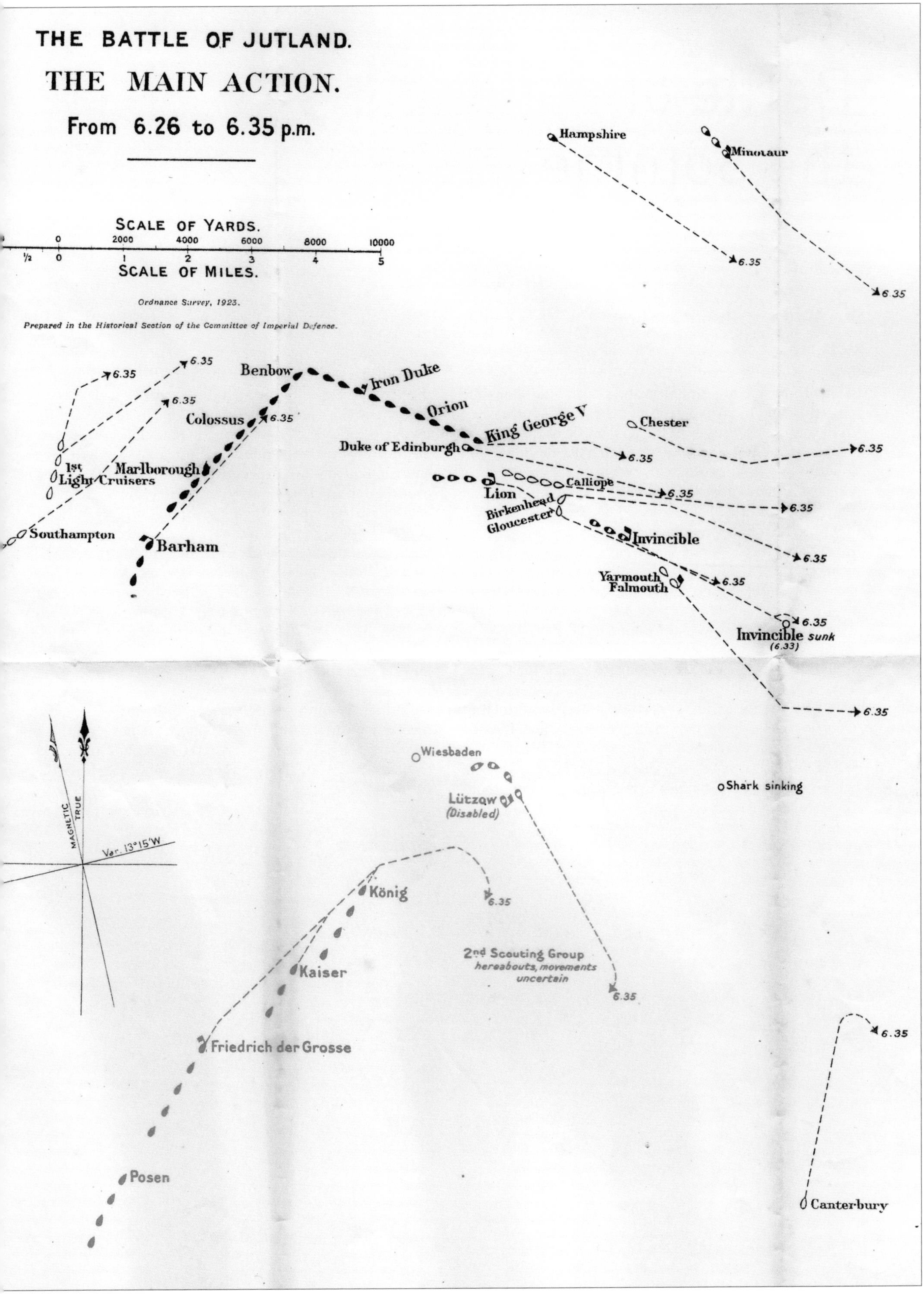

THE BATTLE OF JUTLAND.
THE MAIN ACTION.
From 6.26 to 6.35 p.m.

SCALE OF YARDS.

| 0 | 2000 | 4000 | 6000 | 8000 | 10000 |

SCALE OF MILES.

½ 0 1 2 3 4 5

Ordnance Survey, 1923.

Prepared in the Historical Section of the Committee of Imperial Defence.

Hampshire

Minotaur

→ 6.35

→ 6.35

→ 6.35

→ 6.35

Benbow

Iron Duke

→ 6.35

Orion

Colossus

→ 6.35

King George V

Chester

1st
Light Cruisers

Marlborough

Duke of Edinburgh

→ 6.35

→ 6.35

Lion

Calliope

→ 6.35

Southampton

Birkenhead

→ 6.35

Gloucester

Barham

Invincible

→ 6.35

Yarmouth
Falmouth

→ 6.35

Invincible *sunk*
(6.33)

→ 6.35

→ 6.35

Wiesbaden

Shark sinking

Lützow
(Disabled)

MAGNETIC

TRUE

Var. 13°15′W

König

→ 6.35

2nd Scouting Group
*hereabouts, movements
uncertain*

→ 6.35

Kaiser

→ 6.35

Friedrich der Grosse

Posen

Canterbury

Battle of the Somme

The map of the sector of the Western Front around the northern French towns of Flers and Courcelette shows the objectives and the actual gains of the British Fourth Army in one of the later stages of the First Battle of the Somme, a protracted set of offensives whose first day on July 1, 1916 saw the British army suffer its worst ever casualties in a single day. Drawn by British military cartographers for the volume of the *Official History of the Great War* covering fighting in 1916 in Belgium and France, it was published in 1938 as part of a series that eventually stretched to 109 volumes and was only complete with the publication of the final one (on the Occupation of Constantinople) in 2010.

The Somme offensive was originally conceived by the Allies as part of a series of simultaneous offensives on the Eastern, Western and Italian Fronts to stretch the Central Powers' resources to breaking point. It was hoped this would resolve the grinding stalemate of the Western Front trench systems, where gains in offensives were hugely costly in lives but rarely resulted in any significant advance. But it also became a way of relieving pressure on the French, whose stubborn resistance at Verdun was bleeding both their and the German army dry.

General Sir Douglas Haig, the overall commander of the British Expeditionary Force, handed the task over to General Sir Henry Rawlinson's Fourth Army, a force mainly composed of raw recruits – the huge casualty rate on the Western Front meant troops rarely survived long enough to gain much experience. On July 1 they were sent over the top in slow-moving waves, preceded by a seven-day bombardment and then a creeping artillery barrage. Despite hurling 1.5 million shells at the opposing trenches, the bombardment had failed to reach the Germans, who were sheltering in deep emplacements, and the result was carnage, as the British, wading through the mire and uncut barbed-wire obstacles were mown down by machine-gun fire. By the end of the day, the Fourth Army had suffered 57,470 casualties, 19,240 of them killed, for gains which were, at best, slight.

Only in the south, near Fricourt and Montauban, did the French units assigned to support the largely British offensive almost make a breakthrough, but they had to pause to let the British catch up, which allowed the Germans to regroup.

The next few months saw slow, methodical and ultimately pointless gains, for ever-mounting casualties. Something more was needed to make advances large enough to be exploited. That something turned out to be the tank, an experimental tracked vehicle that could cross uneven ground, and, it was hoped, be impervious to enemy small-arms fire. By September 1916 some 150 of the first Mark I versions were dispatched to the Western Front under the command of Major Hugh Elles. At 28 tons, they were a formidable sight but were not as bullet-proof as hoped and suffered from slow off-road speeds of just 4 miles per hour, limited ability to steer and poor suspension, while the engine heated the insides to an unbearable 50C, and if hit by a shell, great slivers of hot metal flew around the crew compartment.

The tanks had their baptism of fire on September 15 at Flers-Courcelette. The briefing notes for operators described them as "Caterpillar" bullet-proof climbing vehicles but advised that their vulnerabilities were such that they should be used only in night advances, only then to point out that without infantry support they would be horribly vulnerable.

On the morning of the offensive 32 tanks made it to the start line, but 13 of them soon broke down, and after their initial shock at these lumbering metal leviathans, the Germans soon put a further ten out of action. The remaining nine Mark Is pushed on ahead of the infantry (against the official tactical advice) and managed to drive the Germans out of Flers. The advance that day, although less than the (rather optimistic) objectives, amounted to about a mile, which in Western Front terms was something of a triumph.

The coming of autumn mired both armies in a sea of mud, bringing the Battle of the Somme to an end by November, together with Haig's hopes of a decisive breakthrough. British losses in the battle had amounted to 420,000, while the French had suffered 194,000 casualties. The Germans, in turn, had taken more than 440,000 casualties, which left the toll for the battle as a whole at over a million. The tanks at Flers-Courcelette, though, had shown a glimpse of a future in which military mobility would be restored and the futile attritional warfare of the trenches abolished.

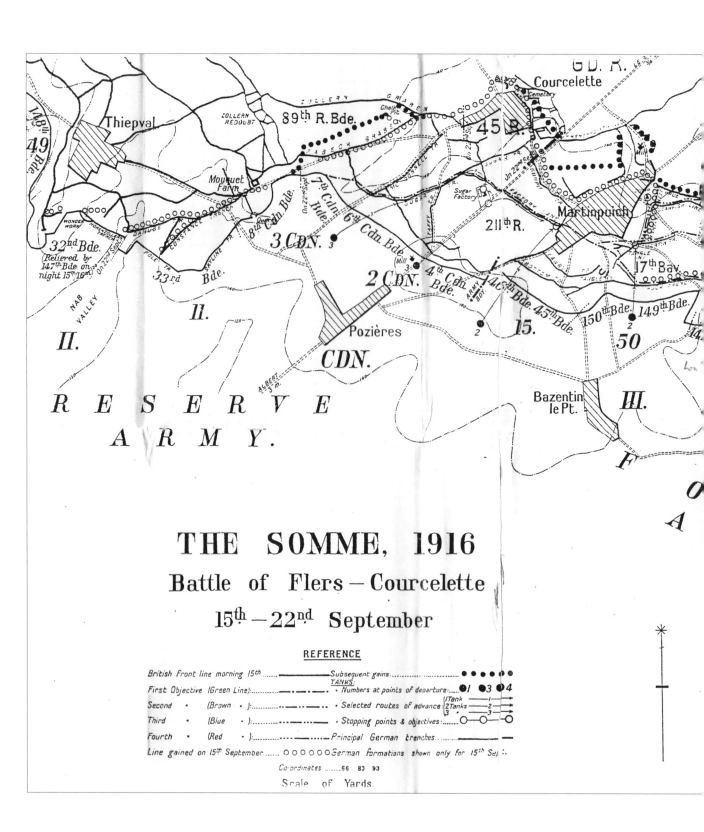

THE SOMME, 1916

Battle of Flers — Courcelette

15th — 22nd September

REFERENCE

British front line morning 15th	Subsequent gains .... ●●●●●
	TANKS:
First Objective (Green Line)	Numbers at points of departure: ●1 ●3 ●4
Second " (Brown ")	Selected routes of advance: 1 Tank —1→ 2 Tanks —2→ 3 —3→
Third " (Blue ")	Stopping points & objectives: ○ ○ ○
Fourth " (Red ")	Principal German trenches ....
Line gained on 15th September .... ○○○○○	German formations shown only for 15th Sep.

Co-ordinates 66 83 93

Scale of Yards

(map labels: Thiepval, Zollern Redoubt, 89th R. Bde., Chalk Pit, Courcelette, Cemetery, G.D.R., 45 R., 148th Bde., 49, Mouquet Farm, 7th Cdn. Bde., 6th Cdn. Bde., 8th Cdn. Bde., 211th R., Sugar Factory, Martinpuich, 32nd Bde. (Relieved by 147th Bde. on night 15th·16th), 33rd Bde., 3 CDN., 4th Cdn. Bde., Army Boy., 17th Bav., 150th Bde., 149th Bde., II., Nab Valley, 2 CDN., Pozières, 45th Bde., 15., 50, III., Bazentin le Pt., RESERVE ARMY, CDN., Albert 3 m., F, A)

Eaucourt l'Abbaye

II BAV.

SEVEN DIALS

Gueudecourt

FIRST

le Transloy

ARMY.

43rd

Flers

Mill

Lesbœufs

18th Bav.

5th Bav.

9th Bav.

2nd N.Z.

N.Z.

122nd Bde.

124 Bde.

14th Bav.

5 BAV.

XII R.

41

41st

Morval

DELVILLE

WOOD

14

PILDEN LANE

7th Bav.

XV.

43 Bde.

1st Gds Bde.

2nd Gds Bde.

21st Bav.

ongueval

Ginchy

THE QUADRILATERAL

GDS.

71st Bde.

185.

R

6.

16th Bde.

28th R.

M Y.

167th Bde.

65th

Frégicourt

XIV.

Guillemont

LEUZE WD.

COMBLES

56.

169th Bde.

54 R.

Falfemont Farm

Priez Farm

2

II

The Meuse–Argonne Offensive

The red lines on the map, which bunch ever more closely together, speak of an offensive which began with great hope but became bogged down in the broken terrain of the Meuse Valley and the dense Argonne Forest of France's northeast. It was drawn up six months after the end of the First World War by Brigadier General Charles Pelot Summerall, commander of the American Expeditionary Force's 1st Artillery Brigade.

The Argonne-Meuse Offensive, launched on September 26, 1918, was the major military operation involving US troops in the First World War, a conflict into which their nation had been inexorably drawn following the decision by Germany in January 1917 to begin unrestricted attacks on shipping (including American vessels) in the Atlantic. The first US troops arrived in Europe that June but did not enter the front lines for four months. Even then, they were confined to relatively small-scale actions until the following summer.

Most of the men of General John Pershing's First Army, therefore, were short on combat experience when they were committed to the Meuse-Argonne operation (though some were transferring, unrested, from an attack on St Mihiel just over a week beforehand). Over 400,000 troops took part in the original attack, which was loosely coordinated with the French and aimed to overrun and surround the German 2nd Army. A huge six-hour-long bombardment – which, it was later said, consumed more ammunition than expended in the entire American Civil War – shook the German lines, and then, at 5.30am on September 26, the infantry stepped out of their trenches to move forward behind 700 tanks, including a regiment of French Renault light tanks.

Although early progress was satisfactory, with advances of up to five miles, the 79th Division crucially failed to capture the strategic Montfaucon Hill, which would have allowed the Americans to pierce the Germans' *Giselher* defence line. Thereafter, the offensive stalled, with few gains the following day (although Montfaucon was finally taken), and German counterattacks on September 29 almost tore the American offensive apart. Three days later, one US unit, the "lost battalion" of the 77th Division, became marooned behind German lines, which led to frantic attempts to save them (which finally succeeded, aided by a heroic flight of the battalion's last carrier pigeon, Cher Ami, which, though badly wounded, delivered a crucial message).

Isolated successes could not conceal the fact that the offensive was floundering. Pershing placed General Hunter Liggett at the head of the First Army, and after a pause to regroup, the Americans resumed their attacks. Despite individual acts of heroism – Corporal Alvin Hunter of the 82nd Division singlehandedly killed 28 Germans and captured 132 more, winning himself a Medal of Honor – progress was grindingly slow. Unit discipline broke down as divisions had to be cannibalised and amalgamated, and tens of thousands of leaderless stragglers clogged up the rear areas.

Liggett tightened discipline and loosened standing orders which had meant units strictly kept to their allotted sections of the line, failing to seize opportunities to exploit advances. On November 1, the offensive renewed with a massive new barrage supported by bombing from the US Air Service. This time the German centre buckled, which allowed the 2nd Division to equal the US gains of the offensive's very first day, advancing five miles. The First Army now surged towards the Meuse, the Germans seemingly powerless to stop them. On November 5, the 5th Division crossed the river, threatening a general American advance on Sedan.

The much-delayed breakthrough fuelled calls in Germany to agree a truce to prevent Allied forces occupying large parts of its home territory. Yet the Americans were still advancing on the morning of the Armistice itself, November 11. Pershing bitterly opposed halting the offensive and believed that, given just ten more days, he could have crushed the German army entirely. In the end, 1.2 million American troops had been engaged, providing the Allies with resources of manpower that the German army, exhausted by four years of combat, could not possibly match. The offensive had cost Pershing 26,277 dead and almost 100,000 wounded, which made it the costliest operation in US military history. Yet, though its beginning had seen stuttering progress and there had been moments when it looked like collapsing, the American Expeditionary Force's gains at Meuse-Argonne had provided the key that unlocked a final end to the mud-soaked, bloodstained trauma of the First World War.

MEUSE-ARGONNE OFFENSIVE
MAP SHOWING DAILY POSITION OF FRONT LINE
Map Room G-3, G.H.Q.
May 24, 1919.

Scale - 1:80.000

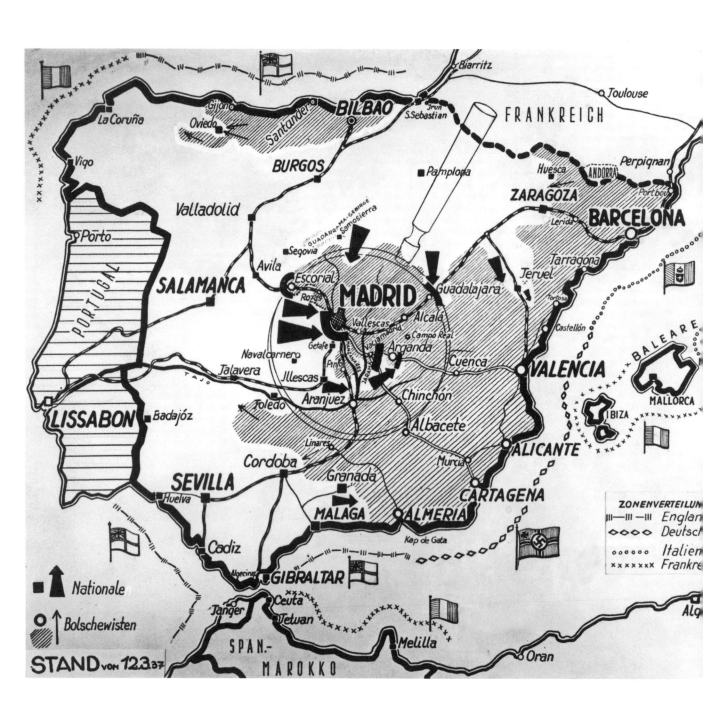

Spanish Civil War

Arrows converge on Madrid and a salient pushes forward from Teruel towards the coast, threatening to cut off the territory ruled by the Spanish Nationalist government in this map of the state of the combatants in the Spanish Civil War on March 12, 1937. It was, appropriately enough, published in the Munich-based *Süddeutsche Zeitung*, since Germany took a close interest in the conflict which became for Hitler's Nazi regime almost a proxy conflict with the Soviet Union and a testing ground for weapons and tactics that would be perfected a few years later during the Second World War.

Spanish political life had become increasingly polarised in the 1930s between conservative Roman Catholic Nationalists and the Republicans, who covered a spectrum of left-wing opinion ranging from middle-class radicals to anarchists, but who relied heavily on urban-based trade unions for support. The election of a left-leaning Popular Front government in February 1936 precipitated a military rebellion which began in Spanish Morocco but spread to the Balearic Islands, much of northern Spain and parts of Catalonia. The Popular Front government, while at first struggling to react, managed to hold onto central Spain, the Basque country, Barcelona and much of the south (apart from Seville, Granada and Cordoba).

The rebellion unleashed spasms of violence, including in the early stages against clerics and others associated with symbols of conservative authority, but enlarging to encompass Nationalist attacks on trade unionists and other activists. Gradually, the war took on a more formal nature, with the Nationalists led by General Francisco Franco marshalling their forces against the Republican government's under Francisco Largo Caballero and Juan Negrin. From the start the Nationalists were aided by the Republicans' internecine squabbling between anarchists and communists who sought to use the war as a means to promote revolutionary change and more moderate socialists and centrists.

Both sides sought foreign allies. Although the Popular Front government of France at first supported their Spanish counterparts, an agreement in August 1936 between France, Britain, the Soviet Union, Germany and Italy to remain neutral in the conflict was honoured only by the first two, which left the Republicans dependent on the Soviets for support, while the Nationalists benefited from a flow of German and Italian equipment and, though not in an official capacity, military personnel.

In November 1936, the Nationalists reached the outer suburbs of Madrid, but stubborn Republican resistance stopped them penetrating any further. By early 1937, however, the Nationalists had swept Republican forces from most of Spain, which left Barcelona and Madrid as the main points of resistance to Franco's armies. The Nationalists had also benefited from an early example of close air support when Ju-52 bombers of the German Condor Legion engaged in a raid on the Basque town of Guernica, killing over 300 civilians and facilitating a Nationalist advance as the Republican garrison's defence fell apart. Both sides also received deliveries of tanks, Soviet T-26s for the Republicans and around 120 German Light Panzer I tanks for the Nationalists, which allowed the USSR and Germany to refine their tank designs and tactics during the early stages of the Second World War (including, for the Germans, mounting heavier guns and thicker armour on subsequent panzer models).

Despite the arrival of around 40,000 foreign volunteers who fought in the International Brigades, the Republicans found themselves increasingly pushed onto the defensive. In April 1938 the Nationalists succeeded in driving their salient east of Teruel and reaching the Mediterranean coast, cutting the Republicans' territory in two. By January 1939 Catalonia, including Barcelona, had fallen, and around a quarter of a million Republican troops fled into France. Only Madrid still resisted, but in early March its defence collapsed as communist and anticommunist factions there began fighting. By the time Franco's troops entered the Spanish capital on March 28, there was virtually no resistance.

Over half a million people died during the Civil War, which became an indirect confrontation between the forces of communism and those of fascism, as moderate democracies averted their gaze. Britain and France failed to realise the peril in which the equilibrium they hoped to maintain in Europe stood, while Hitler learnt much about both the limits of the democracies' willingness to act against force and the performance of German military technology. Ironically, though, when a continent-wide war did break out in September 1939, in a curious mirroring of the Spanish Civil War, it was Spain and Franco who stood on the sidelines and remained neutral.

German Invasion of Poland

"It was a grey day, with gentle rain," began a story in *Time* magazine's September 11, 1939 edition. This seemingly innocuous phrase preceded a report on the beginning of the most devastating conflict the world has known, as Germany's invasion of Poland on September 1, code-named Case White, unleashed the horrors of the Second World War.

The map, from a French publication, includes only the very first German thrusts into Poland; the lines of their attack are clear. German intelligence had prepared the way for the absorption of Silesia, with its large German-speaking population, and the capture of the land corridor which blocked German-held East Prussia from the main body of the Reich, with a series of "false flag" attacks, hoping to put the blame on the Poles for the outbreak of the war. On the night of August 31, German intelligence operatives dressed as Polish insurgents attacked the radio tower at Gleiwitz (then in Germany, but now Gliwice in Poland), west of Katowice, providing the ammunition Adolf Hitler needed for his speech next day declaring war on Poland.

Britain and France, which had guaranteed Poland's independence against any German aggression the preceding March, should have been forewarned. Clare Hollingworth, the intrepid *Daily Telegraph* correspondent, had managed to cross the German border on August 29 and reported "1,000 Tanks Massed on Polish Frontier; Ten Divisions Reported Ready For Swift Stroke". Three days later, when those tanks and the first of 1.5 million troops of the invasion force crossed the frontier, accompanied by 900 bombers and 400 fighter planes, Hollingworth phoned the British embassy to inform them. On being disbelieved, she simply held the telephone receiver out of the window so the sceptical diplomats could hear the roar of tank engines racing into Silesia.

In the north of the country, fighting had started a few hours earlier, with a bombing raid on Puck and a naval bombardment by the German warship *Schleswig-Holstein* of the Polish munitions dump at Westerplatte near Gdansk. The German plan, which came to be termed *Blitzkrieg* ("lightning war"), was to support their infantry with spearheads of armour and close ground support from attack aircraft, disorienting and destroying the enemy before they had time to react. In Poland, this achieved rapid results, assisted by the Polish High Command's own war plan, which insisted on strong defence at the frontier, rather than a more flexible approach which would have allowed the army to regroup further back in Polish territory.

With over a third of Poland's forces in the "Polish Corridor" around Danzig and another third stationed uselessly between Łódź and Warsaw, the Germans had ample strategic options for breakthroughs and encirclements. By September 3, General Günther von Kluge's 4th Army had crossed the Vistula river. Further south, General Walther von Reichenau's 10th Army tanks reached Łódź by September 5 and three days later the outskirts of Warsaw.

Although the Poles resisted bravely, their air bases had been destroyed within 48 hours and they had few planes left to counter the onslaught of the Luftwaffe. On September 10, with his army's resistance reduced to uncoordinated fragments, the Polish commander-in-chief, Marshal Edward Rydz-Smigly, ordered a retreat to the southeast of the country. The Polish government hoped that the declarations of war which Britain and France had made against Germany on September 3 would result in concrete aid to their country, but they were to be disappointed. Morale-boosting words and generalised promises of assistance did nothing to help them when the final hammer blow struck. Unbeknown to Poland and her Allies, the German–Soviet Non-Aggression Pact signed on August 23 had included a secret clause allowing those two countries to dismember Poland. On September 17, Josef Stalin sent the Red Army into eastern Poland, shattering all Polish hopes of victory or even stalemate. The following day the Polish government retreated into Romania, and on September 28 Warsaw fell. Within a week all organised Polish resistance had ended, the army having suffered nearly 70,000 dead and 700,000 taken prisoner, many of whom would die in prison camps.

For the rest of Poland, the suffering did not end when the fighting stopped. Some six million (around half of them Jewish) would be murdered during the war in the zones occupied by Germany, and around 150,000 in the Soviet sector. The hope which the *Time* article expressed that "France and Britain may give Poland blood transfusions via the Mediterranean" was never realised, and when Warsaw's liberation finally occurred in January 1945, it was at the hands of a Soviet regime which had no interest in granting Poland real freedom. Only in 1989 did the country escape the shadow of the Second World War and hold free elections. It had been a grey, rainy six decades for Poland.

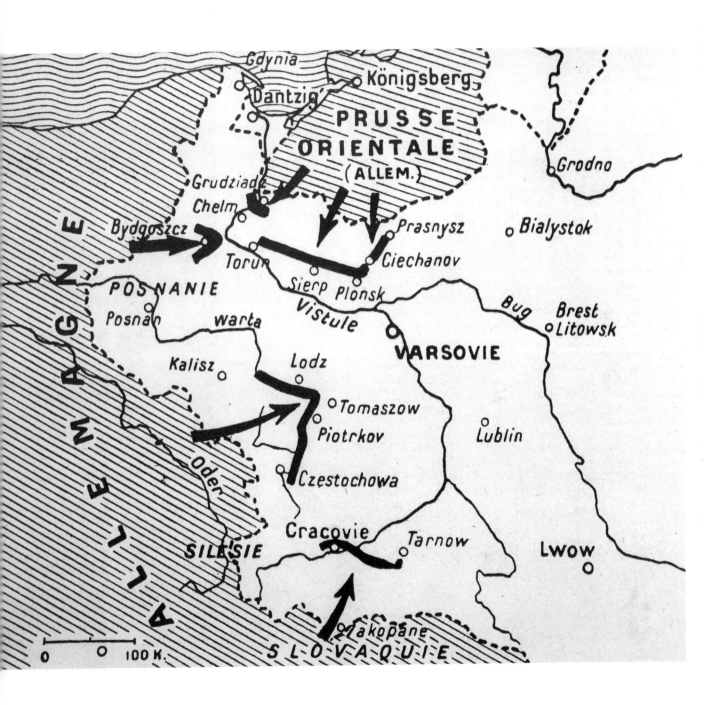

N.f.D.

Middle Wallop

GB 10890 a

Flugplatz

Engl. Bl. 33 c

K. 1:100 000

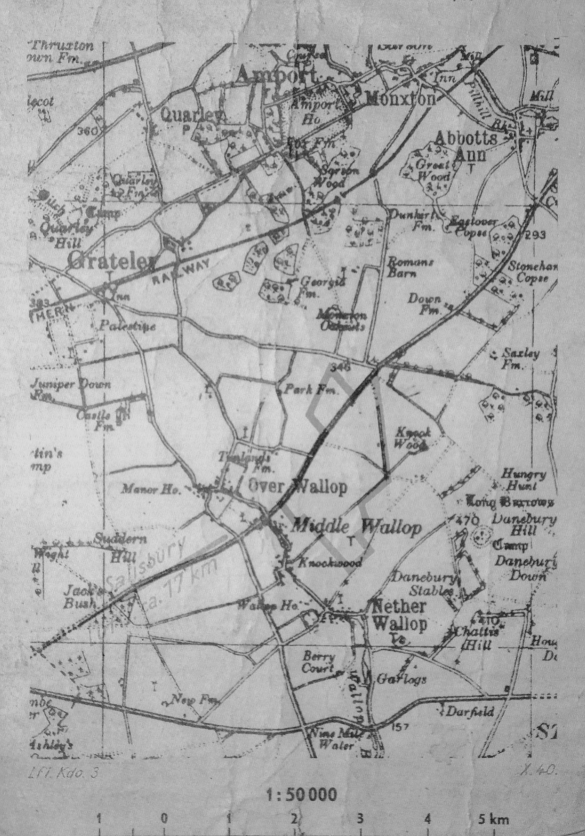

1 : 50 000

| 1 | 0 | 1 | 2 | 3 | 4 | 5 km |

Battle of Britain

At first sight the faded map seems to cover an unassuming plan of a section of rural Hampshire, but the addition of a red ring around Middle Wallop and of the German label "Flugplatz" (airfield) show its part in the German attempt to knock Britain out of the war in the summer of 1940.

The Battle of Britain, as the world's first large-scale aerial battle became known, should not by rights have taken place, as the Versailles peace treaties which ended the First World War forbade Germany from possessing an air force at all. Nonetheless, Adolf Hitler sanctioned one in 1935, entrusted it to Reichsmarschall Hermann Göring to develop and saw it as the lever that would prise open British defences after the fall of France in June 1940 and then clear the way for Operation Sea Lion, his planned invasion of Britain.

The attacks by German fighters against Royal Air Force airfields began in a sporadic way in June, but they ran up against a combination of organisation and technology which allowed the British to overcome their initial lack of numbers compared with the German Luftwaffe's and eventually to turn the tide of the battle. Devised by Fighter Command's commander-in-chief Sir Hugh Dowding, the RAF's system employed an array of radar stations, a technology adopted by the British and of whose precise details the Germans were only hazily aware. The country was divided into four geographical areas or Groups, which were further divided into Sectors each of which had a principal fighter airfield – the Sector Station – from which operations were planned. Middle Wallop was the Sector Station for Sector Y, which covered a large area of southwest England.

German raids were detected by the radar network as they crossed Britain's coastlines and warnings passed to a central command headquarters at Bentley Priory in North London, from where they were disseminated to the relevant Sector Stations. As a result, RAF squadrons gained vital time to scramble, avoided being destroyed on the ground and had a rough idea of the size of the enemy formations they would have to face.

Early German attacks had concentrated on coastal targets, but in August Göring ordered the raiders – Messerschmitt Bf109 fighters and Heinkel He 111 bombers – to move inland and destroy the RAF's airfields and command centres. The campaign was launched on "Adlertag", August 13, when the Luftwaffe despatched nearly 500 bomber sorties (supported by 1,000 fighter sorties) in an attempt to overwhelm the British defences. Some of them passed through Hampshire, intending to attack targets at Farnborough and Odiham, and Middle Wallop's 609 Squadron scrambled to intercept them, shooting down at least 13 German planes (although some bombs were unleashed and fell on the village of Nether Wallop). The hangars at Middle Wallop were targeted the next day, when two of them were damaged.

The raids continued relentlessly through August and early September, taking a terrible toll on the young fighter pilots of the Supermarine Spitfires and Hawker Hurricanes which formed the RAF's principal line of defence. Between August 26 and September 6, the RAF lost 248 planes, although 322 Luftwaffe aircraft were destroyed, and the ratio of losses turned favourable to the British as September progressed. From September 7, a frustrated Hitler ordered a change of tactic, with raids beginning on Britain's cities. London was hardest hit, suffering bombing for 56 of the next 57 days, but though the Blitz, as the bombing campaign was nicknamed, caused mass casualties (with around 40,000 civilians killed) and damaged or destroyed millions of homes, it marked the effective end of Hitler's ambitions to destroy the RAF and of his ability to launch an invasion. Planning for Sea Lion petered out, although it was not officially cancelled until February 13, 1942.

Middle Wallop ceased to be a target for German bombing, instead becoming a base for Allied raids against targets in German-occupied Europe. It was the base from November 1943 to July 1944 of the US 9th Fighter Command, one of the main American air units in western Europe, whose Mustang fighters played a key role during the D-Day landings in Normandy. Truly, the tables had been turned.

Operation Barbarossa

The commemorative map shows the progress of the German 7th Panzer Division – marked by a red line snaking through the western Soviet Union – during Operation Barbarossa, the largest offensive in military history. In one sense an act of betrayal of Germany's Soviet allies (the German–Soviet non-aggression pact in August 1939 had enabled both countries to dismember Poland), the invasion was also the logical conclusion of the German Führer Adolf Hitler's search for *Lebensraum*, new territory for an expanding German population, and of his visceral hatred of the Soviet communist ideology.

The attack sent 3.3 million German troops east towards Moscow on June 22, 1941, and despite the massive build-up of troops on its borders – involving 19 panzer divisions with around 3,000 tanks and over 2,500 aircraft – the Soviet Union was caught by surprise. Three spearheads thrust into its territory: one under General Wilhelm von Leeb advanced towards the Baltic States and Leningrad, another in the south under General Paul von Kleist moved into Ukraine and Kiev, while in the centre General Fedor von Bock's army group aimed at Smolensk and then Moscow, hoping to decapitate the Soviet state.

The 7th Division formed part of this central force. An elite unit, it had been commanded by General Erwin Rommel during the German invasion of France but was now led by General Hans von Funck, a First World War veteran who had twice been awarded the Iron Cross. Racing beyond its start position near Bialystok, the division advanced 60 miles towards Vilnius and then joined a vast encircling movement around Smolensk, which finally fell in mid-September.

The 17,500 officers and men of the division had by then suffered a reduction in their daily bread ration from 850 to 600 grams, as supply units could not keep up with the rapid advance, an ominous sign of the collapse in logistics which would ultimately undo Barbarossa. By July 18 the unit had reached Mogilev, still 600 miles short of Moscow, from where its quartermaster sent back an order for 20,000 socks to protect the division's weary feet. Discipline broke down as heavy rain in July turned the Russian roads into a quagmire that held the tanks' tracks fast like cloying glue, and the Soviet tactic of burning crops and evacuating every last piece of factory equipment meant the Germans could neither forage nor make use of captured industrial facilities.

By late August, the division was stationed at Jelnia on a bend of the Disna river south of Smolensk, weathering repeated counterattacks by the Red Army. One soldier in the 7th wrote in his diary of the ferocity of the fighting: "there are no rules of war here". Winter, though, was approaching, and German efforts to accelerate the advance on Moscow grew ever more desperate. The 7th Division took part in Operation Typhoon, launched on October 1, which captured over half a million Soviet troops around Vyazma (Wjasma on the map) and breached the Soviet capital's outer defences by the middle of the month.

However, the Soviets had more reserves to throw into the battle, and civilian resistance to the German occupation was growing – at Vereya (Wereja on the map overleaf) the unit arrested the entire male population between 17 and 65. As plunging temperatures made transportation next to impossible, the advance slowed but still reached the Minsk to Moscow road, 50 miles from the city centre, on November 30. Sickness and desertion rates rose, and of those notionally fit to fight, most had inadequate equipment; only one in six even had overcoats.

On December 5 the Red Army began its counteroffensive, a million men and 700 tanks crashing into a German army weakened by months of fighting, extended supply lines and strategic blunders. The 7th Division held fast at first, enduring a Christmas dinner of frozen potatoes in between fending off Soviet attacks, but then began a retreat towards Vyazma. Six months after the start of Barbarossa, it had suffered over 2,000 dead and 5,700 wounded, and in May 1942 its shattered remnants were withdrawn and sent to southern France to recuperate.

Barbarossa had failed, and Hitler's dream of a rapid defeat of the Soviet Union had evaporated. The next three years saw the steady destruction of the Wehrmacht and of the Third Reich, as the Red Army steadily pushed westwards towards Poland and then Germany itself. The 7th Division experienced all this as, in a reprise of its earlier hellish campaign, it was sent back to the Eastern Front in 1943, its last remnants trapped on the Hel Peninsula in April 1945, from where some escaped to surrender to the British Army northwest of Berlin. This latter part of the 7th Division's war, unsurprisingly, was not celebrated in a commemorative map.

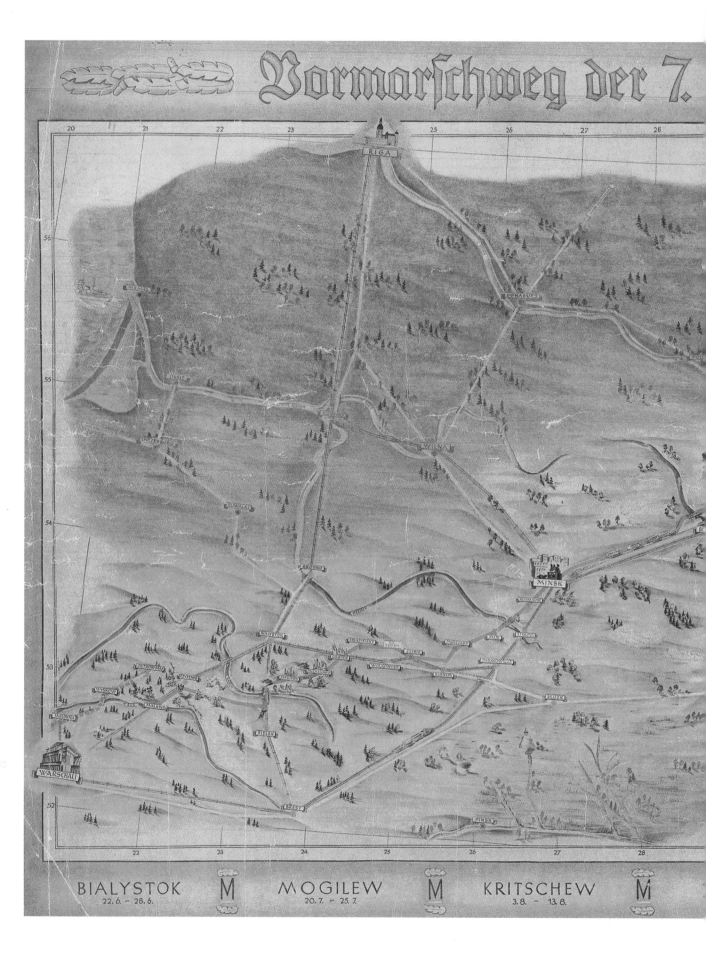

ision in Rußland 1941

 WEREJA
13.10. – 23.10.

 SCHELKOWKA
25.10. – 2.11.

 NARA-SEENENGE
7.11. – 26.11.

Attack on Pearl Harbor

The map, showing United States warships moored in the naval base at Pearl Harbor in Hawaii, depicts a moment of deceptive calm. Drawn up by Lieutenant Welbourn Kelley and Commander Walter Karig as part of their 1944 *Battle Report: Pearl Harbor to Coral Sea*, it captures the deployment of the US Pacific Fleet just before the Japanese attack on December 7, 1941 that precipitated the United States's entry into the Second World War and the nearly four years of combat that ultimately led to Japan's defeat.

The US president, Franklin D Roosevelt, wary of Japan's ambitions in China and its quest to secure supplies of oil to fuel its military advances, had ordered the US Pacific fleet to transfer to Pearl Harbor in April 1940 to deter Japanese aggression. Instead, military planners in Tokyo, alarmed at America's growing naval power in the Pacific, began to plot a pre-emptive strike that aimed to knock the United States out of the war before it had even entered it.

On November 26, 1941, a massive Japanese attack fleet headed by six aircraft carriers left Hitokappu Bay and began a stealthy more than 3,500-mile journey towards Hawaii. Although the United States had cracked Japan's military and diplomatic codes, there were no clear indications of what the Japanese were planning. Despite the fact that the US Navy had been unable to locate the Japanese carriers for over 50 days, many of the ship's crews were on shore leave on the evening of December 6 when a new radio intercept indicated the Japanese were about to launch some kind of attack.

That message took time to reach senior politicians, including the president, and they concluded the Japanese would strike French Indochina. So, when Japanese captain Mitsuo Fuchida issued the coded message "Tora, Tora, Tora" after flying over Pearl Harbor to check the Americans were not prepared, a first wave of 183 fighters, bombers and torpedo planes was unleashed against the unsuspecting US fleet. The first real warning the Pearl Harbor base had came at 7am, when the radar station at the northern tip of Oahu detected a mass of blips heading their way, but by then it was too late. The airbase at Wheeler Field was battered by 1,760-pound armour-piercing bombs, which destroyed the 127 American warplanes that could have mounted a defence.

With air supremacy guaranteed, the Japanese warplanes, and six midget submarines which were also launched into the waters around Pearl Harbor soon swarmed around the American warships, which stood little chance. Six torpedoes struck the *Nevada*, nearly crippling her, while a gaping hole torn by a bomb in its side sank the *Oklahoma* within minutes. Three torpedo strikes dealt a similar blow to the *California*, while a bomb that struck the forward magazines of the *Arizona* caused it to ignite in an inferno of sparks and metal. The light cruiser *Helena* and minelayer *Oglala* took heavy damage, while, on the other side of Ford Island, the *Utah* was crippled.

The first Japanese wave departed from a near-apocalyptic scene, the early morning lit up by fire and obscured by smoke. There was little relief for the Americans, as a second Japanese wave hit an hour after the first. Though a few US planes had managed to get airborne, and a flight of B-17 bombers made it over from California, they could not prevent further devastation, both to the land installations and to the fleet, as the *Cassin* and *Downes* were severely damaged and the *Shaw* took three direct bomb hits.

The attack had destroyed or damaged 323 American planes and killed more than 2,300 Americans. Twenty-one naval vessels, including seven of the Pacific Fleet's largest battleships, were sunk or damaged, at a cost to the Japanese of just 29 planes, five of the midget submarines, and around 100 men. The only consolation for the US Navy was that their two aircraft carriers were not at the base at the time the Japanese struck and that eventually all but two of the sunken battleships were refloated and repaired. More importantly, the unprovoked attack galvanised public opinion in the United States, which had been distinctly ambivalent to becoming involved in the war against the Axis. President Roosevelt termed the day of the attack "a date which will live in infamy" and the next day secured Congress's approval to declare war on Japan. Although the Japanese continued to expand their control in the Pacific until a naval defeat at Midway in June 1942 and US landings on Guadalcanal the same August began to turn the strategic tide, the seeds of their eventual military destruction were sown at Pearl Harbor. The attack had failed to destroy key elements of the US fleet and, rather than breaking American resolve, stiffened it.

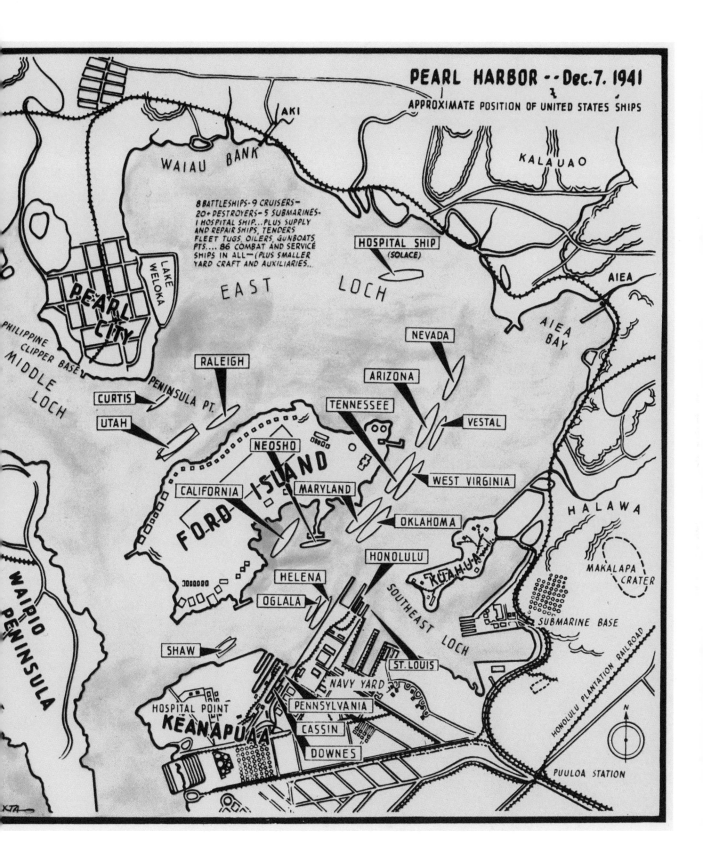

PEARL HARBOR -- Dec. 7, 1941

APPROXIMATE POSITION OF UNITED STATES SHIPS

KALAUAO

WAIAU BANK

AKI

8 BATTLESHIPS - 9 CRUISERS -
20+ DESTROYERS - 5 SUBMARINES -
1 HOSPITAL SHIP... PLUS SUPPLY
AND REPAIR SHIPS, TENDERS
FLEET TUGS, OILERS, GUNBOATS
PTS.... 86 COMBAT AND SERVICE
SHIPS IN ALL — (PLUS SMALLER
YARD CRAFT AND AUXILIARIES...

HOSPITAL SHIP
(SOLACE)

EAST LOCH

AIEA

AIEA BAY

LAKE WELOKA

PEARL CITY

PHILIPPINE CLIPPER BASE

MIDDLE LOCH

PENINSULA PT.

RALEIGH

NEVADA

ARIZONA

CURTIS

UTAH

TENNESSEE

VESTAL

NEOSHO

CALIFORNIA

FORD ISLAND

MARYLAND

WEST VIRGINIA

HALAWA

OKLAHOMA

MAKALAPA CRATER

HONOLULU

KUAHUA

WAIPIO PENINSULA

HELENA

OGLALA

SOUTHEAST LOCH

SUBMARINE BASE

SHAW

ST. LOUIS

NAVY YARD

HONOLULU PLANTATION RAILROAD

HOSPITAL POINT

KEANAPUAA

PENNSYLVANIA

CASSIN

DOWNES

PUULOA STATION

N

KTA

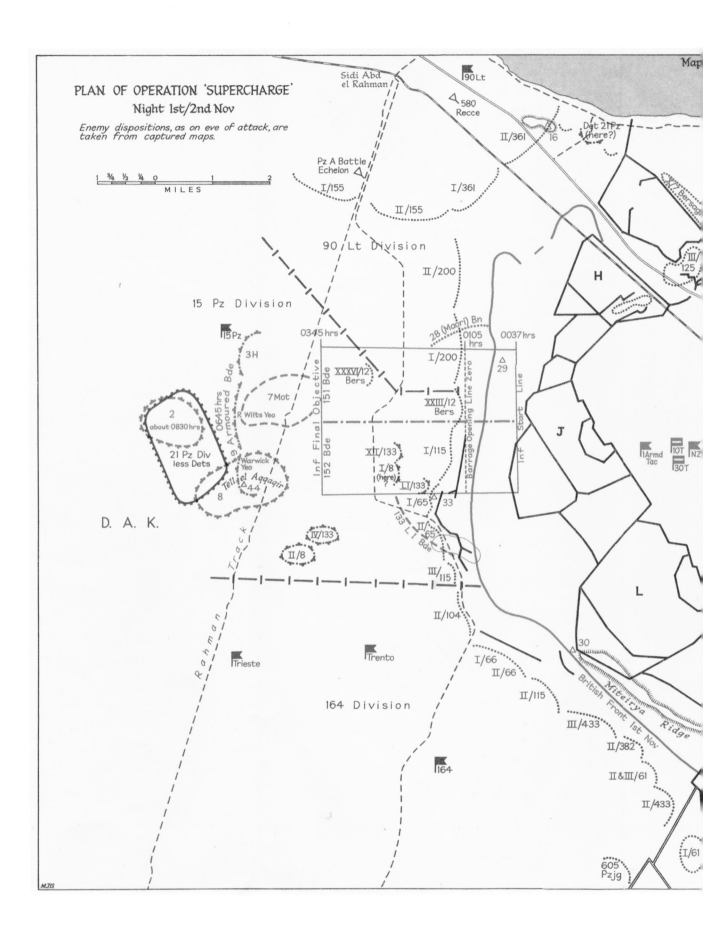

PLAN OF OPERATION 'SUPERCHARGE'
Night 1st/2nd Nov

*Enemy dispositions, as on eve of attack, are
taken from captured maps.*

1 ¾ ½ ¼ 0   1   2
MILES

Sidi Abd
el Rahman

90 Lt

△ 580
Recce

II/361   16   Det 21 Pz
(here?)

Pz A Battle
Echelon △

I/155   I/361

II/155

90 Lt Division

II/200

III/
125

H

15 Pz Division

15 Pz

3 H

28 (Maori) Bn   0105   0037 hrs
                     hrs
0345 hrs   △ 29

I/200

XXXVI/12
Bers

7 Mot   I/115

R Wilts Yeo   XXIII/12
                     Bers

2
about 0830 hrs

21 Pz Div
less Dets

Warwick
Yeo
△ 44   XII/133   I/115

Tell el Aqqaqir   I/8
8   (here)
                     ?   II/133

I/65
△ 33

D. A. K.

II/
65

IV/133   II/
                     65
                     133 Lt
II/8   Bde

III/115

II/104

Trieste   Trento

I/66
II/66

II/115

164 Division

III/433

II/382

164

II & III/61

II/433

605
Pzjg

I/61

1 Armd
Tac   10T
           30T   NZ

△ 30

British Front 1st Nov

Miteirya Ridge

J

L

Inf Final Objective

151 Bde

152 Bde

Barrage Opening Line Zero

Inf Start Line

Armoured Bde

0645 hrs

Rahman Track

MJG

Second Battle of El Alamein

The map, taken from the official British *History of the Second World War*, shows the British plan for Operation Supercharge, the final breakthrough in the Second Battle of El Alamein between Lieutenant General Bernard Montgomery's Eighth Army and the mixed force of the German Afrika Korps and Italian troops led by General Erwin Rommel. The successful Allied advance through the central box marked north of Miteirya Ridge forced Rommel into a retreat that did not end until the Axis forces had been pushed out of North Africa in a devastating blow to Adolf Hitler's Mediterranean ambitions.

Earlier in the summer of 1942 the prospects for the two sides had seemed very different. Rommel's divisions stood only 60 miles west of Alexandria and in a position to menace Cairo. Were Egypt lost, the whole British position in the Middle East would crumble. Although Rommel's relentless advance was held back at a new defensive line at El Alamein in July, it seemed only a temporary reprieve and General Claude Auchinleck, the British commander-in-chief in the Middle East, was removed by an impatient British prime minister, Winston Churchill, when he hesitated to go on the offensive to reverse Rommel's momentum.

Montgomery was given the Egyptian part of Auchinleck's command, but rather than attack immediately, he took his time to rebuild the confidence of a bruised Eighth Army and prepare for an encounter he hoped would deliver a decisive victory. The Germans had not come out unscathed from their rapid advance through the North African desert and by September had only 211 panzers and about 280 Italian tanks, far outnumbered by the Eighth Army's armour. On September 23 too, Rommel, exhausted by the rigours of the previous six months, went on sick leave, leaving the Axis forces under inferior leadership when the crisis broke.

The Germans and Italians had to defend a line from the coastal road to the Qattara Depression in the south, a distance of 75 miles, which allowed Montgomery to choose where to focus his attacks and where to conduct feints to draw the enemy. To conduct these he had over 190,000 men, 1,000 tanks and more than 2,000 artillery pieces and anti-tank guns. The main initial problem was penetrating the "Devil's gardens", the dense network of minefields Rommel had ordered to be laid to defend the German line.

On October 23 Montgomery unleashed Operation Lightfoot, so named in the hope that the infantry which spearheaded it would be light enough not to set off the antitank mines and would secure a perimeter behind which channels could be cleared of mines to allow the tanks to advance. The main attack was carried out by the Australians to the north and the South Africans to the south, who pushed four corridors as far as Miteirya Ridge, but over the next two days the advance stalled. German counterattacks began to inflict serious casualties, though the loss of Rommel's replacement General Georg Stumme, after he had a heart attack, blunted German resistance.

Although in the end Montgomery managed to advance over half a mile beyond Miteirya Ridge, the cost was growing too high, so he ordered a partial withdrawal to regroup. Operation Supercharge involved attacks by the 151st and 152nd Infantry Brigades along a two-and-a-half-mile front, supported by the 9th Armoured Brigade, which would punch a hole in the Axis line for the following armoured units to exploit. The artillery barrage which preceded the attack was intense and allowed the infantry, which began their advance early on November 2, to reach their objectives. In other circumstances they would have been vulnerable to rapid counters by German panzers, but by that evening the Afrika Korps had only 35 operational tanks, and a shortage of fuel threatened to immobilise those.

Rommel, who had returned to North Africa on October 25, felt he had to pull back, but a direct order from Hitler prolonged his resistance, effected by a small force of anti-tank guns which held the Allied tanks at bay. On November 4 even this broke, and Montgomery's infantry broke through near Tel el Aqqaqir, followed rapidly by the 1st Armoured Division, which then raced forward to catch the retreating Germans. Only the Italian armoured divisions continued to fight, but they were almost destroyed by nightfall.

Rommel paused several times, but on November 13 the British were in Tobruk and by January 23, 1943, had taken Tripoli, unravelling nearly all the German gains of the preceding year. Although the British had lost 200 tanks at El Alamein, almost all the Afrika Korps' armour had been destroyed, and the boost to Allied morale after years of reverses was profound. The desert terrain might offer ideal conditions for tank warfare and armoured advances, but the Germans no longer had the forces to take advantage of it.

Guadalcanal Campaign

The blue lines on the map show the landings and advance of the US Marines on Guadalcanal in the southern Solomon Islands on the morning of August 7, 1942. It was a deceptively successful start to what would become a gruelling and for both sides a very costly six-month campaign to control the strategic island. The map was drawn for *The War in the Pacific*, part of the official history of the Second World War supervised by the Historical Division of the US Department of the Army. It hoped to "offer the thoughtful citizen material for a better understanding of the basic problems of war and the manner in which these problems were met, thus augmenting his understanding of national security", a laudable, though largely unattained objective.

As Japan expanded its perimeter in the Pacific following the attack on the US naval base at Pearl Harbor (see page 184), its high command sought bases from which to launch further thrusts towards New Guinea and ultimately Australia, while shielding its existing gains from any American counterattacks. In July 1942 the Japanese army began constructing an airfield near Lunga Point in northern Guadalcanal. The danger this presented to US naval operations and the opportunities it would provide for new Japanese advances prompted the Americans to launch Operation Watchtower to retake the Solomon Islands (and to build their own airbase there).

A flotilla of 75 naval vessels under Vice Admiral Frank Fletcher disembarked nearly 15,000 troops on the morning of August 7. While landings on the smaller islands of Tulagi and Gavutu-Tanambogo were stoutly resisted, on Guadalcanal the Japanese were caught by surprise and the 11,000 men of the US Marine 1st Division under Major General Alexander Vandegrift soon pushed out of the beachhead. Before the day was over, they had occupied the airfield zone. Hopes that Watchtower would end in an easy victory, however, were dashed, when Fletcher withdrew the naval task force after attacks from Japanese planes based on Rabaul and the loss of a destroyer in a naval engagement at nearby Savo Island.

Vandegrift's Marines were left without much of their heavy equipment and most of their supplies. Although they managed to complete the part-finished Japanese airfield (which they renamed Henderson Field), they suffered constant harassing attacks from Japanese army units. Only the "Cactus Air Force", a scratch squadron of Marine, US Army and Navy planes which operated from Henderson and shot down over 150 Japanese planes, saved them from disaster. The tenacity of the Marines, including a two-day defence of Henderson Field on September 13–14 against ferocious assaults, also frustrated the Japanese, who by October had been reinforced to 36,000 troops. The decisive action came a month later on October 23–24, when the Japanese commander Lieutenant General Harukichi Hyakutake, his force boosted by a new landing of 4,500 men a week before, unleashed two full regiments against the airfield. The desperate US defenders were reduced to placing dead comrades in foxholes and shooting their Browning machine guns in rotation to deceive the Japanese into thinking that the ridge which was the final obstacle to taking Henderson was still fully manned.

It earned a Medal of Honor for Platoon Sergeant Mitchell Paige, who held the ridge, and resulted in over 2,000 Japanese casualties, marking the end of serious Japanese ground operations. Instead, the Americans went over to the offensive, steadily gaining ground, particularly from early December, when the long-suffering 1st Marine Division was finally replaced by the 2nd Marine Division and the US Army's 25th Infantry Division. Concerned about possible US losses, the new commander, Major

General Alexander Patch, chose not to impede the Japanese evacuation of the island which began in late January 1943, and on February 9 he was able to declare that Guadalcanal was secure and that "The Tokyo Express no longer has terminus on Guadalcanal."

Japan's expulsion from the Solomon Islands meant that it was less able to threaten Allied shipping to and from Australia, and the losses in manpower and materiel were not easily replaced. The grinding war of attrition which had characterised the Guadalcanal campaign also demonstrated to US commanders that they would need to develop effective combat air transport if they were to win the Pacific War. It also helped focus resources on that theatre, pushing the United States away from its previous "Germany First" policy of privileging action against Germany over the war against Japan. The first day's landing on Guadalcanal might have been a false dawn, but the final victory, albeit at the cost of 1,600 combat deaths (and several thousand more lost to malaria and other tropical diseases), was the first major American ground success, proving that, ultimately, an island-hopping strategy might win the war against Japan.

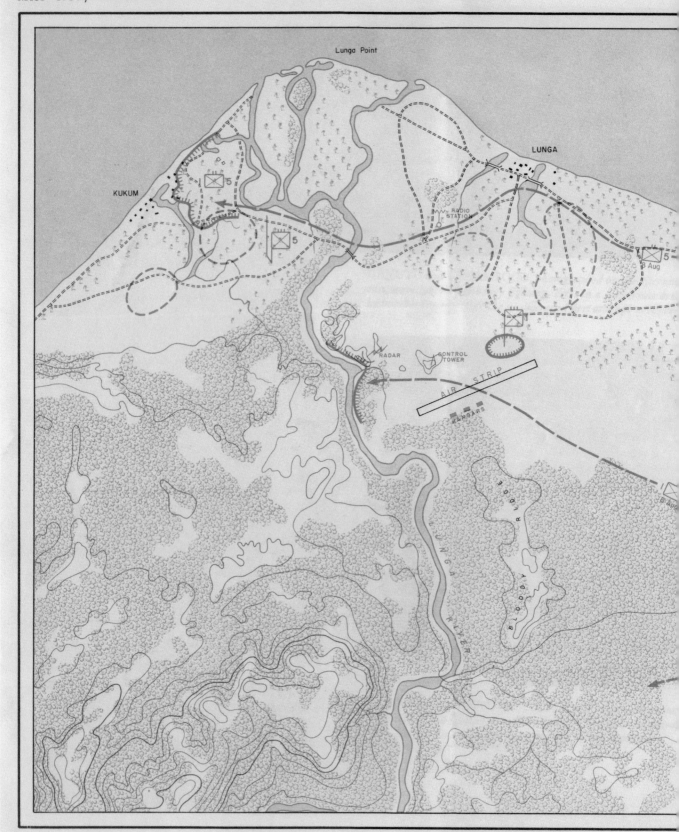

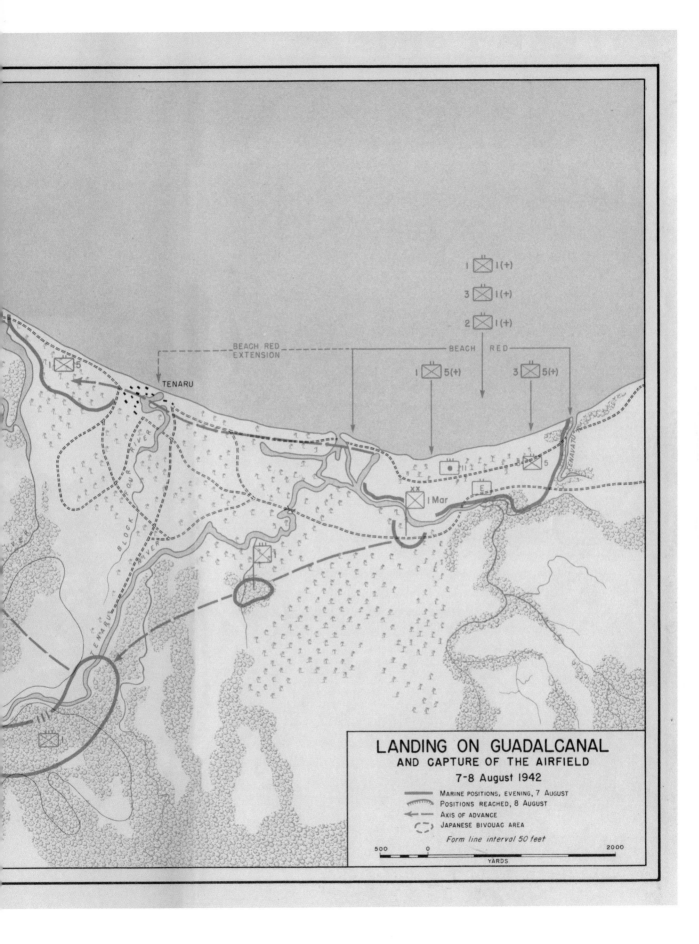

1 ☒ 1(+)

3 ☒ 1(+)

2 ☒ 1(+)

BEACH RED
EXTENSION

BEACH RED

TENARU

1 ☒ 5

1 ☒ 5(+)

3 ☒ 5(+)

5

BLOCK FOUR RIVER

☒

XX
1 Mar

E

☒

TENAVATU

TENARU RIVER

☒

LANDING ON GUADALCANAL
AND CAPTURE OF THE AIRFIELD
7-8 August 1942

———— Marine positions, evening, 7 August

⌒⌒⌒ Positions reached, 8 August

←-- Axis of advance

⌒‿⌒ Japanese bivouac area

Form line interval 50 feet

500   0   2000

YARDS

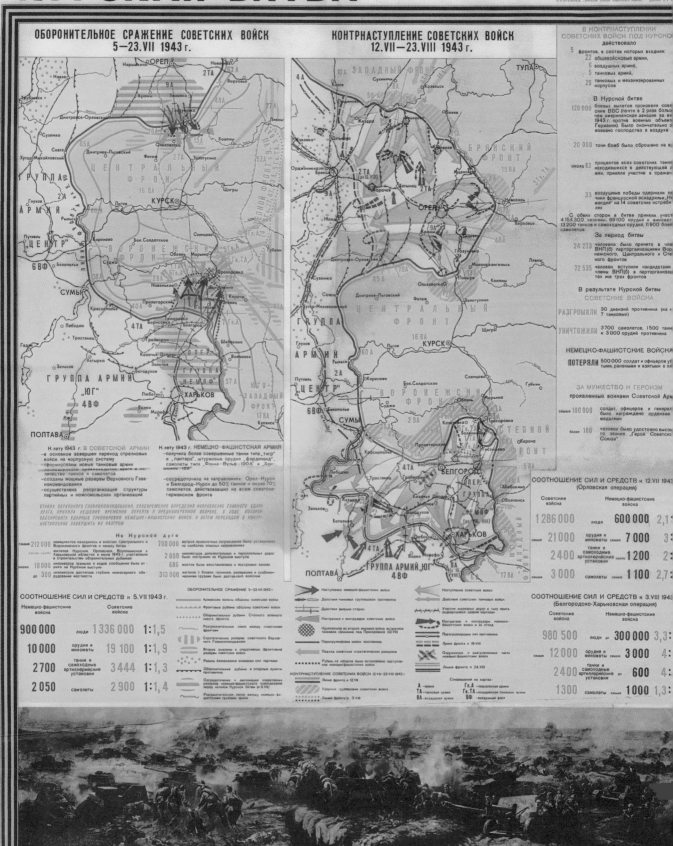

КУРСКАЯ БИТВА

Battle of Kursk

Before 1943, Hitler twice had victory against the Soviet Union within his grasp – or so he thought: at the gates of Moscow in 1941 and at Stalingrad in 1942. It was the Red Army's ability to soak up almost unimaginable levels of casualties and still to retain the capacity to strike back that had thwarted him both times. The map, published by the Soviet Department of Topography and Cartography in 1978 for use in schools, shows a third occasion, at Kursk in the summer of 1943. The Soviet victory there halted Germany's final large-scale strategic offensive on the Eastern Front, closing off Hitler's last avenue to victory.

The battle came about after the surrender of German forces at Stalingrad in February 1943 allowed the Red Army to thrust over 400 miles into southern Russia, in the process creating a bulging salient around Kursk. The commander of German Army Group South, Field Marshal Erich von Manstein, saw an opportunity to pinch out the salient, decisively returning the momentum to the German Wehrmacht. Adolf Hitler was enthusiastic when presented with the plan, declaring that "Victory at Kursk must serve as a beacon to the world."

Unfortunately for the Germans, British intelligence intercepts and the Soviet leader Josef Stalin's own spies, gave him forewarning of the massive build-up to the offensive Manstein called Operation Zitadelle ("Citadel"). The Red Army commander, Marshal Georgi Zhukov, devised a counterstrategy of defence in depth to wear down the German assault and then throw in fresh reserves against a by then exhausted enemy. He built up a force of 1,500,000 men in the Kursk area and directed the digging of 3,000 miles of defensive trenches and anti-tank ditches – anything that would blunt the German attack and prevent a breakthrough.

Stalin's luck held, as Hitler delayed the launch of the offensive several times, which allowed Zhukov precious extra time to prepare for the onslaught. When finally it came, the Germans had assembled around 650,000 men and nearly 2,500 tanks, close to three quarters of their armour on the Eastern Front. General Walter Model's Ninth Army was to break through the Soviet defences north of Kursk, while General Hermann Hoth's Panzer Army would deliver a crushing blow to the south, aiming to reach Kursk within a week.

The first stages of the attack are shown in the map on the left. Early that afternoon, German Stuka dive bombers pulverised a section of the Red Army's lines in the north, while in the south Hoth's panzers smashed against Soviet positions at Zavidovka. Although the Luftwaffe gradually achieved air superiority, the land offensive was less successful. Clearing the Soviet minefields proved time-consuming, and the slowing rate of advance made the German armoured vehicles sitting ducks. By July 9 the advance had ground to a halt, and three days later the Soviets were even able to launch a limited counter-offensive, capturing Orel.

The real disaster for the Wehrmacht unfolded in the south. While at first Hoth's panzers advanced 10 miles in a day, gradually the apex of the advance grew narrower, and the Red Army's tactics of laying new minefields by night in the path of the offensive took a terrible toll: the Grossdeutschland Division began with 118 tanks, but five days into the offensive it was down to only 20 operational. As reinforcements from the Soviet Steppes Front began arriving in the Kursk area, on July 12 Hoth threw all his remaining reserves into an attack on Prokhorovka, just at the moment the Soviet 5th Guards Tank Army launched its own counteroffensive. The resulting clash between nearly 300 German tanks and twice that number on the Soviet side made it the second largest tank battle in history (after an engagement at Brody during Operation Barbarossa in June 1941) and also the most mythologised. Far from it being a resounding Soviet victory, as the Red Army commanders claimed, the Soviets lost half their tanks, as many became trapped in their own anti-tank ditches, to be blown apart, helpless, by the German Tigers.

Disaster was averted because the depth of the Soviet defensive lines and the disparity in the two sides' ability to muster reserves made it clear to the German High Command that the offensive was failing. News of the Allied invasion of Sicily on July 10 caused Hitler to doubt the wisdom of continuing, when resources would have to be devoted to the defence of Italy. On July 17 Zitadelle was called off, and, far from being pushed out of the Kursk salient, as Manstein had hoped, the Soviets expanded it, capturing Kharkov on August 23. From there, until the final capture of Berlin in May 1945 (see page 202) the Red Army's advance was almost uninterrupted. Kursk had not proved a new dawn for Hitler, but an eclipse.

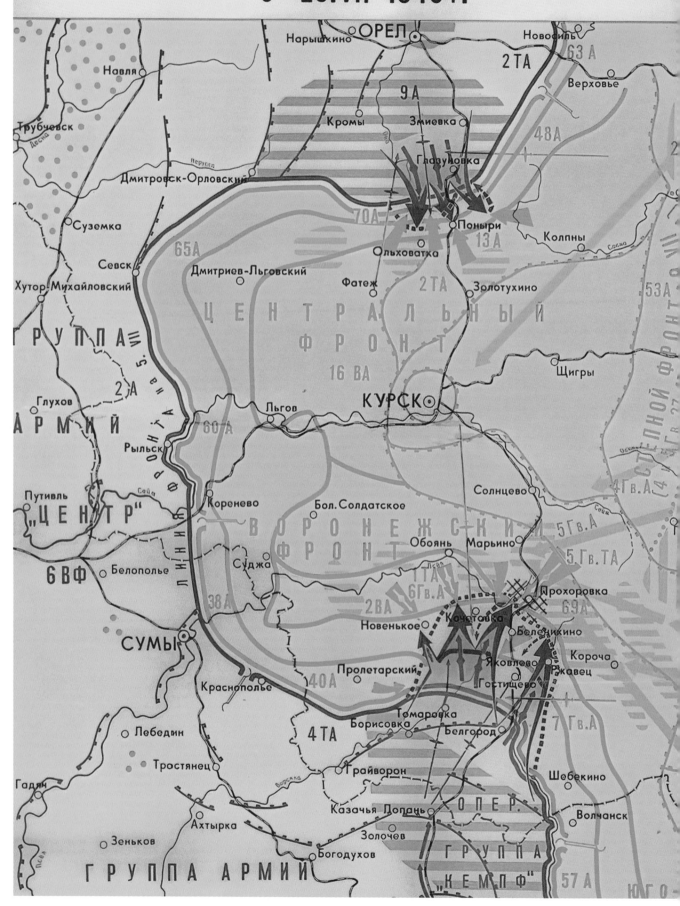

ОБОРОНИТЕЛЬНОЕ СРАЖЕНИЕ СОВЕТСКИХ ВОЙСК
5—23.VII 1943 г.

ОРЕЛ

Нарышкино

Новосиль

2 ТА

63 А

Навля

9 А

Верховье

Кромы

Змиевка

48 А

Трубчевск

Глазуновка

Дмитровск-Орловский

70 А

Поныри

Суземка

Колпны

13 А

65 А

Ольховатка

Дмитриев-Льговский

Севск

Фатеж

2 ТА

Золотухино

53 А

Хутор-Михайловский

Ц Е Н Т Р А Л Ь Н Ы Й

Г Р У П П А

2 А

Ф Р О Н Т

Глухов

Льгов

16 ВА

Щигры

А Р М И Й

60 А

КУРСК

Рыльск

"Ц Е Н Т Р"

Путивль

Солнцево

Коренево

Бол. Солдатское

4 Гв. А

В О Р О Н Е Ж С К И Й

5 Гв. А

6 ВФ

Белополье

Ф Р О Н Т

Обоянь

Марьино

5 Гв. ТА

Суджа

Прохоровка

38 А

1 ТА
6 Гв. А

69 А

СУМЫ

2 ВА

Кочетовка

Беленихино

Новенькое

Яковлево

Короча

Пролетарский

Ржавец

40 А

Гостищево

Краснополье

Томаровка

7 Гв. А

Лебедин

Борисовка

Белгород

4 ТА

Тростянец

Шебекино

Грайворон

Гадяч

О П Е Р.

Казачья Лопань

Волчанск

Ахтырка

Золочев

Зеньков

Г Р У П П А

Богодухов

Г Р У П П А   А Р М И Й

"К Е М П Ф"

57 А

ЮГО-З

КОНТРНАСТУПЛЕНИЕ СОВЕТСКИХ ВОЙСК
12.VII—23.VIII 1943 г.

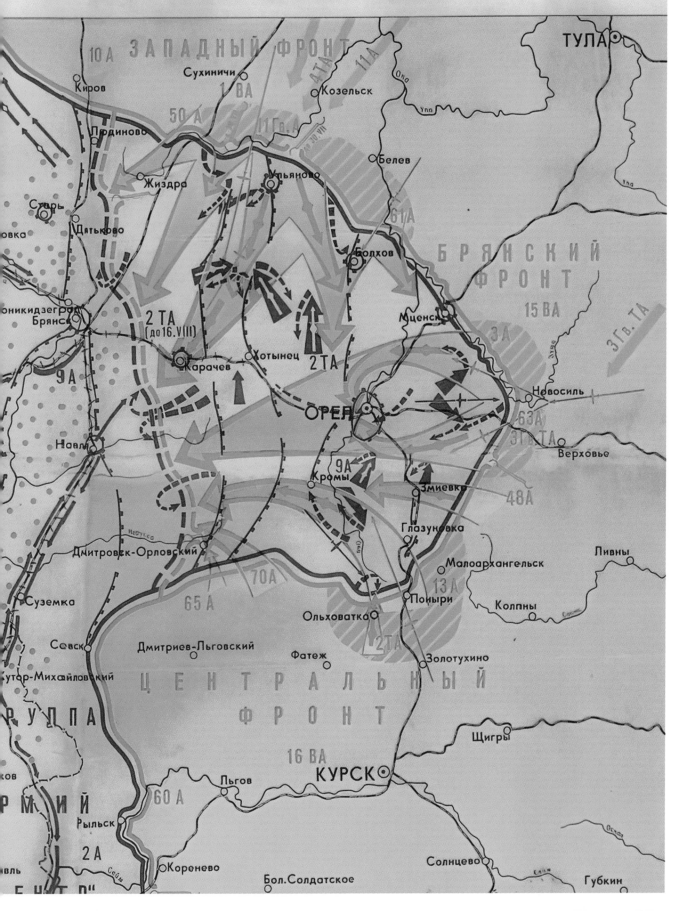

D-Day

The red line snaking from the northern French coast and through the inland towns and dense hedgerows of rural Normandy marks the path of the US Army's 743rd Tank Battalion during the first seven weeks after they came ashore at D-Day. The landing, on June 6, 1944, was the largest amphibious assault in military history, with thousands of landing craft delivering 156,000 US, British and Canadian troops to five beaches along a heavily fortified 50-mile stretch.

The D-Day landings had been months in the planning, involving an extensive deception campaign (Operation Fortitude) to fool the Germans that the long-awaited opening of a second front in western Europe would take place in the Pas-de-Calais, together with the launching of large-scale preliminary air assaults to neutralise the threat from the Luftwaffe. The 743rd were an independent tank battalion, tasked with supporting the 116th Infantry Combat Team, rather than forming part of an armoured division. Their designated landing site was Omaha, the more easterly of the two American beaches, which they were to secure rapidly and then link up with the neighbouring British troops at Gold Beach and the American landing at Utah Beach to the west.

Little went to plan. The defenders, the German 352nd Infantry Division, were amongst the most experienced in Normandy, and even before they made it to dry land, the LCTs (Landing Craft Tanks) in which the 743rd's tanks were being transported were subjected to a devastating rain of artillery shells, mortars and heavy machine-gun fire. It was 6.24am on June 6, H –6 – or six hours before the main landings were due to take place – that the M4 Shermans, the first Allied tanks to reach the Normandy beaches, began to lumber forward across the sand. There followed a day of severe trial, as the infantry and tanks of the 743rd were pinned down on the beach, unable to break out to their first-day objectives in the villages beyond. Among the tales of heroism was that of Lieutenant Harold Beavers, who dismounted from his tank in the middle of a firefight to retrieve a wounded officer whom he then drove through a German minefield to the safety of a first-aid post. The battalion's commander, Lieutenant Colonel John Upham, continued to direct his armour's determined assaults on enemy strongpoints, despite his shoulder being shattered by a hit from a German sniper. In recognition he received a Distinguished Service Cross, one of nine won by the battalion for the day's action (as well as a Presidential Unit Citation ribbon given to the whole unit).

By nightfall, German resistance had slackened. At about 10.30pm the first Shermans drove off Omaha Beach to begin the link-up with the British, and at mid-morning the next day they destroyed their first German tank, a Mk-IV Panzer near the village of Formigny. There followed an unfortunate case of friendly fire, as units of the 115th Infantry mistook the Shermans for enemy tanks. Other such misadventures are chronicled on the map, which documents the 743rd's campaign with wry, dark humour, including one incident near Pont Hebert where US planes bombed them by mistake several times over a 48-hour period. The culprits are labelled the "American Luftwaffe". The map ends with the 743rd at St-Lô, whose capture on July 19 (after a ferocious bombardment in which over 90 per cent of the town was destroyed by American artillery) marked the point at which the German cause in Normandy was effectively lost.

The 743rd had suffered terribly. They were often outgunned in fights with German armour and had to plough their way through the *bocage*, the Normandy terrain of thick hedgerows that in places created an impenetrable labyrinth which could only be escaped by dynamiting a way through. They lost 96 Shermans and 131 men killed, with over 400 wounded, which represented almost the full operation strength of the unit. They carried on fighting through Belgium and the Netherlands, took part in the Battle of the Bulge in January 1945, crossed the Rhine in March and reached their final positions on the Elbe river facing the advancing Soviet Red Army in mid-April. As the rest of the battalion waited to meet the Russians, one man whose talents as an artist had been spotted (and employed to design the battalion Christmas card) was held back. Private First Class Norman E Hamilton, an artist from Chicago, spent the day drawing full-colour maps of the battalion's progress during the war. D-Day must have seemed so long ago, but his map and its lively annotations brought it all back to life again.

N·OR·M·A·N·D·Y — D·DAY

THE INVASION AND THE FIRST 48 DAYS OF ACTION
WITH THE 743rd TANK BATTALION IN FRANCE

People who didn't go through the war with us may not understand this pictorial history. It looks gay and light-hearted. They may say it isn't a true record because it isn't somber, grim, heroic, and tense . . the way war is supposed to be. Perhaps they're right. But after it's all over and we're back home, this is the way we'll tell about the war. We know about the terror, the grief, the violence, the hatred, the pride, and the bitterness of battle. But when we talk about the 743rd and what we did, we will laugh and speak fondly, as these drawings do. The rest is too deeply buried in us for words and pictures, though perhaps now and then it will show through in little symbols. Here is one of them:

This is the Presidential Unit Citation ribbon. We won it on the 6th of June, 1944 - D-Day - at Omaha Beach, Normandy, France. We landed 20 minutes before H-Hour, the first American tanks in the invasion, leading the beachhead assault. This little blue ribbon is a symbol of a 16 hour battle on a thin strip of sand, with a furiously fighting German army in front of us and with the waters of the English Channel in back of us, rising gradually and certainly with the tide, threatening more each minute to swallow us, drown us, and finish the invasion. Then we made the break. We punched out an exit, blasted through enemy strongpoints, and with elements of the Rangers, and the 29th and 1st Infantry Divisions, established an apron of Allied-held land from which the tedious and terrible hedgerow fighting of Normandy was developed.

This sheet shows our part in that fighting. It traces our long course. It plots the towns to be remembered. It sketches the life we led. It is a picture of the land we were in and some of the details of why we were there and what we did and what was done to us. It is a part of what is behind another simple, tiny symbol - the Normandy Campaign Battle Star.

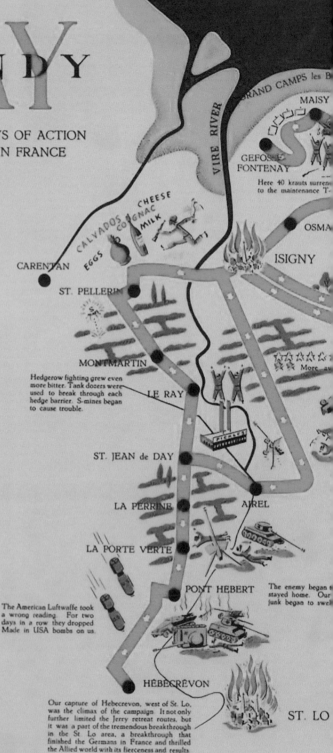

GRAND CAMPS les B...

MAISY

GEFOSSE FONTENAY

Here 40 krauts surrendered to the maintenance T-...

OSMA...

ISIGNY

VIRE RIVER

CALVADOS EGGS CIDER COGNAC CHEESE MILK

CARENTAN

ST. PELLERIN

MONTMARTIN

Hedgerow fighting grew even more bitter. Tank dozers were used to break through each hedge barrier. S-mines began to cause trouble.

LE RAY

...More aw...

ST. JEAN de DAY

LA PERRINE

AIREL

LA PORTE VERTE

PONT HEBERT

The enemy began t... stayed home. Our... junk began to swel...

The American Luftwaffe took a wrong reading. For two days in a row they dropped Made in USA bombs on us.

HEBECREVON

Our capture of Hebecrevon, west of St. Lo, was the climax of the campaign. It not only further limited the Jerry retreat routes, but it was a part of the tremendous breakthrough in the St. Lo area, a breakthrough that finished the Germans in France and thrilled the Allied world with its fierceness and results.

ST. LO

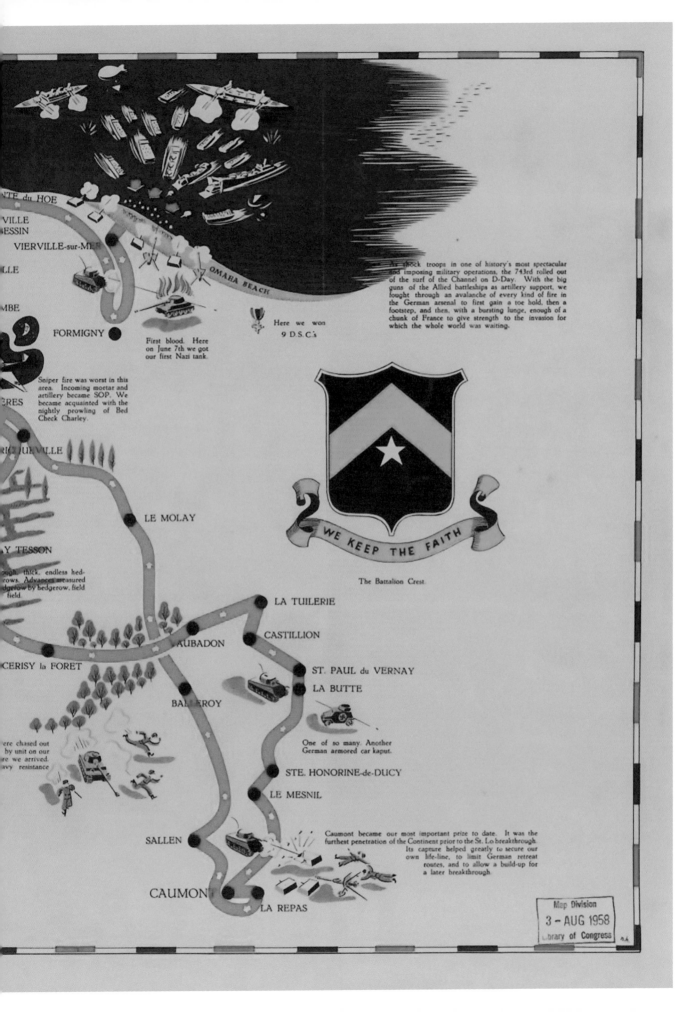

NTE du HOE

VILLE
ESSIN

VIERVILLE-sur-MER

ILLE

MBE

FORMIGNY

OMAHA BEACH

Here we won
9 D.S.C.'s

First blood. Here
on June 7th we got
our first Nazi tank.

As shock troops in one of history's most spectacular and imposing military operations, the 743rd rolled out of the surf of the Channel on D-Day. With the big guns of the Allied battleships as artillery support, we fought through an avalanche of every kind of fire in the German arsenal to first gain a toe hold, then a footstep, and then, with a bursting lunge, enough of a chunk of France to give strength to the invasion for which the whole world was waiting.

Sniper fire was worst in this
area. Incoming mortar and
artillery became SOP. We
became acquainted with the
nightly prowling of Bed
Check Charley.

ERES

RIZIUERVILLE

LE MOLAY

Y TESSON

ough, thick, endless hed-
rows. Advances measured
dgerow by hedgerow, field
field

WE KEEP THE FAITH

The Battalion Crest.

LA TUILERIE

CASTILLION

AUBADON

CERISY la FORET

ST. PAUL du VERNAY

LA BUTTE

BALLEROY

One of so many. Another
German armored car kaput.

ere chased out
by unit on our
re we arrived.
avy resistance

STE. HONORINE-de-DUCY

LE MESNIL

SALLEN

Caumont became our most important prize to date. It was the
furthest penetration of the Continent prior to the St. Lo breakthrough.
Its capture helped greatly to secure our
own life-line, to limit German retreat
routes, and to allow a build-up for
a later breakthrough.

CAUMONT

LA REPAS

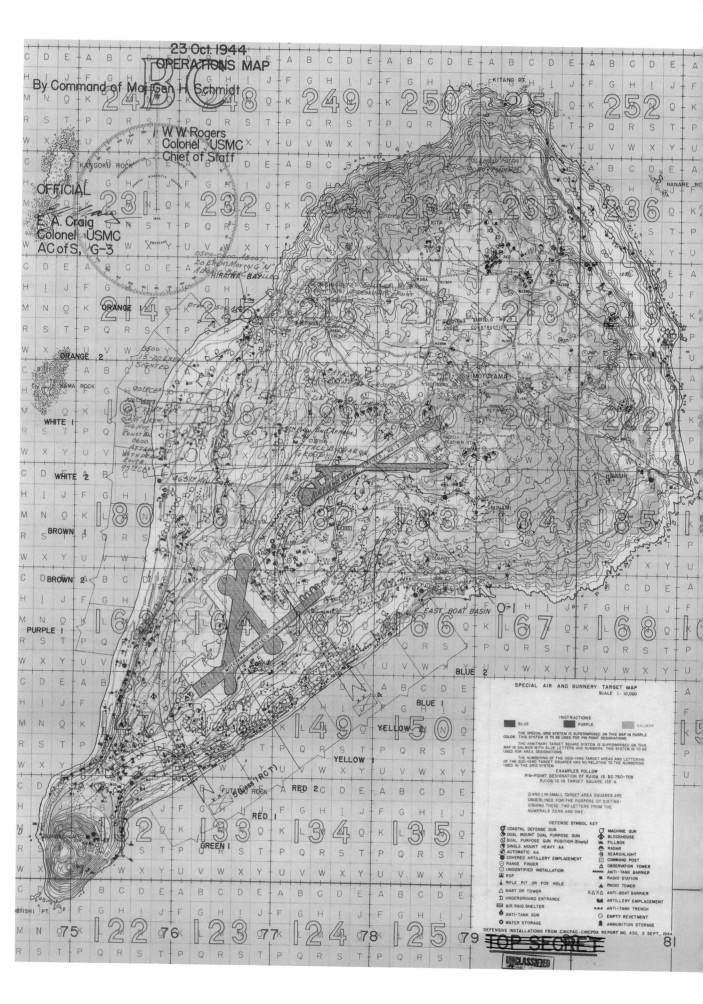

SPECIAL AIR AND GUNNERY TARGET MAP

SCALE 1 : 10,000

Battle of Iwo Jima

The map, prepared for the United States Marine Corps in autumn 1944, shows the defences on the Japanese-held island of Iwo Jima in the Volcano Islands, 750 miles south of Tokyo. Dotted with military installations and dominated by the 169-metre-high bulk of Mount Suribachi, an extinct volcano in the south of the island, Iwo Jima offered a possible staging post for American P-51 Mustang fighters which could provide escort cover to the B-29 bombers that by early 1945 had begun devastating raids on the Japanese home islands.

The job of taking the island was given to Major General Harry Schmidt's V Amphibious Corps under the overall command of a naval task force led by Admiral Raymond A Spruance. Allied intelligence indicated that Iwo Jima was only lightly defended, but in reality its Japanese commander Lieutenant General Tadamichi Kuribayashi had constructed a formidable system of bunkers connected by a network of tunnels to allow the rapid reinforcement of strongpoints under enemy attack.

For 74 long days, Iwo Jima was pounded by American B-24 Liberator bombers, and for three more days with naval gunfire, before Marines from the 4th and 5th Divisions came ashore on the southeast of the island at just before 9am on February 19. The pre-invasion bombardment of unprecedented ferocity should have decimated the defenders, but Kuribayashi's bunker system had done its work, and the Japanese emerged to inflict heavy casualties, forcing the Marines to clear each strongpoint in a grinding, methodical advance. By February 23, though, the Marines managed to reach the top of Mount Suribachi, where they raised the Stars and Stripes, providing an iconic photographic image that did wonders for American morale. Yet this early success was illusory. The soft volcanic sand of the landing beaches made it hard for the Marines to dig foxholes, and the tunnels meant that no sooner was a bunker cleared than the Japanese could send fresh troops to retake it. Heavy fighting around the airfields north of Suribachi yielded only tiny advances for the Americans, who endured a hail of fire from pillboxes, trenches and dug-in tanks. By February 24, the Marines had suffered 8,000 casualties, and Schmidt ordered a brief pause while reinforcements from the 3rd Marine Division were brought in.

When operations resumed the next day, there was little respite. Bitter fighting around Hill 382 and Turkey Knob won so little ground, at such high cost, that the area came to be nicknamed "the Meat Grinder". Gradually, the use of Sherman tanks armed with flamethrowers and close air support burned and blasted the Japanese from their strongholds. Although the Marines took huge casualties, gradually the Japanese defences were worn down. On March 8, a suicidal Japanese attack headed by General Sadasue Senda, one of Kuribayashi's deputies, cost them 800 dead and failed in its intent to punch a hole in the Marines' advancing perimeter.

From then, Japanese resistance became sporadic, if no less bitter. Even after the island was declared secure on March 16, Kuribayashi still held a final stronghold in a gorge on the island's northwest tip. It took a further ten days to clear it, with the Japanese commander, whom the Imperial Headquarters in Tokyo had promoted to full general just days before as a reward for the damage he had inflicted on the Americans, dying in a final charge near Airfield No. 2. Even then, Japanese stragglers held out in isolated positions, emerging to carry out hit-and-run attacks. Few were willing to surrender, and throughout June the US Army forces killed 1,600 of them in an extended epilogue to the campaign. The very last Japanese soldiers to give themselves up did so only in 1951.

The capture of Iwo Jima had been hugely costly for the Marines, who lost nearly 7,000 dead and 19,000 wounded (though the Japanese death toll was close to 20,000, almost 90 per cent of the original defenders). Securing it provided the much-needed platform for B-29 bombing operations, though the limited capacity of its airfields made many question whether Iwo Jima had been worth the price. The operation also yielded important lessons for the last major operation of the war, against the island of Okinawa, which began on April 1, just days after the end of that on Iwo Jima. Even so, the Americans suffered 50,000 casualties there, which, combined with the toll on Iwo Jima, heightened fears of what an invasion of the Japanese home islands would cost and helped boost the case of those who argued that the deployment of the newly developed atom bomb against Japan was the best way to end the war.

Battle for Berlin

The plan of Berlin shows the arrows of the Soviet Red Army's advance pressing from all directions into the central defence district during the final stages of the city's capture in late April 1945. By May 2, when General Helmuth Weidling, the Berlin commandant, finally surrendered, the German army controlled just a few streets of what had once been the Europe-spanning Third Reich.

The tide had turned against Germany in eastern Europe in 1942, as its forces were pushed back from Stalingrad, Kiev, Minsk and other key Soviet cities by the steamroller of Josef Stalin's increasingly confident Red Army, and then inexorably through Poland into Germany itself. By April 1945 the fighting had reached the environs of Berlin, with the more than two million men of Georgy Zhukov's 1st Belorussian Front and Konstantin Rokossovsky's 2nd Belorussian Front massed to the north and Ivan Konev's 1st Ukrainian Front advancing from the south. Facing them were roughly 800,000 German defenders made up of a rag-tag collection of regular army units, SS formations and tens of thousands of Hitler Youth and Volkssturm militia units, whose fanatical adherence to the Nazi cause had to make up for a lack of training, discipline and weaponry.

On April 16 the storm broke, beginning an apocalyptic fortnight in which over 130,000 died. Hitler's stubborn refusal to countenance surrender meant every suburb, every street, every house and in many cases every room was fought over in some of the most intense urban fighting of the war. It took Zhukov four days to storm the Seelow Heights to the east of the city, which allowed Konev to the south to gain an advantage in the race for the honours of capturing the Nazi capital. In Berlin itself increasingly frantic communications to the commanders of the German 9th and 12th Armies ordering them to relieve the capital were met with disbelief in the field, where the 9th found itself surrounded and the 12th blocked by a mass of Soviet divisions.

Directing the dwindling theatre of war from a bunker near the Reich Chancellery, Hitler fired his commander in Berlin and replaced him with Helmuth Weidling, who led the final stages of a hopeless defence. The remaining German panzers held up the Soviet advance in places, and the large government buildings of the central zone were hard for the Red Army to clear except through costly hand-to-hand fighting. By April 27, the outer suburbs had fallen, and two days later the Soviets pushed across the Moltke Bridge over the River Spree and began attacking the Interior Ministry. Nearby, their prime target was the Reichstag (the German parliament building), which the Soviet leader Josef Stalin wanted to capture in time for the May Day celebrations. Finally, at some point on April 29 or 30, the Soviet Red Flag was hoisted on top of the Reichstag, but even then it took one or two more days to flush out the last defenders.

Among the final positions to fall was a defensive Flak Tower in the Tiergarten (zoological gardens), and there was chaos as escaped lions, jackals and monkeys ran around the zoo. By now it was clear that no rescue was coming and on the evening of April 30 Hitler and his wife killed themselves, followed the next day by the propaganda minister Josef Goebbels and his wife. In his last testament Hitler handed over charge of the Reich to Admiral Karl Dönitz, who controlled a sliver of territory near Hamburg in Germany's northwest, but there was really nothing worthwhile left to command. Final desperate attempts to break out through the Soviet lines consumed the last organised military units, and most who tried it died or were captured.

Finally, on May 2, the Soviets captured the Reich Chancellery, which put them very close to the German command bunker. At 6am, having negotiated all night, Weidling capitulated and ordered the remaining defenders to surrender. Virtually the last large unit to lay down their arms were the 350 defenders of the Zoo Flak Tower, and it took until late in the afternoon for word to reach isolated hold-outs. Many troops surrendered, some tried to blend in with the civilian population or escape past the Red Army lines, but by the end of the operation the Soviets claimed to have taken 480,000 prisoners (though it had cost them over 350,000 dead and wounded and the loss of about 2,000 tanks). The Battle for Berlin was over, and with it the nightmare of the Third Reich was consigned to history.

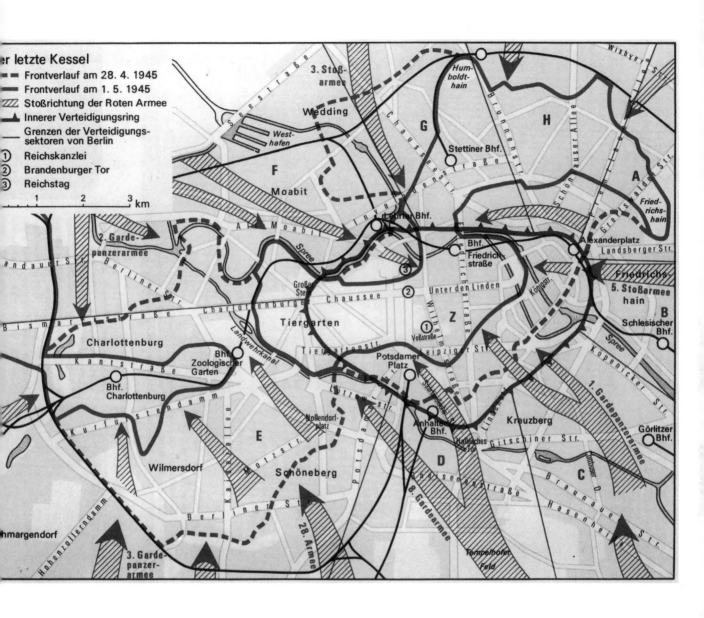

Der letzte Kessel

- ▬ ▬ Frontverlauf am 28. 4. 1945
- ▬▬▬ Frontverlauf am 1. 5. 1945
- ▨ Stoßrichtung der Roten Armee
- ◄ Innerer Verteidigungsring
- ── Grenzen der Verteidigungs-
  sektoren von Berlin
- ① Reichskanzlei
- ② Brandenburger Tor
- ③ Reichstag

0 1 2 3 km

3. Stoß-
armee

Wedding

Humboldt-
hain

West-
hafen

Stettiner Bhf.

G

H

Wisbyer Str.

A

Friedrichs-
hain

F

Moabit

2. Garde-
panzerarmee

Alt Moabit

Spree

Lehrter Bhf.

Bhf.
Friedrich-
straße

Alexanderplatz

Landsberger Str.

Berliner Str.

Charlottenburger

Chaussee

Großer
Stern

Tiergarten

③

Unter den Linden

Z

Königstr.

Friedrichs-
hain

5. Stoßarmee

Bismar straße

②

B

Schlesischer
Bhf.

Charlottenburg

Kantstraße

Bhf.
Zoologischer
Garten

Landwehrkanal

Tiergartenstr.

①

Voßstraße

Leipziger Str.

Spree

Köpenicker Str.

1. Gardepanzerarmee

Bhf.
Charlottenburg

Kurfürstendamm

Potsdamer
Platz

Lützowstr.

Nollendorf-
platz

E

Motzstr.

Schöneberg

Anhalter
Bhf.

Hallesches
Tor

Kreuzberg

Görlitzer
Bhf.

Gitschiner Str.

D

Braunauer Str.

C

Wilmersdorf

Berliner Str.

Potsdamer

28. Armee

8. Gardearmee

Großbeerenstraße

Hasenheide

Schmargendorf

Hohenzollerndamm

3. Garde-
panzer-
armee

Tempelhofer
Feld

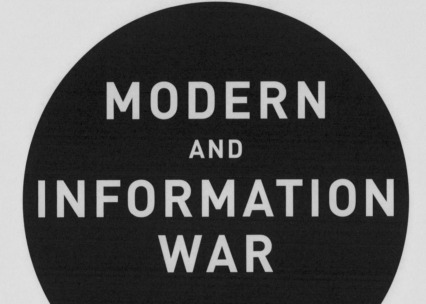

MODERN
AND
INFORMATION
WAR

1950–PRESENT

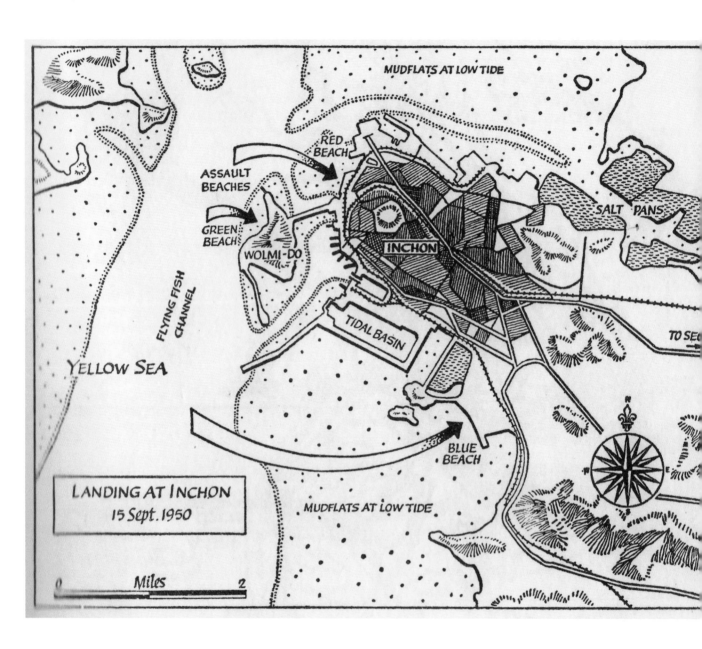

MUDFLATS AT LOW TIDE

RED
BEACH

ASSAULT
BEACHES

GREEN
BEACH

WOLMI·DO

SALT PANS

INCHON

FLYING FISH
CHANNEL

YELLOW SEA

TIDAL BASIN

TO SEO

BLUE
BEACH

LANDING AT INCHON
15 Sept. 1950

MUDFLATS AT LOW TIDE

0   Miles   2

The Inchon Landings

In 1950, the Cold War turned hot and by September of that year the United States and its allies faced a crisis, as North Korean forces threatened to overrun the entire Korean Peninsula and unite it under a communist regime, so becoming the first domino to topple in what might then be a complete collapse of pro-western regimes in the region. The map from General Matthew B Ridgway's *The War in Korea* shows the landing of UN forces (principally composed of American troops) at Inchon halfway up Korea's western coast, which unexpectedly turned the tide.

As commander of the US 8th Army there from December 1950, Ridgway understood well the roots of the Korean conflict. The country, which had been occupied by Japan since 1910, fell apart into a communist-aligned north and a pro-western south following the Japanese defeat in 1945. Protracted skirmishing between the two sides exploded into a full-scale invasion of the south, when North Korean forces crossed the 38th parallel on June 25, 1950. The United Nations Security Council rapidly passed resolutions condemning the invasion and authorising military force to reverse it. Under the auspices of these, the US president Harry S Truman sanctioned the dispatch of US troops to contain the North Koreans. These formed the main bulk of a 140,000-strong UN force which also included contingents from Britain, Australia, Canada, New Zealand and 11 other nations. This combined force was, however, steadily pushed back and by August 4 was penned into a 150-mile defensive perimeter around the southeastern port of Pusan. In the face of massive attacks by the NKPA (North Korean People's Army), it looked as though that too might fall, and with it Korea.

General Douglas MacArthur, the commander-in-chief of the UN forces, had other ideas. He persuaded Truman to authorise an audacious plan. Operation Chromite, an amphibious landing at Inchon, 110 miles behind NKPA lines, would force the North Koreans to pull back from Pusan, which would allow the UN forces penned there to advance northwards. Significant cuts to the US Marines since the Second World War, which had reduced their numbers to around 27,000 and scrapped most of their landing craft, made mounting the operation a severe logistical challenge, while Inchon's topography with two easily defensible and heavily mined approach channels (Flying Fish and Eastern), rapid currents and a tiny harbour meant MacArthur had to overcome considerable

scepticism such as that of Admiral James H Doyle, who was tasked with landing the marines and who remarked "The best I can say is that Inchon is not possible."

The first elements of the 13,000-strong US X Corps landed on Green Beach on Wolmi-Do island at 6.30am on September 15. They took the island within five hours at the cost of just 14 casualties (while killing 200 of the NKPA defenders). Shelling and bombing from the US navy and airforce suppressed any possible North Korean counterstrike, while a second assault force landed in the late afternoon at Red Beach on the mainland. The Marines were forced to climb a sheer seawall, some of them literally hurling their comrades over the top in a bid to secure a foothold. Having driven off the NKPA defenders, they opened the causeway leading to Wolmi-Do, which allowed the Green Beach contingent's tanks to cross over and complete the clearing of Inchon. Only at the third landing point, at Blue Beach to the south, was there significant North Korean resistance, but by September 17 US forces had pushed six miles out of Inchon, and reinforcements from the US 7th Infantry were being landed to expand the beachhead.

The North Korean forces at Pusan were, as MacArthur had hoped, forced to pull back, beginning a retreat which only ended when UN troops crossed the Yalu river in Korea's far north, prompting a massive Chinese intervention to save Kim Il Sung's North Korean government. The war, then, being far from over by Christmas, as the Americans had hoped after MacArthur's Inchon triumph, by July, they found themselves pushed back close to the 38th parallel. MacArthur, whom President Truman blamed for invading the north and prolonging the war, had by then been replaced by Ridgway, who presided over the next two years of bloody but inconclusive fighting, during which the lines of control barely moved. Only on July 27, 1953, was a truce finally signed at Panmunjom which established a demilitarised zone between the two sides along the 38th parallel, though a final peace settlement was never signed. Inchon remains one of the most daring and successful amphibious operations in military history but in the end, despite the roughly 750,000 soldiers and two million civilians who died during the Korean War, the division between the two Koreas at its end lay more or less where it had been before it began.

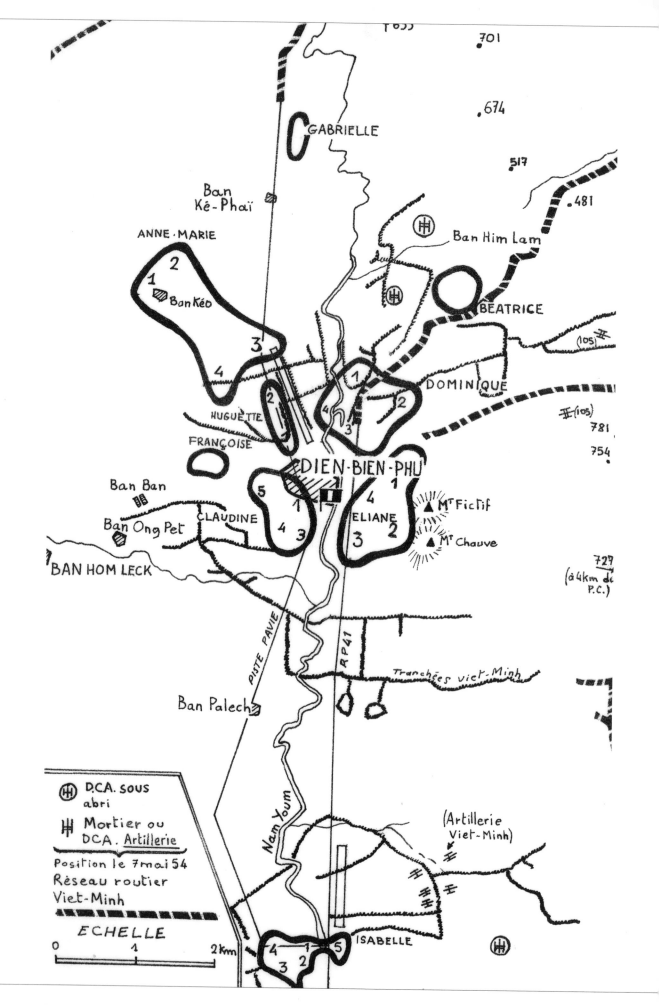

Dien Bien Phu

The lines of attack converging on the imaginatively named bastions around the French-held airstrip at Dien Bien Phu mark one of France's worst modern military disasters. The hand-drawn map shows the final stages in the assault by the forces of the Vietnamese communist revolutionaries against what had been assumed to be an impregnable position.

France had struggled to regain full control of its colonial possessions in Indochina after their occupation by Japan during the Second World War, and an uprising led by the Soviet- and Chinese-trained communist leader Ho Chi Minh grew more intense from 1950, when supply routes opened up from Laos and Beijing began more active training and supply of his Viet Minh guerrillas. As arms seeped over the border from Laos and Viet Minh activity increased, General Henri Navarre, the French military commander in Vietnam, grew frustrated. It had proved impossible to entice the Viet Minh commander, General Vo Nguyen Giap, into a large-scale engagement in which the French superiority in numbers and weaponry would have given them an advantage. Instead, hit-and-run attacks and ambushes were steadily undermining the colonial power's authority.

To counter this, Navarre adopted the *hérisson* ("hedgehog") strategy, by which he would establish strongly fortified bases astride the Viet Minh supply lines, forcing them to assault it, whereupon the French air and artillery support would cut them to pieces. The first location chosen was at Dien Bien Phu, ten miles from the Laotian border, where a pre-existing airstrip would be reinforced with nine bastions (each given a female name in alphabetical order from Anne-Marie to Huguette and each containing several strongpoints) to shield the airstrip and provide a cordon the Viet Minh would not be able to penetrate.

On November 20, 1953, Operation Castor began, in which the French flew in around 10,000 troops to the area and then, under the command of Colonel Christian de Castries, they set about reinforcing the airstrip and building the bastions. Far from being lured into a trap, however, General Giap realised at once that Castries had walked into one himself. Giap later characterised the position at Dien Bien Phu as a "rice bowl" in which the French were stuck in the bottom, while the Viet Minh occupied all the surrounding high points. He rapidly moved additional Viet Minh divisions into the area, until he had five there, totalling 50,000 men, significantly outnumbering the French.

De Castries' and Navarre's fatal mistake, however, was in assuming that the Viet Minh did not possess heavy artillery and certainly not anti-aircraft guns. It turned out that the Chinese had supplied the Viet Minh with these (including some American howitzers captured during the Korean War). As a result, Giap was able to interdict the airfield, preventing French planes from landing and gradually starving de Castries of supplies. His guns were also able to pound the bastions from camouflaged positions, which made the job of holding the French perimeter harder, while the construction of a system of trenches brought his troops ever closer to the French positions.

Beatrice, to the northeast of the airstrip, was the first to fall after a Viet Minh assault on March 13, 1954, after its defences were suppressed by the Vietnamese 75mm artillery. Although the Viet Minh lost almost 2,000 dead and wounded, it proved that Giap's strategy could succeed. Two days later Gabrielle fell to a similar attack, followed by Anne-Marie which was surrendered by the Tai troops, members of a Vietnamese ethnic minority who had been defending it.

After a two-week lull the Viet Minh began their final assaults on the central bastions (Huguette, Claudine, Dominique and Eliane). By May 1 parts of all of these had fallen, which left only Eliane 1 and 2, Dominque 3, and Huguette 5, as well as the central command bunker in French hands. On May 7 the final mass assault came, as 25,000 Viet Minh rushed the remaining 3,000 French defenders. De Castries promised his superiors in Hanoi that "We will fight to the finish," but by late evening they were overwhelmed. A few French troops managed to break out, and a handful reached Laos, but de Castries was forced to surrender, leaving 11,700 of his men as prisoners.

The blow to French morale was profound. Peace talks opened at Geneva the next day, leading to an agreement in July which partitioned Vietnam into two zones along the 17th parallel, the northern one of which would be a communist state led by Ho Chi Minh. From there, eventually, a second insurgency would be nurtured which sparked a new war and ultimately led to the unification of the whole country under communist rule in 1975. Navarre's hedgehog had proved far more damaging to its makers than to the independence movement it was intended to crush.

Six-Day War

Israeli troops are already positioned east of Jordan and in occupation of Jerusalem as they advance in the northeast on the Golan Heights border with Syria in this map of the final stages of the Six-Day War in June 1967.

During that summer, tensions between Israel and its Arab neighbours had risen to boiling point. Relations between them had always been difficult since the 1948 Independence War which had squashed hopes of an independent Palestinian state and resulted in hundreds of thousands of Palestinian refugees being crowded into camps in Syria, Lebanon, Gaza and Jordan. Attacks by Palestinian guerrillas against Israeli border positions, skirmishes between the Israeli and Syrian air forces and a warning from Soviet intelligence led the Egyptian president Gamal Abdel Nasser to become convinced that the Israelis would retaliate. He mobilised Egyptian forces stationed in the Sinai Desert, expelled the UN monitoring force there, and on May 22 closed the Straits of Tiran to Israeli shipping, effectively blockading Israel's Red Sea port of Eilat.

As a small nation surrounded by hostile powers, the Israelis felt they could not stand by and wait for a blow to strike: within 48 hours Prime Minister Levi Eshkol had ordered the mobilisation of 250,000 reservists. As diplomacy stuttered along and Jordan, on May 30, agreed to join in any Egyptian military action against Israel, the Israeli high command prepared an audacious plan. It depended on rapid, surgical strikes to knock out Egypt's combat potential and then deal with Jordan, while holding the Syrians at bay until the two other Arab nations had been defeated. At 7.40am on June 5, the Israeli air force struck Egyptian positions in the Sinai without warning. Extensive reconnaissance had yielded results, and much of the Egyptian air force was destroyed, with the Jordanian and Syrian air forces suffering the same fate, their Soviet Mig-21s more than outclassed by the Israeli French-supplied Mirage III fighter jets.

Meanwhile, Israeli tanks raced across the Sinai, rushing to secure the Suez Canal and then fanning out south and west to take the whole peninsula. Retreating Egyptian units were pummelled by Israeli artillery and jets, many abandoning their equipment and, with their vehicles destroyed, forced to walk 125 miles back to the borders of Egypt proper. Israeli Sherman, Patton and Centurion tanks decimated their Egyptian rivals, and within two days Nasser's army and air force had been comprehensively defeated. By then,

the Israeli Defense Forces (IDF) had moved against Jordan, which had ignored warnings that Israel would hold back from attacking if King Hussein remained neutral. On the afternoon of June 5, IDF units began an enveloping manoeuvre around Jerusalem, the east of which, including the Old City, had not been allocated to Israel in the 1948 armistice. Despite dogged resistance in intense street-fighting, the Jordanians could not hold back the three Israeli brigades deployed against them, and although the Israeli commander Moshe Dayan paused before risking the destruction entering the Old City would cause, by the evening of June 7 both it and virtually the entire West Bank were in Israeli hands.

It was now the turn of Syria to face the full fury of the IDF. There had been sporadic shelling by the Syrian army against Israeli positions near the Golan Heights plus a few skirmishes, but on June 9 with forces released from the successful operations in the Sinai and West Bank, the Israelis attacked in force. Massive aerial bombardments knocked out Syrian air defences and artillery batteries, while the IDF's infantry pushed forward into the Golan, reaching the central plateau by the end of the day. With its resistance broken and Syrian forces streaming back towards Damascus in disarray, Hafez al-Assad, then the Syrian regime's defence minister, signed a ceasefire on June 10, joining Egypt and Jordan in accepting a UN-brokered peace that left Israel in possession of the Sinai, the Gaza Strip, East Jerusalem, the West Bank and the Golan Heights.

Israel's victory was absolute. It had proved that professional forces with modern armour, if well led and with clear tactical and strategic goals, could defeat apparently superior forces if they prevented those forces from coalescing (a lesson successful generals from Alexander the Great to Napoleon had taught). In the longer term, however, Israel's massive extension of its borders proved a mixed blessing. Its Arab neighbours signed a declaration at Khartoum in September pledging that there would be "no peace, no recognition and no negotiations with Israel". They too had learnt that planning and surprise were key to winning a war in the region, so that when they embarked on a joint attack on Israel in October 1973 (this time involving Lebanon), the outcome, though the war ended in a far less resounding Israeli victory, was a much closer-run affair.

מלחמת ששת הימים
קרבות רמת הגולן
9-10 ביוני 1967

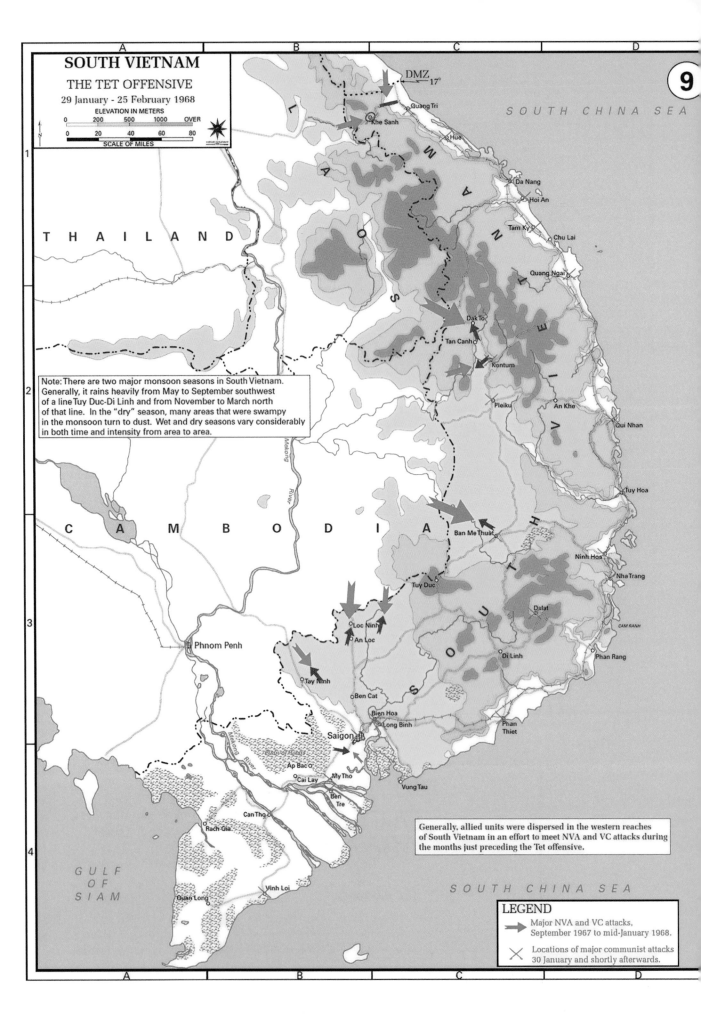

SOUTH VIETNAM
THE TET OFFENSIVE
29 January - 25 February 1968

ELEVATION IN METERS

| 0 | 200 | 500 | 1000 | OVER |

| 0 | 20 | 40 | 60 | 80 |

SCALE OF MILES

SOUTH CHINA SEA

DMZ 17°

Quang Tri

Khe Sanh

Hue

Da Nang

Hoi An

Tam Ky

Chu Lai

Quang Ngai

THAILAND

LAOS

Dak To

Tan Canh

Kontum

Pleiku

An Khe

Qui Nhon

Note: There are two major monsoon seasons in South Vietnam.
Generally, it rains heavily from May to September southwest
of a line Tuy Duc-Di Linh and from November to March north
of that line. In the "dry" season, many areas that were swampy
in the monsoon turn to dust. Wet and dry seasons vary considerably
in both time and intensity from area to area.

CAMBODIA

Mekong River

Ban Me Thuat

Tuy Hoa

Ninh Hos

Nha Trang

SOUTH

Tuy Duc

Dalat

CAM RANH

Phan Rang

Loc Ninh

An Loc

Di Linh

Phnom Penh

Tay Ninh

Ben Cat

Bien Hoa

Long Binh

Phan Thiet

Saigon

Binh of Reeds

Ap Bac

Cai Lay

My Tho

Mekong River

Ben Tre

Vung Tau

Can Tho

Rach Gia

Generally, allied units were dispersed in the western reaches
of South Vietnam in an effort to meet NVA and VC attacks during
the months just preceding the Tet offensive.

GULF
OF
SIAM

SOUTH CHINA SEA

Quan Long

Vinh Loi

LEGEND

→ Major NVA and VC attacks,
September 1967 to mid-January 1968.

✕ Locations of major communist attacks
30 January and shortly afterwards.

The Tet Offensive

Sometimes, a defeat ends in victory and a war is won in the homeland of an army's adversary, far from the battlefield. The Tet Offensive, an attack by North Vietnamese forces on over 100 urban centres in South Vietnam, was one such battle, shown on this map compiled by the United States Military Academy at West Point, in New York State.

The defeat of the French at Dien Bien Phu in 1954 (see page 209) and the subsequent partition of Vietnam into a communist North and Western-aligned South had not brought peace. Instead, a chronic low-level war rumbled on, aggravated by the inflammatory and oppressive antics of the US-backed president Ngo Dinh Diem (who was finally deposed in 1963). Step by step the Americans were sucked into greater involvement, first with the dispatch of military advisers and then, after a North Vietnamese attack on a US naval vessel in the Gulf of Tonkin, with combat troops. By 1968, there were almost 550,000 troops stationed there but despite their overwhelming superiority in firepower, the Americans and their South Vietnamese allies could not break a stalemate in which, no matter the tactical losses suffered by General Vo Nguyen Giap's North Vietnamese Army (NVA) and their southern allies, the Viet Cong, the insurgents would re-emerge hydra-like in another province.

Giap and his political master Ho Chi Minh were frustrated too and in early 1968 resolved on a change of tactic. They loudly signalled an offensive at Khe Sanh, close to the Laotian border, beginning on January 21 with a huge artillery bombardment of the US Marine garrison there. The attack was a ruse, designed to pull US troops away from the real North Vietnamese targets. Convinced that a show of massive force would unleash a popular revolution in South Vietnam, Giap sent out 80,000 NVA and Viet Cong troops against more than 100 towns and cities, including 33 of the 34 provincial capitals. They struck on the night of January 30–31, when the traditional Lunar New Year holiday left the defenders off-guard. In Saigon, the North Vietnamese managed to enter the US embassy compound, and in the old royal capital of Huế they seized virtually the entire city and held it for nearly three weeks of intense conflict that left around 670 of the defenders dead (including more than 200 Americans) and over 5,000 North Vietnamese casualties.

Elsewhere the Tet Offensive gained little traction and by the second week in February the North Vietnamese had been largely driven out. On the face of it, Giap's transition from guerrilla warfare to all-out assaults had been a failure: there had been no rising in favour of the communists and tens of thousands of his troops had been killed. Yet in the United States, things were perceived very differently. Images of the fighting in Huế and Saigon and the request soon after the offensive by the US army commander in Vietnam, General William Westmoreland, for 200,000 more troops contributed to a feeling that South Vietnam was only being propped up by ever-greater sacrifices of American blood and money. Whereas in 1965 only about one in seven Americans opposed their country's involvement in Vietnam, soon after the Tet Offensive the figure rose to become a majority. Previously supportive journalists became openly critical of government policy and antiwar demonstrations began to break out on university campuses.

In March, President Lyndon B Johnson recalled Westmoreland, and his replacement General Creighton Abrams began a policy of "Vietnamisation" that slowly reduced the number of US troops there to reach a level of just 27,000 by the end of 1972. Hopes that the South Vietnamese military could step in and hold the line against the North Vietnamese proved wildly overoptimistic. Only the fear that a full-scale attack would invite renewed American intervention held the communist forces back, but in spring 1975 a final NVA offensive swept through the country's central provinces, and on April 30 they entered the South Vietnamese capital Saigon.

The images of the final US Marines who had guarded the embassy being evacuated in a chaotic scramble by helicopter seared into the American political imagination and scarred the country's foreign policy for decades. The seeds of that final humiliating defeat had been sown in the apparent victory of the Tet Offensive.

Operation Desert Storm

The map of Operation Desert Storm shows arcs of blue arrows punching into Iraq, marking one of the most effective battlefield envelopments of modern times and the first major conflict of the post-Cold War era, when it had looked for a time as though the United States's dominant military position following the implosion of the Soviet Union might lead to a period of international peace.

The victory and the hopes that accompanied it were short-lived. Yet at first the international community had reacted decisively to the invasion of Kuwait on August 2, 1990, by the Iraqi dictator Saddam Hussein, who claimed it as Iraq's "19th Province". Within hours, the US president George Bush had ordered the largest build-up of American forces since the Vietnam War, dispatching the US 82nd Airborne Division with 300 aircraft and adding to them until by September there were 200,000 US service personnel in Saudi Arabia. He also assembled an international coalition that eventually amounted to 34 countries, and helped engineer UN Security Council Resolution 678, which authorised the use of force if the Iraqis did not withdraw by January 15.

Saddam refused to do so and on January 16, Bush unleashed a ferocious air campaign against Iraq. Tomahawk cruise missiles saw action for the first time as the United States deployed a range of hi-tech weapons, sophisticated anti-missile systems, stealth bombers and drones that began the age of "smart" warfare. The coalition air campaign included more than 100,000 sorties over 43 days, pulverising Iraq's air campaigns, its Scud missile sites (which it had used to strike at Israel, hoping to widen the conflict) and its military infrastructure. By the time the ground campaign began in the early hours of February 24, the ability of the Iraqi army to defend itself had been seriously degraded. The Iraqis also faced around 750,000 coalition troops (including 540,000 from the United States alone, with smaller contingents from the United Kingdom, France, Germany, Japan, Egypt and Saudi Arabia).

The US commander Norman Schwarzkopf designed an attack with three nesting encirclements, one aimed at Kuwait City, a second one to the west to strike the Iraqi flanks and a third one far in the desert to loop north and cut off the Iraqi forces. Within a day the first advance had reached halfway to Kuwait City, and in the west the Iraqi army had simply dissolved, with whole units deserting.

By the third day of the attack, US M1A1 Abrams tanks engaged the Iraqi Republican Guard, supposedly the elite units of Saddam's army, in the largest tank battle in history. It turned out to be a duck shoot; at one engagement at Medina Ridge, the 1st Armored Division destroyed over 300 enemy tanks and armoured vehicles, for the loss of a handful of its own. All that was left to the Iraqis was vengeance as they set light to over 700 Kuwaiti oil wells, creating a pall of thick smoke over the road from Kuwait to Basra on which US aircraft bombed the fleeing Iraqi forces relentlessly, giving it the nickname "the Highway of Death".

The United States forces had suffered fewer than 150 combat deaths, as against the Iraqi death toll of over 20,000 in one of the most unequal military contests in history. The total destruction of the Iraqi army was only averted by President Bush's decision to declare a ceasefire on February 28, after precisely 100 hours. Kuwait had been liberated, though Saddam still remained in power until a second Iraq War in 2003, fought over US claims that he had developed weapons of mass destruction, finally unseated him. The advanced technology deployed by the United States in Operation Desert Storm raised the prospect that wars might one day be won by purely technological means with drone pilots in air force bases thousands of miles from the conflict replacing "boots on the ground". That turned out to be as much of a mirage as the idea that the United States's involvement in Iraq could end in 100 hours and with a few hundred casualties. Instead, after Saddam's deposition, the Americans became entangled in an occupation and counterinsurgency war that lasted a decade and destabilised the whole region, with nearly 4,500 US military deaths and around 25,000 insurgents and hundreds of thousands of civilians meeting violent ends. Operation Desert Storm had demonstrated how wars could be won swiftly and at low cost (for the victor), but it showed nothing of the price of peace.

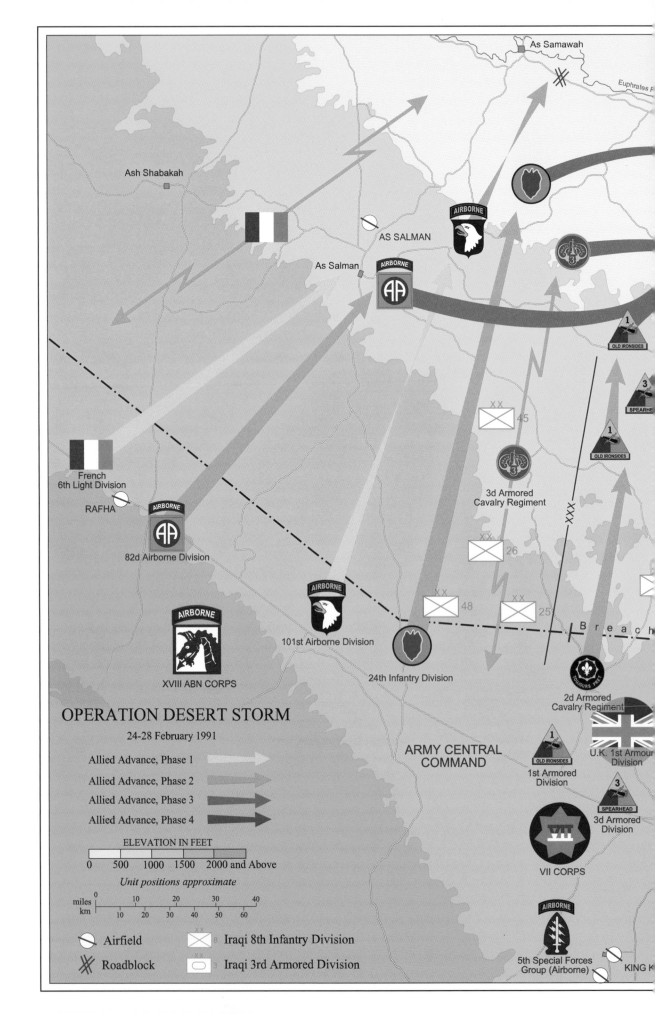

As Samawah

Euphrates ...

Ash Shabakah

AS SALMAN

As Salman

AIRBORNE
AA

AIRBORNE

AIRBORNE
AA

French
6th Light Division

RAFHA

82d Airborne Division

AIRBORNE

101st Airborne Division

AIRBORNE

XVIII ABN CORPS

24th Infantry Division

XX 45

3d Armored
Cavalry Regiment

XX 26

XX 48

XX 25

B r e a c h

1
OLD IRONSIDES

3
SPEARH...

1
OLD IRONSIDES

2d Armored
Cavalry Regiment

1
OLD IRONSIDES

1st Armored
Division

U.K. 1st Armour...
Division

3
SPEARHEAD

3d Armored
Division

VII

VII CORPS

AIRBORNE

5th Special Forces
Group (Airborne)

KING K...

ARMY CENTRAL
COMMAND

OPERATION DESERT STORM

24-28 February 1991

Allied Advance, Phase 1 ➤

Allied Advance, Phase 2 ➤

Allied Advance, Phase 3 ➤

Allied Advance, Phase 4 ➤

ELEVATION IN FEET

| 0 | 500 | 1000 | 1500 | 2000 and Above |

Unit positions approximate

miles 0 10 20 30 40
km   10 20 30 40 50 60

⊘ Airfield

※ Roadblock

XX
8 Iraqi 8th Infantry Division

XX
3 Iraqi 3rd Armored Division

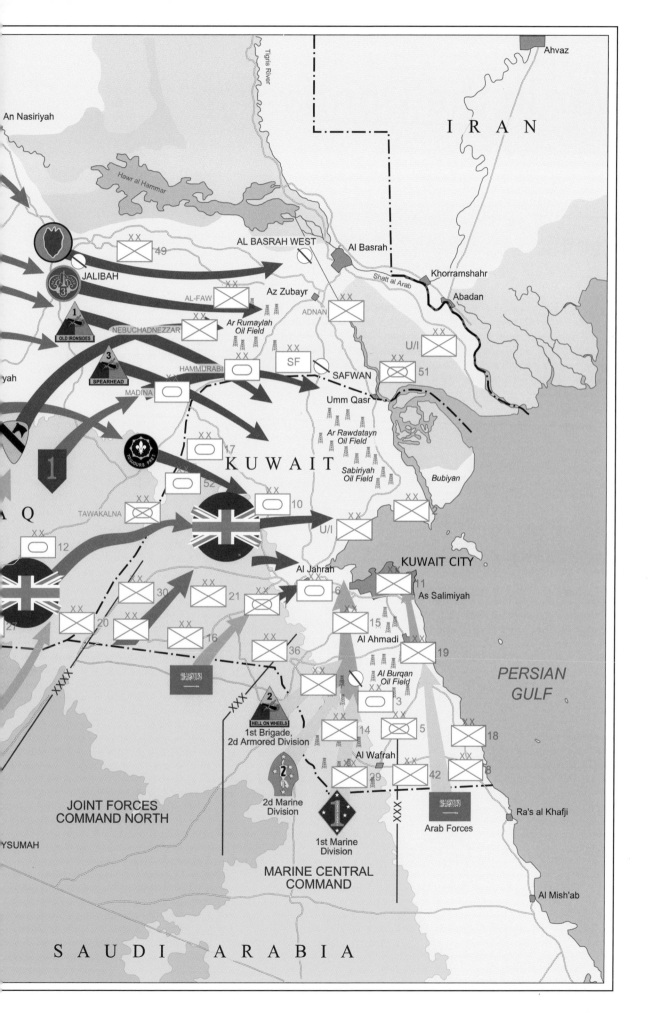

War in the Donbas

Modern wars occur at all levels of scale and intensity, the line between war and peace ever more blurred as chronic low-level violence merges with full-scale armed conflict, involving forces from local militias and proxy combatants to formally constituted armies. The map, issued by the Ministry of Defence of Ukraine in July 2015, shows the lines in one such war, in the country's eastern industrialised Donbas region, where Russian-backed separatists launched an uprising in 2014.

Russian nationalists had long sought to suck the independent nations which had arisen from the break-up of the Soviet Union in 1991 back into Moscow's orbit. Ukraine, as the most populous of these and with almost a third of its people having Russian as their mother tongue, was a particular target of this revanchist nostalgia. Many Ukrainians, however, looked westwards, aspiring to membership of the European Union, and when the country's pro-Russian president Viktor Yanukovych abrogated a proposed EU–Ukraine Association Agreement, their anger exploded into the Euromaidan Revolution, which led to Yanukovych fleeing the country in February 2014.

Russia's president Vladimir Putin, who had never made any secret of his ambition to bind Ukraine more closely to Moscow, responded angrily. Within days mysterious militia units operating without insignia began occupying government buildings in Crimea, a region to which Russia laid especial claim (maintaining that Nikita Khrushchev had added it to Ukraine as a mere administrative convenience). On March 1, 2014 all pretence was dropped as official Russian military units moved into Crimea, and by the end of the month, to international condemnation, Russia had annexed the peninsula and held a referendum of dubious legality to affirm its control.

Soon after, pro-Russian protests erupted in the Donetsk and Luhansk oblasts, areas which Russian nationalists claimed to be part of *Novorossiya*, a region which encompassed much of southern Ukraine and which formed part of the industrial heartland of the country. Militias similar to those which had formed the spearhead of Moscow's Crimean annexation began occupying government facilities in cities such as Donetsk, Luhansk and Sloviansk. There were growing suspicions that these "little green men", as they were called by both Russian and Ukrainian reporters, were in many cases actually serving Russian army personnel "on leave" from their posts. On April 15, the government of Ukraine launched an "anti-terrorist operation" (ATO) to regain control of a region which was rapidly slipping from its grasp, but a lack of preparedness and the ambiguities of a war in which it was not entirely clear who the enemy was meant that progress was initially very slow.

By August, however, despite injections of Russian military supplies, the separatists had been driven back, and the cities of Donetsk and Luhansk looked close to recapture by the Ukrainian army, which had also taken back the key railway junction at Debal'tseve. Then, on August 23, regular Russian army formations began crossing the frontier into Ukraine, and Russian artillery commenced shelling Ukrainian government positions from across the border. Unable to contain this new onslaught and after thousands of Ukrainian troops were trapped in a pocket near Ilovais'k, the Ukrainians fell back, ceding almost all of their gains from the previous month's combat.

Although a ceasefire agreed in the Belarusian capital of Minsk on September 5 brought a temporary end to the fighting and demarcated a line between the two sides, it was only ever partial. Behind its shelter and with backing from Moscow, the separatists constituted themselves as the Luhansk and Donetsk People's Republics (the LPR and DPR), bodies which were not internationally recognised and which were clearly under the thumb of Russia. The next seven years were punctuated by almost thirty further ceasefires, as localised fighting flared up and both sides manoeuvred to improve their positions. The opposing forces settled down into systems of trenches and fortified positions which made it seem likely that Donbas would turn into the sort of "frozen conflict" that had emerged in other regions of Russia's frontier with the post-Soviet world: in Georgia and Moldova, where Moscow's tactic of judicious intervention, support of separatists and undermining of any government which made overtures to the West created a landscape of chronic instability.

In war, however, if there is one guiding principle for strategists it is to expect the unexpected, and after months of increasingly bellicose statements, on February 24, 2022, Vladimir Putin ordered a full-scale invasion of Ukraine, with the apparent aims of toppling the Ukrainian government, installing one more favourable to Moscow, and possibly annexing further regions of the country. What had seemed set to be a protracted frozen conflict, gnawing slowly away at Ukraine's integrity, was now suddenly a very hot one and the largest war on the European continent since the end of the Second World War.

▶

THE SITUATION IN THE EASTERN REGIONS OF UKRAINE

23 July 2015 (00:00)

UKRAINE

KHARKIV OBLAST

DNIPROPETROVSK OBLAST

ZAPORIZHIA OBLAST

DONETSK OBLAST

LUHANSK OBLAST

Tanushivka
Biloluts'k
Nov
Bilokurakyne
Svatove
Star
Kreminna
Sieverodonetsk
Lysychansk
Tr'okhizb
Krasnyi Lyman
Yampil'
Siversk
Hirs'ke
Slov'
Donets'kyi
Sloviansk
Popasna
Pervomais'k
Kramatorsk
Kalynove
Oleksandrivka
Artemivs'k
Stakhan
Druzhkivka
Troits'ke
Svitlodars'k
Alch
Kostyantynivka
Pere
Dobropillia
Dzerzhyns'k
Vuhlehirs'k
Debal'tseve
Horlivka
Panteleimonivka
DNIPROPETROVSK OBLAST
Krasnoarmiisk
Avdiivka
Kirovs'ke
K
Yasynuvata
Mi
Pisky
Khartsyz'k
Shakhtars'k
Snizhne
Krasnohorivka
Makiivka
Ilovais'k
Savur-Mohyla
M
Kurakhove
Donetsk
Velyka Novosilka
Maryinka
Amvrosiivka
Uspe
Dokuchajevs'k
Starobesheve
Shramko
Novotroits'ke
Marfi
Starohnativka
Volnovakha
Hranitne
Telmanove
Chermalyk
Volodarske
Krasnoarmiis'ke
Maksimov
Talakivka
Mariupol
Novoazovsk
Shyrokyne
Manhush

Prosyane

Milove

odsk

Voloshino

Krasna
Talivka

okyi

anytsia
hanska

Derkul
Elan'

nansk

● Novosvitlivka

Izvaryne

Krasnodon

Kamensk-
Shakhtinsky

Sverdlovsk

ky

Chervonopartyzansk

Gukovo

Dovzhansky

Novoshakhtinsk

RUSSIA

Rostov-on-Don

Control over settlements:

 Under control of Ukraine

Positions of Ukrainian military

 Existing

 Combat's location

 Territory of the pro-Russian militants shelling

 The direction of attacks of Ukrainian troops

 Pro-Russian militants attacks

The border

 Border areas under the control of Ukraine

 Border areas not under control of Ukraine

 Humanitarian corridors through ceasefire demarcation line

Main check-points on Ukraine-Russia border

 Working

 Controlled by pro-Russian militants

 Seven task forces (ships and coast guard motorboats) are continuing to guard the Azov Sea to prevent the penetration of sabotage and intelligence groups on the coast of Donetsk and Zaporizhia oblasts, and to guard the raids of the Mariupol and Berdyansk ports

 The location of military units of the Russian Federation

 Boeing 777 crash site July 17, 2014

 **Ministry of Defense of Ukraine**

http:www.mil.gov.ua

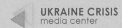 UKRAINE CRISIS media center

The Future of War

At the dawn of warfare, the maximum range at which an opponent could be killed was the span of an outstretched arm or the distance a rock could be hurled; a span extended with the invention of the bow and arrow around 70,000 years ago to a hundred feet or more. Handheld gunpowder weaponry gradually lengthened it to around 300 yards by the mid-19th century, until in 2017 a Canadian army sniper in Iraq recorded a kill at a distance of over two miles.

Artillery and, in the 20th century, aeroplanes and intercontinental ballistic missiles added to the general's arsenal for the infliction of death at a distance, but the chimera remained a means of close targeting of an enemy without risking the lives of one's own forces. The development of unmanned aerial vehicles (UAVs) or drones offered the prospect of this becoming a reality. Although arguably dating from the use of bombs launched from balloons sent by the Austrians against an uprising in Venice in 1848, they first saw widespread service as reconnaissance vehicles during the Vietnam War. By the early 21st century, UAVs such as the United States' Reaper drones were able to carry bomb payloads of up to 3,000 pounds and read a number plate at two miles, their operations all carried out by pilots safely ensconced in the Nevada desert, thousands of miles from the battlefields in which they were "operating". US drone strikes were carried out in Somalia, Yemen and northwestern Pakistan between 2002 and 2013, all regions in which American ground forces would find it extremely difficult to operate.

The targeted killing of adversaries seems to provide a relatively risk-free means of achieving combat objectives, but is this the future of war? The evidence is that it is not and cannot be. Drones depend on the intelligence provided to them and may kill as many innocent bystanders as the targets at which they are aimed, often escalating support for insurgencies rather than subduing it. Drones also cannot physically occupy territory, so that while they can create a highly hostile environment for enemy forces, they cannot eradicate them or establish a politically stable solution without injections of conventional forces.

Wars in the 21st century are becoming more fragmented, more varied and more complex. The prevalence of civil wars, as opposed to classic state-against-state wars, has spiralled, so that by 2017 there were around 40 civil wars being conducted, an increasing proportion of them aggravated by the intervention of outside countries in favour of one side or the other. The involvement of organised crime groups, drug traffickers and religious extremists in these conflicts, as states fray and dissolve in the world's most troubled regions, has created almost intractable problems that no drone strike, peace conference or military assault alone can solve.

Wars are becoming more hybrid affairs, fought not only by state armies provided with increasingly sophisticated technology but by local militias, mercenary groups and in ways that blur the line between war and peace. The increasing dependence of modern economies on technology has left them vulnerable to cyberattacks: the Stuxnet worm which damaged Iran's nuclear industry in 2010 or the mass attack on Estonia's computing infrastructure in 2007 highlight grey areas where it may be unclear when the threshold of war has been crossed, an ambiguity which an opportunistic aggressor may use to confuse an opponent.

In contrast, the eruption of the Russia–Ukraine War in 2022 showed that, far from being a thing of the past, replaced by hybrid, asymmetrical and shadow wars, armed conflict between major states is still very much a phenomenon of the 21st century. The truth is that, rather than being fought at a touch of a button, at little cost to its main players, wars in the future will be more complex, conducted in an ever-wider spectrum of operations, from urban streets to mountainous refuges, from cyberspace to outer space. They will use as full a range of weaponry as each side is able to deploy, from knives to nanobots, from cyberstrikes to missile strikes. The wars of the future will be genuinely total wars.

Acknowledgements

Note from the author

A complex book such as this is the work of many hands other than those of the author. I am very grateful to Jethro Lennox at HarperCollins for commissioning the title, to follow on in a series that began with *History of the World in Maps* in 2015 and to Harley Griffiths for overseeing the first editorial stages of the book. Robin Scrimgeour has been a capable and patient editor and of huge assistance in tracking down some of the trickier maps in the book. Thank you also to Karen Marland for her acute and sympathetic copy-editing which improved my initial manuscript enormously. Thanks also to Kevin Robbins for the beautiful cover design. My final thanks go to Cara Jones, my wonderful agent at RCW and to the staff at the London Library, in which much of this book was written, and whose capacious collections include many 18th-, 19th- and 20th-century accounts of war which contain some of the maps which appear in this volume.

Front cover unknown / Alamy Stock Photo

p7 Philip Parker collection

p8 Wetdryvac / Alamy Stock Photo

p9 Ministry of Defense of Ukraine / Ukraine Crisis Media Center

pp12–15 World History Archive / Alamy Stock Photo

pp16–17 Antiqua Print Gallery / Alamy Stock Photo

pp18–19 Asar Studios / Alamy Stock Photo

pp20–21 Topographical Collection / Alamy Stock Photo

pp22–23 CC BY-SA 4.0, https://commons.wikimedia.org/wiki/File:Mawangdui_Military_Map.jpg

pp24–27 Philip Parker collection

pp28–29 Asar Studios / Alamy Stock Photo

pp30–33 Gibon Art / Alamy Stock Photo

pp34–35 Philip Parker collection

pp36–37 incamerastock / Alamy Stock Photo

pp38–39 Antiqua Print Gallery / Alamy Stock Photo

pp40–43 Alex Ramsay / Alamy Stock Photo

pp44–45 Artokoloro / Alamy Stock Photo

pp48–49 CC BY-SA 4.0, https://en.wikipedia.org/wiki/File:The_Battle_of_Pavia,_1525_(by_Rupert_Heller)_-_Nationalmuseum,_Stockholm.jpg

pp50–51 Hulton Archive / Getty Images

pp52–53 Royal Collection Trust / © Her Majesty Queen Elizabeth II 2022

pp54–57 CC BY-SA 4.0, https://commons.wikimedia.org/wiki/File:Sekigahara_Kassen_By bu-zu_(Gifu_History_Museum).jpg

pp58–59 Archivac / Alamy Stock Photo

pp60–63 Royal Collection Trust / © Her Majesty Queen Elizabeth II 2022

pp64–67 Royal Collection Trust / © Her Majesty Queen Elizabeth II 2022

pp68–69 World History Archive / Alamy Stock Photo

pp70–73 Heritage Image Partnership Ltd / Alamy Stock Photo

pp74–77 Artokoloro / Alamy Stock Photo

pp78–79 The History Collection / Alamy Stock Photo

pp80–81 Royal Collection Trust / © Her Majesty Queen Elizabeth II 2022

pp84–87 Asar Studios / Alamy Stock Photo

pp88–89 Antiqua Print Gallery / Alamy Stock Photo

pp90–91 PRISMA ARCHIVO / Alamy Stock Photo

pp92–93 incamerastock / Alamy Stock Photo

pp94–95 Maidun Collection / Alamy Stock Photo

pp96–99 Asar Studios / Alamy Stock Photo

pp100–103 Philip Parker collection

pp104–105 incamerastock / Alamy Stock Photo

pp106–109 Lordprice Collection / Alamy Stock Photo

pp112–115 The Print Collector / Alamy Stock Photo

pp116–119 Artokoloro / Alamy Stock Photo

pp120–123 Wetdryvac / Alamy Stock Photo

pp124–125 Wetdryvac / Alamy Stock Photo

pp126–127 unknown / Alamy Stock Photo

pp128–129 Classic Collection 3 / Alamy Stock Photo

pp130–133 Map reproduction courtesy of the Norman B. Leventhal Map & Education Center at the Boston Public Library

pp134–135 duncan1890 / Getty Images

pp136–137 The History Collection / Alamy Stock Photo

pp138–141 VTR / Alamy Stock Photo

pp142–145 CC BY-SA 4.0, https://commons.wikimedia.org/wiki/File:River_War_2-7_Omdurman_Battle_10.15am.jpg

pp146–147 The Print Collector / Alamy Stock Photo

pp148–149 Philip Parker collection

pp152–155 Philip Parker collection

pp156–157 Philip Parker collection

pp158–159 Philip Parker collection

pp160–163 UtCon Collection / Alamy Stock Photo

pp164–165 The Print Collector / Alamy Stock Photo

pp166–167 Philip Parker collection

pp168–171 Philip Parker collection

pp172–173 History and Art Collection / Alamy Stock Photo

pp174–175 Sueddeutsche Zeitung Photo / Alamy Stock Photo

pp176–177 World History Archive / Alamy Stock Photo

pp178–179 BoBman / Alamy Stock Photo

pp180–183 Heritage Image Partnership Ltd / Alamy Stock Photo

pp184–185 GRANGER - Historical Picture Archive / Alamy Stock Photo

pp186–187 Antiqua Print Gallery / Alamy Stock Photo

pp188–191 Philip Parker collection

pp192–195 Philip Parker collection

pp196–199 Dipper Historic / Alamy Stock Photo

pp200–201 CC BY-SA 4.0, https://commons.wikimedia.org/wiki/File:Iwo_Jima_Historical_Map_(Poster).jpg

pp202–203 Sueddeutsche Zeitung Photo / Alamy Stock Photo

pp206–207 Philip Parker collection

pp208–209 © Tallandier / Bridgeman Images

pp210–211 PJF Military Collection / Alamy Stock Photo

pp212–213 PJF Military Collection / Alamy Stock Photo

pp214–217 CC BY-SA 4.0, https://en.wikipedia.org/wiki/File:DesertStormMap_v2.svg

pp218–221 Ministry of Defense of Ukraine / Ukraine Crisis Media